MW00623050

He Is My Brother

The Bonding of a Priest and a Rabbi Over 25 Years

Father William Treacy
&
Rabbi Raphael Levine

CLASSIC DAY PUBLISHING

Seattle, Washington
Portland, Oregon
Denver, Colorado
Vancouver, B.C.
Scottsdale, Arizona
Minneapolis, Minnesota

Copyright © 2007 by Father William Treacy

ISBN: 978-1-59849-037-4

Printed in the United States of America

Editor: Deb Caletti
Design: Soundview Design Studio
Scripture quotations are taken from The New American Catholic Bible
© 1976 Catholic Publishers, Inc., A Division of Thomas Nelson Inc.

All rights reserved. No part of this book may be transmitted in any form or by any means, electronic or mechanical, including photocopying, recording, or by any information storage or retrieval system, without the written permission of the publisher, except where permitted by law.

Requests for such permissions should be addressed to:

Classic Day Publishing
2925 Fairview Avenue East
Seattle, Washington 98102
877-728-8837
info@peanutbutterpublishing.com

Dedication

Dear Rabbi,

I am dedicating this book to you. It is about my priesthood for 63 years, but my priesthood has been influenced by you ever since I walked into your office in May, 1960, to plan our weekly interfaith TV program "Challenge" which lasted for 14 years.

Your vision and enthusiasm for harmony in the human family ignited a similar fire in me. My book is being published as we celebrate the 40th anniversary of Camp Brotherhood. Before you left in death on November 5, 1985, I promised you to continue Camp Brotherhood which we co-founded in 1966. It has grown and prospered with the help of devoted benefactors and with your influence and is host to thousands of people each year.

Recently, I read of the research done in 1982 by Professor Bohm, a physicist at London University. He amazed scientists by proving that subatomic particles can communicate instantaneously regardless of distance apart. Is this a clue to how loved ones cannot be separated even by death? I sense your presence and support as I carried on without you for the past 22 years. I thank God for uniting me, an Irish born priest, with you, a rabbi from Eastern Europe, so that we became like brothers.

Your brother,
William

Preface

Dear Friends:

In a personal Christmas message in 2005, Archbishop Brunett of Seattle writes: "You have had some wonderful experiences and they should not be forgotten." These kind words of the Archbishop inspired me to share some of my experiences of sixty-three years as a priest in Seattle. I present them in the spirit of St. Paul who wrote in II Corinthians 4:7 concerning our Christian faith in Jesus: "This treasure we possess in earthen vessels, to make it clear that its surpassing power comes from God and not from us."

Blessings,
Father William Treacy

Acknowledgments

I am grateful to all the people who helped to make this book possible:

- Deb Caletti for her editorial assistance. For her book, *Honey, Baby, Sweetheart,* she was a finalist for the National Book Award.

- Pam Morrison and Penny Howell who typed the manuscript.

- Roger Yockey and his wife Marilyn for many helpful suggestions.

- Jennifer Caravalho who carefully proofread the manuscript.

- David Marty and Amy Vaughn for creating an artistic layout.

- Elliott Wolf of Classic Day Publishing, Seattle, for overseeing the printing and publishing.

May the road rise with each one of them, and the wind be always at their back, and may God keep them in the palm of His hand.

Father William Treacy

Table of Contents

Part 1
Father William Treacy

Chapter 1

The Saggarth Aroon

The climb began in a home in central Ireland where I was born May 31, 1919. I remember as a child being taught the Our Father and felt proud when I recited it one evening for an American guest. As a student in the local public school, I was prepared for my First Communion by Miss Sarah Campion, the first grade teacher. On May 2, 1926, I received my First Communion in the local church where I was baptized as an infant. There were twelve of us kneeling at the communion rail holding a candle in our right hand. It was springtime in Ireland, and we had primroses and daisies decorating the candles. Next to me was a classmate with brown paper wrapped around his candle. The picture of him so out of step with the rest of us moved me with compassion for him when his parents could easily have gathered some of the beautiful wild flowers around their home for his candle.

In 1931, I came face-to-face with a bishop who was to change my life. The meeting took place in the parish church where I was confirmed. The bishop's name was Patrick Collier, who as part of the ceremony at that time, gave me a slight slap of his hand on the cheek to remind me that to follow Christ meant I must be prepared for the negative that would probably arise for me.

Six years after I met the bishop at my confirmation, I finished high school in St. Kieran's College, Kilkenny. This was not just an academic accomplishment but also a financial one. I was born just when the British evacuated Ireland after about one thousand years of governing occupation; they had left the country with few high schools and fewer universities. It was only possible for me to attend high school because my family could pay the tuition for me to be a boarder. The school was about thirty miles from home, and I seldom got to visit my family when I was a student between the ages of thirteen and eighteen. They were lonely years marking a gradual drift away from family.

At age eighteen, I decided to enter a seminary to prepare for priesthood. Fortunately, I received a scholarship to the National Seminary, St. Patrick's, Maynooth.

In September, 1937, I joined a freshman class of seventy-five candidates from all over Ireland who entered the Seminary at Maynooth. It could house more than five hundred students. Built in two squares with a beautiful chapel, its spire stood 254 feet to welcome generations of students. The Seminary began as a single residence in 1795.

Prior to that time, there was not a single seminary in Ireland due to the anti-Catholic laws passed by the Irish Parliament. Students for the priesthood risked arrest and death as they made their way to a seminary in Rome, France or Spain. When they returned, they took more than a passing interest in the political and economic status of their people. They founded schools, and protested against injustice and cruelty of the Penal Laws, as they were known. The British Government took a bold step to try to discourage priests who seemed to be a threat to British occupation and exploitation. The Parliament in London agreed to finance the building and staffing of an Irish seminary. The few bishops in Ireland in the 1790's agreed to the British conditions, namely, that the Government of Britain should be presented with the names of priests who were candidates for bishops in Ireland and submitted for review with the right to veto at least one. The agreement was secret at the time the seminary opened in 1795. It became public in 1813. Irish Catholics protested strongly against this attempt to interfere with the leadership of the Church. Rome had approved the veto but, following the protests of the Irish, it was withdrawn in 1813. Catholics rallied in support of the statement, "Our religion from Rome, our politics from home." In spite of the removal of the veto, the British Government supported the Seminary until 1869. Then to conclude the arrangement, a considerable sum of money was given to the Irish bishops and invested by them. My scholarship came from this British money!

The first priests to staff the Seminary were from France. The French Revolution of 1789 took a very anti-Catholic attitude, especially toward clergy. Many priests met death because of their connection with the status quo. Others escaped, such as those who staffed my Alma Mater. About that time, a very virulent strain of Catholicism arose which began in Holland. It was named after a Dutch bishop who helped spread it. His name was Jansenius, and the virus was called Jansenism. It robbed Christianity of the joy Jesus promised us.

Jansenism centered its energy on sin and the human tendency to do wrong, especially in regard to sex. Through the French priests who pioneered the education of the Irish clergy, this negative approach to human life was overlaid on a Celtic spirit that tended to celebrate life, human love, and God's love, which like that of a parent was full of compassion and understanding for human frailties. Irish priests carried some of this negative understanding of Christianity to foreign mission fields with them.

One of the tragic effects of this theology to which I and so many others were exposed was the fear it gave of God and the great possibility because of sin of being separated from God forever in hell. As a child, I recall a dream of my grade school class being judged by God. I was a failure, excluded from heaven by this God of judgment and punishment. Finally, after wondering if God would choose me to be a priest, I walked out of the Seminary Chapel, Maynooth, on June 18, 1944, with tears of gratitude after being ordained a priest by John Charles McQuaid, the Archbishop of Dublin.

During seminary years I was expecting to be a priest in Ireland. The vision of the priest closely connected to his people inspired me to begin my journey to the priesthood. I inherited some of the Celtic vision of the priest as expressed in "The Saggarth Aroon."

It is difficult to translate these words. Literally they mean the "beloved priest." But the tone of voice can convey the affection of the speaker for a person who had a special place in the hearts of the Irish.

This affection was fostered in the 18th century. During this century, the harsh anti-Irish, anti-Catholic laws passed by the anti-Catholic Irish Parliament forbade the practice of the Catholic Faith. If a priest was captured by a priest hunter, he received twenty pounds for the head of the priest. A person who met a priest and did not report it had his ears cut off because of his silence.

One of the great Irish poems of the 18th century is entitled, *The Priest Hunters.* Some English soldiers surprised a priest, Fr. Farrell, as he celebrated mass in the woods. The Irish had sentries to watch out for such surprise raids. Quickly the sentry, Phelim O'Carroll, put the priest on his horse and together they raced away from danger. Phelim put the priest in a safe hiding place and then faced his pursuers. The last verse of the poem reads:

"And there some hours later his own comrades found him,
With a dozen grim troopers strewn lifeless around him;
They thought of his young bride the fond Rosaleen,
As they bore his cold corpse o'er fair Rosnacreena.
They dug his lone grave amid tears of deep sorrow,
As they laid him to rest in wild Cappanarrow.
In the cave in the hollow, poor Father O'Farrell
said a Requiem Mass for young Phelim O'Carroll."

[The place names in the poem are near my home in Ireland.]

The attitude of people to the "Saggarth Aroon" was expressed by a modern writer, Leonard Cohen, in his book, *The Purpose Driven Life.* He wrote, "Forget your perfect offering. There is a crack in everything. That is how the light gets in." A friend commented, "That is also how the light gets out."

A story, typical of the compassion for the priest in Ireland, is that of a parishioner who found a priest lying helpless beside the road, a victim of alcoholism. The response was not one of condemnation, but compassion. The parishioner took off his coat and silently placed it on the priest. He did not even awaken the priest to save him embarrassment before a parishioner.

Recently a friend recalled this story of the helpless priest, adding an inspiring insight based on the words of St. Paul. Through the compassion and love of a parishioner for his frailties, the priest could say, "Blest are they whose iniquities are forgiven, whose sins are covered over. Blest is the man to whom the Lord imputes no guilt." Romans 4:7-8

This love of the Irish for the "Saggarth Aroon" is being tested by a people with no religious persecution and with the best economy in Europe.

The sex scandal has also strained the relationship. But the Book of Sirach tells us, "For in fire gold is tested and worthy men in the crucible of humiliation." Sirach 2:5, and then adds, "Trust God and he will help you."

The prophet Malachi in Chapter 3 compares God to the refiner of silver. In his time, the refiner placed the mined silver on a platform and lit a fire under it to purify it. When the soil and stain were burnt away, the refiner could then see his image as in a mirror in the silver. Malachi pictured God refining all of us by our sufferings in life until we reflect the image of God. The Irish person putting a cloak over the priest on the roadside was purifying his heart from judgment and condemnation. Perhaps on awakening and discovering a parishioner's cloak around him, the priest felt God had touched him and fostered in him anew the spirit of the Saggarth Aroon.

There are other stories which illustrate the love of the Irish for the Saggarth Aroon. One is told by Canon Sheehan, a priest and well-known novelist in the last century in Ireland. In a small village in Ireland, a man, known as an alcoholic, is charged with murder. The defense concentrated on proving that the accused was not in the area where the murder took place at approximately 6:00 p.m. in the evening. During the trial, the mother of the accused attended court each day and stood by her son.

The defense lawyer put the local priest on the stand. He began by asking where the priest was on the date of the murder. He answered, "In my study."

Question: "Was anyone with you?"

Reply: "Yes, the accused."

Question: "Are you sure of the time he was with you?"

Reply: "Yes."

Question: "Why can you recall the time so exactly?"

Reply: "Because the Angelus rang at 6:00 p.m. and I recited it."

Question: "How did the accused act?"

Reply: "He did not recite the Angelus."

Question: "What did you say to him?"

Reply: "I rebuked him."

Question: "What was his response?"

The priest remained silent. The attorney demanded an answer. Finally the priest answered, "When I rebuked him for not praying, he struck me when the bell rang and broke my glasses." At this moment the mother of the accused stood up in court and screamed at the judge, "Your honor, if my son hit the priest, hang him."

The final story to give insight into the relationship of the Irish to the priests going back to the time of persecution is illustrated by a namesake of mine, a Fr. William Treacy. He served as pastor in my home parish and built the first school there just prior to his death in 1839. When he decided to study for the priesthood there was no seminary in Ireland. He was smuggled to France with the help of friendly Protestants, and he was ordained prior to the French Revolution. Some of the anti-Catholic revolutionaries discovered where he was living and came to arrest him, and he faced certain death. While they were at the front door, he jumped out of a window and escaped in the rear of the house. I have read this story in local history and also heard it from an elderly relative. The priest's life, his dedication to priesthood, led him to face death in France. Many others risked their lives to minister to their people, making them the Saggarth Aroon.

My climb up the mountain of the Lord during seminary days was far from easy. Our association with classmates was limited. Tradition called for us to take recreation primarily with those from the diocese for which we were to be ordained. This limited my contact to seven or eight students out of seventy-five. The morning bell rang at 6:00, and we were trained to see in this the call of God to begin a new day and to arise at once. By 6:30, all were in chapel for a half hour of prayer. Mass was at 7:00 and breakfast at 7:45. We were free until class began at 9:00 and continued until lunch at 12:00. Class began again at 1:00 p.m. until 2:45. Then there was a fifteen-minute visit to the chapel, with dinner following at 3:00 and recreation until 5:00. Study from 5:00 to 7:00, with supper at 7:00, evening prayer at 7:45 and further study from 8:00 to 10:00 brought the day to a close. No one needed medication to sleep at the end of the day. During the war, we had no rationing except in regard to electricity for heat.

During my fourth year, I contracted pleurisy and was in the infirmary for six weeks. Then in mid-March I was sent to St. Vincent's

Hospital, Dublin, for an x-ray, as I was suspected of having TB. Before leaving for the hospital, I was told that if there was any sign of TB, I was not to return to the seminary. TB was common in Ireland at this time.

On March 16, 1941, I was taken to a basement room in St. Vincent's Hospital, Dublin, for a chest x-ray. I still recall the chill of the x-ray machine pressed close to my chest. The procedure took about ten seconds but that ten seconds was to determine my life. Again I struggled to believe God wished me to be a priest and waited for the result. It came that evening. Literally, it was all clear. Again I was on the road to priesthood — still climbing.

Climbing the Mountain of the Lord, artwork by Jana Sparks, 2006.

Chapter 2

By Bicycle, Train, Troopship to America

Following ordination, June 18, 1944, I had been appointed to assist a senior pastor in my native area in Ireland. The only transportation I had was a bicycle. Every other Sunday, rain or shine, with no breakfast, I cycled three miles to a local church for Mass. Then after Mass I cycled to another church for a second Mass. Church law at the time required priests to be fasting when they celebrated Mass. The pastor at this second church gave me breakfast, and I cycled another three miles back to my residence. It was no exaggeration to say I was drenched to the skin from exposure to wind, rain and cold in Ireland. The wind at times in Ireland was so strong that I recall going to visit a man who was dying. I simply could make no progress against the wind on my bicycle and almost turned back, but a final push kept me going, and I am grateful that I reached his home before he died.

Prior to my ordination, the bishop of Seattle had written to the seminary requesting volunteers to come for the war years to assist because of the population growth in Seattle. My Irish bishop, Patrick Collier, gave me permission to serve temporarily in Seattle for five to ten years.

During the year 1944, the Seattle bishop, Gerald Shaughnessy, was making efforts to obtain a visa and transportation for me to America in wartime. After waiting until the beginning of 1945 for a reply from Seattle, Bishop Collier informed me that if I did not get to travel to America in the near future, he was planning to send me to a place called Newcastle, a coal mining area in Northeast England.

Finally, at the end of January 1945 a telegram arrived telling me to proceed to London and to contact the Military Transport Service. After crossing from Dublin to Holyhead, England, by boat, I took a train to London. My family knew I was subject to departure at a moment's notice. Since I did not know what would happen in London, I did not say a final goodbye to them when I left. I had been saying goodbye to my family since I was thirteen, leaving home for school. Totally inexperienced in travel, I arrived in London with no place to stay. A senior priest in Dublin told me to go to the Sisters of Nazareth in Hammersmith, London, and they would find accommodations for me. My travel instructions required me to report at 9:00 the next morning to the Military Transport Service office in downtown London. The senior priest in Dublin gave me the impression that Hammersmith was a "village" outside London. Perhaps it was a hundred years ago, but now it was part of greater London.

I took a subway to Kings Cross Station where I was to change for Hammersmith. As the train came to a stop, I placed a small suitcase inside the door with my passport and ticket inside. I hesitated briefly to obtain another suitcase with clothes. As I turned around, I saw the train move quickly away from the station. I ran to the office of the stationmaster and requested him to call someone at the next station to remove my small brown suitcase. He told me there was no hope of ever finding it. He pointed out that people had to step over it and since there was little security on the train, it was "certain" to be stolen. "Make your plans without it," was his advice, telling me he had been retired from the underground and returned to help during the war. I went and set down somewhere on a seat and began to ponder my future.

Suddenly God had appeared to me telling me that I had to surrender my future to God's Providence. Before me I saw my hopes to go to America vanish in an instant unless the suitcase was found that night. If not, with the little money I had, it would be necessary to phone my bishop in Ireland, confess my stupidity and request an assignment in Newcastle. Having come to this conclusion, I experienced a deep, deep peace. I went back to the stationmaster to see if anything could be done to locate my baggage. Again, he offered no hope. It was now 9:25 p.m. He told me to return after 11:00 p.m. After praying for two hours to receive the strength to accept God's will, wandering alone in the darkness of the London streets in wartime, I returned to King's Cross Station, at 11:20 p.m. A young woman replaced the elderly stationmaster. As soon as I arrived she looked at me and said, "You must be the priest that lost his luggage." I said, "Yes, I am." She hugged me, saying I must be "holy" because a miracle happened for me. My suitcase had traveled the London circle in two hours, arriving back at 11:10 to King's Cross Station. She had just arrived on duty when the train stopped. She was not searching for my lost luggage, but something about a single small suitcase all by itself attracted her attention. She removed it and matched it to my name. Then God told me at 11:20 p.m., on Valentine's Day in 1945, that Seattle, America, and not Newcastle, England, was my destination.

Then I realized I was homeless in London at midnight. I made my way by train to Hammersmith. The first big building I saw was this police station. Entering, I asked if they could recommend accommodations in the area. The officer on duty was courteous and made some phone calls and then told me he could find nothing. There was a bench in the office. It was a cold February night, and I asked if I could sit there until morning. He agreed, and with my passport and ticket close to me, I rested. About 1:00 a.m. the duty officer came to me and said he could improve on my accommodations and to follow him with my luggage. He put me in a single cell and gave me a rubber mat to sleep on the floor. I slept well.

The next morning, an officer opened the cell door and directed me to a washroom with the other inmates. There were about twelve of us with a small washbasin each. The gentleman next to me asked, "When did they bring you in?" Not wishing to lie to him I said, "I came in last night." His next question was, "What did they have on you?" Again, vaguely, I said, "It has to be sorted out." He said, "I am in again for being drunk, what should I say to the judge?" I asked him if he had any children in the service. He said he had a son in the British Army in North Africa. I said to him, "Tell the judge you are suffering under emotional stress for your son in the army." Very pleased he patted me on the back and then I was released in time to be in downtown London by bus at 9:00 a.m. to complete travel plans to Seattle.

That evening, I left London at 7:00 p.m. on a troop train for an unknown destination. For security reasons, we were kept in the dark. Fourteen hours later, we arrived at Grenock outside Glasgow and boarded one of the biggest trans-Atlantic liners, the Ile de France. It could transport 14,000 soldiers. On its return trip to New York, we had about

5,000 troops. Hundreds of them had frozen feet from the Battle of the Bulge. Others had been overseas so long that they qualified for a ninety-day furlough. There were Red Cross people, diplomats, entertainers and about five hundred war brides also on board.

We sailed on Friday, Feb. 17. For the first day, we had a destroyer at each side of the ship. Then we relied on radar to find submarines and on superior speed to escape. Day and night we wore life jackets and had a daily drill on how to get to lifeboats in case of emergency. Finally, on a beautiful Sunday morning, February 25, 1945, we sailed up the Hudson, past the Statue of Liberty. Returning soldiers wept tears of gratitude. I thanked God for bringing me safely this far.

Chapter 3

Growth in Faith

I experienced my first crisis in faith when I was about seven years old. From my earliest years I believed strongly in Santa Claus and looked forward to hanging up my stocking for the gifts he brought each year. I discovered the truth about Santa Claus at about age seven, and felt betrayed by all the stories I heard about him. In my shock and disappointment I recall studying a crucifix in my room. I checked the hands of Jesus and felt the tip of nails. I felt what seemed thorns on his head. Then I concluded the story of Jesus and his death on the cross was not a Santa Claus story but was for real. My faith in Jesus was renewed at that time.

About the same time, age seven, I received my first communion. Like any child, I was told about a great person called God, the Church, etc. As I look back on the day of my first communion in a small country church, I observed all the adults in the church receiving communion and unconsciously their example strengthened my faith.

Even farther back, I remember when a priest came to bless our newly built house. The family had to gather in the kitchen for the house blessing. A workman whom I admired joined us and knelt while the priest blessed the house. The workman impressed me as he prayed with the family. On the wall in the kitchen was a framed certificate with the date of the blessing. I was three years old that day.

As I look back, faith begins as a tiny seed in the heart of a child. With faith, the child with a pain or problem turns to a mother. My parents slept on the second floor. One night, probably again when I was around three, I developed a bad headache and climbed a dark stairway for comfort and assurance from my mother. As I grew older, I realized that faith is a positive acceptance of the unseen, needing no visible proof. The love of a mother by the child is faith. This faith grows stronger day by day due to manifold acts of love, by the mother. This love is communicated with words, hugs, kisses, food, etc. Such acts of love help us as children to realize that love needs expression. When we perform any action in love the invisible in us finds expression. At a retreat for couples preparing for marriage, one remarkable young woman said to me, "I totally reject the phrase 'making love.' Only God can give love, as only the sun gives light." "When I love," she said, "I simply give expression to a fountain of love bubbling in my heart from the hands of a Loving God." Our lives, our work, (call it our ministry) should through faith be an expression of love. Once I visited a faith-filled grandmother in a hospital as death approached. She was at peace. "I have one more assignment to carry out," she said, "to show my children and grandchildren how to face death."

My paternal grandmother, a woman of great faith, died when I was about three months old. When a neighbor was seriously ill or dying, the family sent for my grandmother and she helped with the grieving and the funeral. During her lifetime she lived through famine and poverty, through eviction with her husband by a cruel landlord. My mother, who cared for her in her final illness, told me that when my grandmother felt in great pain she asked that I, three months old, be placed beside her in bed. Later my mother explained that my lying silently next to her strengthened my grandmother's faith in God. She realized God had given her the privilege of being a partner with her husband in giving five boys to the human family and now was blessed with the first grandchild. The story of my ministry to my grandmother when an infant, as told by my mother, has been a reminder of her great faith in God and her love for me.

As I grew up, my Catholic faith was strengthened every Sunday morning when I joined all my neighbors for Sunday Mass. As the church was surrounded by the cemetery where generations who believed and worshipped before me were buried, I can still recall the individual family plots.

Another milestone in my faith journey took place when I was eleven years old. My maternal grandmother died suddenly. I recall my mother calling me and telling me, "Grandmother has gone to heaven." It was my first experience with death. For months I reflected on the words of my mother and pictured my grandmother looking down from heaven at me. My childish imagination allowed me to continue speaking to her.

Later I realized that this was what the Creed calls faith in The Communion of Saints, the spiritual faith bond between the living and the dead.

Perhaps it was at the time of the death of my grandmother that my mother sent a donation to an orphanage in England dedicated to a young French Carmelite nun who died in 1897 and was canonized in 1925. My mother received much literature from the orphanage about their patroness St. Therese. I read everything about her and felt I had another friend in heaven.

In fact, I fell in love with this saint. Six times I made a pilgrimage to the town of Lisieux in France where she lived and died. I read her autobiography, *The Story Of A Soul*, a bestseller. She was deeply attached to her father. Yet, a call to be a Carmelite nun led her to tell him, at age fourteen, that she wished to follow two of her sisters into the local Carmelite convent in Lisieux. There is a statue of her in the garden of the family home still preserved in Lisieux. The young daughter is represented as whispering to her father of her desires to be a nun. The sculptor captured the anguish in the face of the father at the prospect of being separated from his youngest daughter that he called "my little Queen."

Therese entered Carmel with special permission at age fifteen in 1888 and died at age twenty-four, Sept. 30, 1897. I read her autobiography again in 1939. In the words of another priest who read it that same year: "She convinced me that someone as ordinary as I could aspire to the love of God, which filled her heart to overflowing."

The book was first published in 1898, exactly one year after her death. Today it can be found in sixty languages worldwide. In the words of one biographer, Bishop Patrick Ahern, "She was very human. She battled with neurosis and in the last moments of a long illness was tempted to suicide...but her life for the most part was ordinary, the kind of life we encounter every day." Her story is not the story of high adventure, but of a life in which she endeavored by faith to do the ordinary extraordinarily well.

The poet Alfred Tennyson said, "Lives of great men all remind us we can make our lives sublime and passing leaves behind us footprints in the sands of time."

Therese, with her great grasp of scripture, with her great personal love for Jesus and for everyone, shows us how to live by faith. Her vocation was especially to pray for priests. Whatever footprints I may leave in the sands of time will owe a great deal to the faith, the prayers, the love and example of St. Therese, as I feel her presence daily as I try to climb the mountain of the Lord.

Chapter 4

Joyful Hope in the Seasons

I grew up on a farm in Ireland. Spring plowing took place on our farm and all the local farms about the same time. Potatoes were placed in the soil and covered during the month of March and wheat was planted about the same time. The seed was thus covered over in the darkness of the earth, invisible but still alive. The farmers waited in joyful hope for the wedding of the seed and the soil to bear fruit when the new potatoes or new wheat began to appear in the fields. In Ireland there was never worry about the rain needed to help bring the new life to the planted seed. Farmers in the Midwest in America where there is drought find it hard to wait in joyful hope as they hope with anxiety for rainfall to nourish the seed they plant.

As there are four seasons of spring, summer, autumn and winter, there are seasons in our inner lives. When we experience pain, sorrow, separation from loved ones, it is like winter. It is advisable to find time to reflect, or as a friend says, "to process." This can be also called winter hibernation practiced by nature and by animals. Bears can live in winter for months without food or water with their hearts slowing to a minimum rate to support life. The bear retires to a cave.

Spiritual writers suggest that in time of great sorrow and pain that we retire within our own souls. It can be done in a retreat with others or alone in some private place.

Growing up in Ireland with long dark winters, I always greeted the lengthening days in spring. With the first flowers I was assured that winter was leaving. Soon there would be wonderful colors in the whitethorn trees and wild flowers. One evening I was riding a bicycle along a country road and I heard a bird sing from the top of a tree. I paused. For fifteen minutes that bird sang to me with such sweetness that I have never forgotten it and can clearly recall the tree where this melody touched me. The first flowers and the first swallows gave me joyful hope that spring was coming and then summer.

Summers in Irish fields had that unique green color. Wild flowers were in abundance. Ireland has been described as a place where "smiling spring its earliest visit paid, and parting summers lingering blooms delayed." Summer was a time to find the beauty of God in an Irish countryside. In summer I have climbed an Irish mountain, relatively small compared to the Cascades or the Olympics, but still revealing a mosaic of fields with crops, cattle and sheep grazing, and houses with smoke ascending to indicate human presence — truly inspiring. All I did was gaze and photograph the scene, not with a camera, but with my memory where I can recall it wherever I am, and it speaks to me of God. John O'Donohue captures this mystic Celtic spirituality of gazing at the wonders of creation. He wrote, "May you realize that holiness is mindful, gazing, feeling, hearing, touching. May your senses gather you and bring you home. May your senses always enable you to celebrate the universe, and the mystery and possibilities of your presence here. May the Eros of earth bless you." Others loved autumn, time of harvest and change of color in nature. Children in particular enjoyed the occasional winter snowfall in Ireland.

As there are changes in the seasons of the year, so there are changes in our personal lives. Cardinal John Henry Newman said, "To grow is to change and to be perfect is to have changed often." Growth will involve the risk of failure. John O'Donohue speaks of the "Beauty of the Flaw" in Anam Cara. This is the strange contradiction of the cross that from apparent failure and suffering comes resurrection when even Jesus experienced spiritual desolation before a spiritual springtime to life where death is no more.

As the seasonal type changes in our spiritual lives we will experience failures and flaws. There is an old Irish saying that, "There is no craftsman without a flaw." People dream of success in marriage, with their children, in politics, in art, and various professions including the service of God. Flaws occur in every profession. One of the best analysts of the flaw in human character that I have met is John O'Donohue in his book, *Divine Beauty.* He writes, "The shape of each soul is different. The shape of the flaw that each person carries is different…Then we stop seeing the flaw as a disappointment and exception to an otherwise laudable life, we begin to glimpse the awkward light and hidden wisdom that the flaw holds." Then we can have joyful hope.

Antonio Machado in his poem, *"Last Night as I Was Sleeping"* reflects on the "flaw" and its effect on character. He begins by saying:

"Last night as I was sleeping
I dreamt — marvelous error,
that a spring was breaking into my heart in water of new life."

Roger Housden, commenting on these lines, tells us the origin of the spring of water is not in your own heart — but comes from outside us. He writes, "Your soul after all, is not yours, but the fresh water clears away the hurts of the past and renews and refreshes us." Machado continued his poem. Again he dreamt,

"that I had a beehive inside my heart.
And the golden bees
were making white combs
and sweet honey
from my old failures"

Again Roger Housden comments that Machado is saying that failures "can soften you, render you more permeable to worlds you may never have countenanced if you had met with success in the world of action." Machado concludes his poem:

"Last night as I slept
I dreamt — marvelous error!
That it was God I had
there inside my heart."

He found joyful hope for every situation of success or failure. He discovered that God's love constantly enfolds us. Living with joyful hope means that every situation in life can be a blessing. As St. Paul states this message in Romans 8:28: "We know that God makes all things work together for the good of those who love him."

Our lives that should radiate as Christians with joyful hope are often robbed of this joy by the fear of death. I have indicated how the Irish experienced each season of the year as an occasion to find joy, find God in each season. This is expressed in an old Irish prayer:

"I am going home with thee, to thy home, to thy home
I am going home with thee, to thy home of winter.
I am going home with thee, to thy home of autumn, spring and of summer
I am going home with thee, thy child of my love to the eternal bed to thy perpetual sleep."

After the Lord's Prayer at each Mass there follows this prayer: "Deliver us, O Lord, from every evil and grant us peace in our day. In your mercy keep us free from sin and protect us from all anxiety, as we wait in joyful hope for the coming of our Savior, Jesus Christ."

Fr. Ron Rolheiser writes, "When we act like God, we get to feel like God and God is never depressed."

A person who lived in joyful hope and anticipation of meeting Jesus was Cardinal Nicholas Patrick Wiseman who lived in the 19th century in England. He was diagnosed with cancer and was told death was fast approaching. From then on he paid no attention to administration but laughed and joked with all who came to see him. Some of his serious-minded staff were worried about his lighthearted approach to life when death was drawing closer and closer. They decided to bring a classmate of the Cardinal to his bedside and to discuss the Cardinal's approaching death. The classmate came and pointedly said to the Cardinal, "Do you know death is very close to you?" The Cardinal smiled and nodded. Next his classmate said, "How do you feel about approaching death?" The Cardinal replied to his classmate, "Do you remember when you and I were in the seminary and how eagerly we awaited a vacation so that we could go home? That is how I now feel — anticipating going home to the God I love with no fear." This is what it means to live in joyful hope in spring, summer, autumn and winter.

Chapter 5

My First View of Seattle

In New York, I spent three weeks with first cousins Catherine and Agnes Treacy, daughters of my father's oldest brother, Joseph. After viewing the St. Patrick's Day Parade from the steps of St. Patrick's Cathedral, I took a train for Seattle. Again, most of the passengers were soldiers. I changed trains in Chicago and enjoyed the journey especially as we climbed the Rockies and observed the ice melting in the rivers beside the tracks.

My first view of Seattle was from a Northern Pacific train that arrived on Friday morning, March 22, 1945, at 8:00 a.m. A priest from the cathedral, Fr. Walter Mortek, met me and drove me to the cathedral giving me my first tour of a city to be my home for the greater part of my life. The Cathedral of St. James dominated the skyline, as the only other tall building in Seattle at that time was the forty-six-story Smith Tower.

At about 11:00 a.m. that Friday morning I had an appointment with Bishop Shaughnessy. The meeting was brief and business-like. He informed me that I was assigned to St. Alphonsus Parish, Seattle, to assist the pastor, John D. McGrath, who was also from Ireland.

My first weekend was Palm Sunday. My assignment was confessions during Mass at 8:00 a.m. and celebrant of the two later Masses. About 1:00 p.m. I had breakfast. Feeling the effects of travel and the busy morning schedule, I told the pastor that after breakfast I would rest for a time. To my amazement he told me there was much work to do on Sunday afternoon. He took me downstairs and gave me the sum total of the collection from all the masses. My instructions were to open the envelopes and to make sure the donation was recorded on the envelope and to count and wrap loose change. I had never held dimes, nickels, quarters, fifty-cent pieces in my life until that time. Skill in placing a roll of 50 dimes in a package was not something I learned in the seminary! Alone by myself trying to wrap various coins for hours, I began to ask myself why I came to Seattle.

Each morning I had Mass at 6:30. There was a high school for girls attached to the parish, Holy Angels High School. The pastor assigned me to teach religion to the freshman and sophomores. Some of them are now senior parishioners here in St. Thomas More Parish and like to recall how they "teased" the newly arrived Irish priest by asking him the most difficult questions they knew or questions that would embarrass a shy new arrival in America.

About the second week, I was playing ball at lunchtime with the children. The pastor, a very dignified, solemn person, a very dedicated, hard-working priest, came over to me and told me to return to the rectory where a non-Catholic gentlemen was waiting for instructions. Suddenly reality set in. I wondered what questions he might ask. Would he query me on justification, indulgences, etc? With such thoughts I entered the parish rectory and met a very kind, gentle person. He was a police officer, married about four years to a Catholic, and had just completed an eight-hour assignment.

Instead of a pupil and teacher relationship, Earl Wymore and I became good friends. He was eventually received into the Catholic Church and remained faithful to his commitment and kept in touch with me during the past sixty years. His wife and he, following his retirement, recited the rosary every day at 9:00 a.m. She died a few years ago and he continued the practice of reciting the rosary daily at 9:00 a.m. On July 22, 2005, I officiated at the wedding of his grandson in St. Brendan's Church, Bothell. At the reception, he and I stood side-by-side for a photo marking my 61st anniversary of ordination and his 95th birthday.

At St. Alphonsus Parish I met a gentlemen who was to have a profound effect on my life. His name was Herb Norris, married to a Catholic woman with three children. He was raised with many negative ideas about the Catholic Church. A confrontation with a Seattle pastor over the baptism of his second child led to his conversion. They had moved to St. Catherine Parish, Seattle, but his wife's family attended St. Alphonsus Parish. They arrived at St. Alphonsus Parish for the baptism of his second daughter. For Herb it was simply an occasion for a family celebration, so his preparation for the baptism was to purchase plenty of beer. When they came to St. Alphonsus Parish, the young priest on duty hesitated to baptize the child of Herb and his wife, Eva, without permission of Fr. Matthew Beglin, pastor of St. Catherine Parish. Fr. Beglin refused permission saying, "I can take care of my own parishioners." The baptism did not take place, and the following Tuesday an angry Herb Norris kept an appointment with a priest he insisted on calling "Mr. Beglin."

Herb explained that as a non-Catholic he was simply trying to do what he promised his wife at their marriage — to raise his children Catholic. Then he said, "You, Mr. Beglin, won't cooperate with me."

Fr. Beglin congratulated Herb on trying to raise his children as Catholics. Then he added, "Wouldn't you like to know what your children, that you love, are being taught?" Herb agreed. Then Fr. Beglin said, "You come to me once a week for a few months and I will tell you what we teach in our Catholic school." Herb took the offer and six months later was received into the church.

He had a very inquisitive mind. After we met he would invite me to his home for long discussions about the Catholic faith, which he accepted with all his heart. Then one evening he said to me, "I was raised with great ignorance about the Catholic Church. As a businessman I advertise my products. Why doesn't the Catholic Church advertise in the newspaper the teachings of the church? I agreed that this was well worthwhile. But at that time I was on a temporary assignment in Seattle and never expected to see his wish come true for a Catholic Advertising Program in which I was to be involved. But again, I believe Providence brought Herb and myself together as friends in 1945, and in 2005 I attended the 69th wedding anniversary of Herb and Eva.

Chapter 6

God, A Loving Friend

During WWII I was in Ireland's national seminary, St. Patrick's, Maynooth, about fifteen miles north and west of Dublin. My approach to priesthood was influenced by the time in which I grew up. I did consider a military career and still recall the ads that appealed to me before and during WWII. One in particular had a picture of a Navy pilot with the words, "Enjoy the beauty of sea and sky." Seminary training with its daily schedule of rising at 6:00 a.m. to lights out at 10:15 p.m. was something like military discipline, and I accepted it as part of my journey to priesthood.

Seminarians usually selected a scripture passage for souvenir cards of ordination. The words I selected were from a letter, the final letter St. Paul wrote to his friend and fellow worker, Timothy. He wrote, "Bear hardships along with me as a good soldier of Christ Jesus." (II Timothy 2:3) My ordination took place on June 18, 1944 as thousands of my contemporaries in military service were dying on the beaches of Normandy in an effort to end the tyranny and evil leadership of Hitler. Their sacrifices inspired me as I accepted ordination to priesthood. Slowly and steadily the concept of priesthood as expressed in the words of Paul to Timothy gave way to an understanding of priesthood as a partnership with God. Words of Jesus to the first priests in his farewell reminded them of his relationship with God, the Father: "It is the Father who lives in me accomplishing his works." (John 14:10) The journey from seeing God to be served and approached with fear and hesitation, to a response to a God of love, compassion, and caring, called for faith and divine assistance, and time.

A young nun revealed to me that she related to God as friend to dear friend. When she read about the sufferings of people from famines, earthquakes, war and violence, she felt sorry for God and for human failure to respond to God's love by our love for one another. Her sorrow was so real that she had to find a quiet place to weep in silence for our insensitivity and lack of appreciation for God's gift of life, of people, of a beautiful universe. She was mindful of a Jewish story about the escape of the Israelites from the pursuing army of the Egyptians, and the joy of the angels when God's special people escaped. To their surprise, the angels saw a tear in the eye of God as he remarked, "The Egyptians who died are also my people." Another friend on a spiritual journey, not in the Catholic Church, feels the word "God" has been so abused and does not use it, instead addressing God in each prayer as, "Loving Friend."

More and more I have reflected on the words of Isaiah in Chapter 55: "God is generous and forgiving. For my thoughts are not your thoughts nor your ways my way." In a sense, these words seemed to put God outside the human realm. But then Isaiah also spoke of God having our names written, "on the palm of his hand." This was an effort by Isaiah to assure us of God's personal love for each person.

Sometime between the seventh and fifth century B.C., an anonymous Jewish writer wrote what has been called, "an exquisite dramatic poem which treats the problem of suffering of the innocent." The book is a masterpiece in trying to answer the question, "Does God care when we suffer?" In the book of Job, we find Job is a chieftain, wealthy and blessed with a wife and family. In a severe tornado, Job loses his wife and family and also his property. To add to his sorrows Job contracts a painful skin disease. He pleads with God to explain why his life has turned upside down with the loss of his family and possessions. God does not give an explanation but calls Job to trust in God's Power, which created the universe, and in God's Wisdom, that governs the universe. Job trusts God and again his health is restored, as are his fortune and happiness in a new family.

Leonard Bernstein pondered on the Book of Job as he experienced great personal loss and also great sadness at the tragic death of President Kennedy in 1963. He set his reflections on Job to music in the *Kaddish Symphony* which had its American debut in the Opera House in Seattle in the sixties. In the Book of Job, the author has Job in Chapter 30 speak against God saying, "I cry to you but you do not answer me, you stand off and look at me. Then you turn upon me without mercy and with your strong hand you buffet me...Yet should not a hand be held out to help a wretched man in his calamity?" These could be the words of Jewish people as they were persecuted across the centuries and especially the cry of the Jews in the concentration camps. They reflect the cries of Christians from the first martyr Stephen to the thousands like Archbishop Romero, the Maryknoll Sisters, and lay workers murdered in recent years in Central and South America because of their faith in Jesus Christ. In the musical, Bernstein has a woman reproach God in the spirit of Job. But the music and singing by the woman is harsh and strident as she questions God in anger: "And you let this happen, you with your manna and pillar of fire. You asked for faith. Where is your faith now? Shall I quote your own words, 'I set my bow in the clouds I will look upon it that I may remember my everlasting covenant.' Tin God, your bargain is tin. It crumbles in my hand. Where is your faith now — yours or mine?" Then the singer addresses God softly and gently. "Sleep my Father. Rest your anger. Dream softly. Let me invent your dream and dream it for you as gently as I can and perhaps by dreaming I can help you find your image again and love him (Job) again." In Seattle the wife of Bernstein, Felicia Monteleagre, gave a magnificent performance.

One evening before the symphony's Seattle performance, the panelists of the the interfaith television show "Challenge," that Rabbi Levine and I co-anchored for fourteen years (along with various Protestant ministers) were asked to discusse the theology of Bernstein in the *Kaddish Symphony.* Rabbi Levine stated that he found it hard to accept the harsh, angry tone of the singer lashing out at God. Dr. Lynn Corson, a Methodist pastor, agreed with Rabbi Levine. I did not find myself in agreement with them. For Job to question God as described was a daring approach for one who was taught as was Moses by God, to "take off your shoes," to empty your mind and heart in reverence and humility when you approached God. To me, the key words of Bernstein were those which referred to the weakness of God, to God needing us. For many years I would have agreed with my colleagues, Rabbi Levine and Dr. Lynn Corson, but a new and different insight had come to me about my relationship to God and the question, "Does God need us?"

This growth in understanding of God came to me from reflections on Genesis I 27: "God created man in his image, in the divine image he created him, male and female he created them and God blessed them." Gazing into the depth of the human heart, my own or others, can reveal selfishness, greed, a tendency to violence, but also a quality that can overshadow everything else in the human heart — the spirit of love, which comes from God present in us. Love is exemplified for me by Jesus willing to surrender everything, even life, under the most painful circumstances, out of his commitment and love and desire to bring about a better world that he called, "The Kingdom of God."

To me this flame of love in the human heart is a spark from the divine Fire of Love — from a God who chose to love us and to dwell in us. Love in my heart calls me to be "patient and kind, never haughty, selfish or rude." St. Paul tells me, "If I love someone I will be loyal to that person no matter what the costs. I will always believe in that person, expect the best of them and always stand my ground in defending that person." (1 Corinthians 13) To love another is to freely give that person a power to bring us great joy but a power also to break our hearts. God freely created us out of love and therefore accepts the pain and joy love gives. If the person I love has Job-like experiences of sadness because of death of loved ones, I grieve with that friend. Believing God loves me, I can also believe that when my life is not a sign of God's love for others, that God weeps. Now I weep for the times I did not accept my partnership with God to love people as God within me seeks to do. But I approach God unburdened by past failures or present weakness because I am conscious of God's power to heal my past, sustain me each day. In Chapter 4 of his letter to new converts in Philippi, Paul writes: "Rejoice in the Lord always. I say it again, Rejoice. Dismiss all anxiety from your mind...that God's own peace, which is beyond all understanding, will stand guard over your hearts and minds in Christ Jesus."

My tears and sorrow now more quickly turn to gratitude to God when I recall that unmarried woman in Luke, Chap. 8, who anointed Jesus, washing his feet with her tears, wiping them with her hair in appreciation of his acceptance of her in spite of the angry looks from others in the room where they met. To her, Jesus spoke the most consoling words he ever uttered, "therefore her sins — and they are many, are forgiven, for she loved me much, but one who is forgiven little shows little love."

Now when I awake in the morning, it is not to carry out a duty, but a call to a partnership to bring God's love to others. The day may bring a call from God to minister to a person about to leave this world, or one who has just entered it and is to be baptized. It may be a call to listen with the ear of God to a story of failure and self-rejection and to endeavor to bring to the speaker the assurance of God's love. Life is more joyful since I have become more conscious of my partnership with God. Time is running out for me in regard to earthly ministry, but I trust my Loving God to allow me to join my patron saint, St. Therese, by "spending my heaven doing good on earth," hoping that God in His Love and mercy will still have some need for me, something to accomplish that no one else can do.

Chapter 7

Duped

"You duped me, O Lord." These are words attributed to the prophet Jeremiah who lived about 700 years before the time of Jesus. He tells us how he received his vocation to be a spokesperson for God in Chapter One of the book we know as Jeremiah. We read, "The word of the Lord came to me thus, before I formed you in the womb I knew you, before you were born I dedicated you, a prophet to the nations I appointed you." Jeremiah protested to God, "I know not how to speak, I am too young." God said to Jeremiah, "Have no fear before them because I am with you to deliver you." (Chapter 4)

In Chapter Two, Jeremiah spoke out against the religious and political leaders of his time in famous words, "Two evils have my people done, they have forsaken me the source of living waters, they have dug themselves cisterns, broken cisterns that hold no water." No wonder he tells us in Chapter 20, "All the day I am object of laughter — everyone mocks me." He was tempted to cease his denunciations of the rich and powerful, "but, then it becomes a fire burning in my heart, imprisoned my bones. I grow weary holding it in; I cannot endure it."

In Chapter 26, Jeremiah is tried as "an enemy of the people" and condemned to death by religious leaders. In the end he was pardoned. But Jerusalem was captured by the Babylonians in 587 BC. Jeremiah lived for a time in the ruins of Jerusalem and according to some was murdered by his own people because of his outspoken criticism of the king and the religious leaders.

Though he lived almost 3,000 years ago, I can relate to the vocation of Jeremiah in my own life and in the life of my friends. When I had finally arrived in Seattle after an adventurous journey facing bombs in London, submarines in the Atlantic and a voyage on a troopship, I was exhausted. When the pastor of St. Alphonsus Parish in Ballard sent me to that basement room to count the Sunday collection on my second day, I felt lonely, tired, and frustrated. I would have handed in my resignation and returned to Ireland except for the hazards of the journey. Counting collections for three to four hours on a Sunday afternoon was not how I saw my vocation as a priest in Seattle. I felt "duped" like Jeremiah in his vocation.

After one year I was transferred to downtown Seattle to St. James Cathedral. Here I was a member of a team of six busy, young priests who ministered to five or six hospitals in the area, to the county jail, and to rest homes. We had many weddings and funerals. Yet, it was a time of camaraderie, a time of shared ministry, of unity and friendship.

Then after one year, the pastor, Monsignor John Gallagher, called me into his office and said there was an urgent need for a priest to help out in the chancery due to illness on the part of the chancellor. He added, "It will only be for a few weeks." It lasted fifteen years. A desk job was never part of my vision of my priestly vocation. Again, I felt "duped," but eventually after sixteen years, I was appointed pastor of St. Patrick's Parish, Seattle. Having served in four different parishes, I have felt this was my vocation and seldom again had the Jeremiah experience of feeling "duped."

During my first year at the Chancery a young woman, a recent graduate in journalism at Washington State University, came to me to discuss her religious vocation. We discussed different religious communities and she decided to be a missionary as a Maryknoll Sister. In her generous spirit, she accepted different assignments willingly. But fourteen years of teaching and being principal of a large high school in Hong Kong gave her the feeling at times of being "duped" especially when she was later assigned to the University of Washington to obtain a Masters in Communication and then was assigned for sixteen years to office work on the editorial staff of Maryknoll Magazine.

I suspect Peter was "duped" when he decided to leave his boat and fishing tackle in Capernaum and follow Jesus, a charismatic neighbor from Nazareth. The idea that this vocation would mean that his new leader and guide would be rejected by his fellow Jews and put to death was totally abhorrent to Peter.

In the sixteenth chapter of Matthew's Gospel, Jesus began to explain to Peter and his immediate followers, "that he must go to Jerusalem and suffer greatly from the elders, the chief priests, and the scribes, and be killed, and on the third day be raised." Peter felt "duped" by his decision to follow this Jesus saying, "God forbid Lord. No such thing shall ever happen to you." Jesus turned and said to Peter, "Get behind me, Satan. You are an obstacle to me. You are thinking not as God does, but as human beings do." Peter was to learn that following Jesus we are never "duped" no matter how painful the journey.

Perhaps what leads all of us to feel "duped" in regard to our vocation, whether in marriage, priesthood, or the single life, is when we are "thinking not as God does but as human beings do."

Fr. Stephen Rosetti, Ph.D., in his book, *When the Lion Roars* gives us practical advice for not feeling "duped" in our vocation. He writes:

> *"But, the key is, in whatever path one is called, to enter it with a full heart and to live as completely as one can for God. We cannot enter the mystical path thinking that it will be a hobby or something to do in our spare time. It must become a life changing and all-embracing totality. There will be trials and tests along the way. If we cling to anything except God, we will not finish the journey. 'No one who sets a hand to the plow and looks to what was left behind is fit for the kingdom of God' (Lk 9:62). Once again, it is important to note that this full conversion to God will take a lifetime. God calls very imperfect people to follow his intimate way."*

There is a spiritual practice that can foster and enhance one's total conversion and self-gift to God. The scriptures admonish us, "Let lay aside every encumbrance of sin which clings to us…let us keep our eyes fixed on Jesus." (Hebrews 12:1-2) Indeed, many great mystics have used this expression, "Fixing one's eyes on God" or, "Focusing one's eye on Christ." This is not simply a metaphor. It speaks of a deep truth in the mystical life. This was a grace Brother Lawrence of the Resurrection, another spiritual teacher, had himself received. He related, "What comforts me in the life is that I see God by faith in such a manner that I can sometimes say: 'I no longer believe, but I see.'"

The more one's inner spirit becomes attuned to and focuses on God, the more one "sees" God. The mystic learns, by grace, to see God constantly. This is a great source of joy and consolation. While this vision is, of course, not the consummation of the beatific vision that will only be possible in the next life, it is a real "but incomplete" vision of God. The inner spirit senses the presence of God and focuses one's spiritual eye on him.

Chapter 8

Get Rid of the Ego

Growing up in what I considered a picturesque part of Ireland, near the Slieve Bloom Mountains in the center of the country, I often spent hours contemplating the beauty of creation. The highest peak of the Slieve Bloom mountains is 2,000 feet. This makes it a dwarf compared to the Cascades. But I shall always remember the view the first time I climbed it. For miles, I could see farmlands, trees, homes, and rivers giving me a perspective I never had before. Something similar, a new perspective, has come to me from years of studying Paul with some help from Sufi Moslems.

Paul wrote a great deal about the flesh and the spirit. Everything I heard from teachers on Pauline theology referred to the "flesh" as "body" which, it seemed, Paul regarded as an enemy of the "spirit" or "soul." But when it was pointed out to me that Paul used the terms "flesh" and "spirit" due to some influence of Plato, then we must turn to find the biblical influence in Paul and to a deeper understanding of his use of these terms. For example, in Corinthians 6:20, Paul tells these first Christians, "Glorify God and bear God in your body." In the same letter, 7:36, he advises, "Be holy both in body and spirit," showing great respect for the body. Again Paul returned to the role of the body in his second letter to the Corinthian Christians. In Chapter 6, verse 16 he reminds them, "You are God's temple, the home of the living God." Paul saw a flaw in people and this was what he called "the flesh." It had nothing to do with the dignity of the body. Rather, flesh for Paul was the tendency toward selfishness or the cultivation of the ego. Psychologists call the ego a system of illusions and selfishness.

The opposite of the ego is a transformation in Christ. Paul described what this transformation calls for in Philippians 2:5. He writes, "Your attitude should be the kind that was shown us by Jesus Christ, who though he was God, did not demand and cling to his rights as God, but laid aside his mighty power taking the disguise of a slave."

This transformation takes years. St. Francis of Assisi began life looking forward to military adventure as the son of a wealthy merchant. Defeat, imprisonment, and illness changed his thinking, leading him to abandon his father's business and to live a life of poverty and service to others. One of his regrets as he died at the age of forty-four was his mistreatment of his body by undue penances, which he inflicted on himself.

Acquiring the mind of Christ is not something we can do for ourselves. It is a gift of the spirit. When Paul contrasts the "flesh" and the "spirit" he has in mind what we call the Holy Spirit, the presence of God. Theology of the third person of the Trinity was not developed at the time of Paul. In John 15:2, Jesus speaks of God as the "vinegrower." He lops off every branch that does not produce. And he prunes the branches that bear fruit for even larger crops." This pruning by God, the transforming of self-seeking to self-giving, takes many forms. Illness is one. St. Ignatius of Loyola experienced transformation in a hospital as he recovered from wounds in battle. St. Thomas More, Lord Chancellor of England, had to sacrifice reputation, family, and life for the sake of fidelity to the Spirit of God, which did not allow him to condone the adulterous conduct of Henry VIII, his boss.

St. Thomas More, the patron of the parish where I served for four years, is an example of what many in church and state must confront for one reason or another, due to others or to human weakness and malice. This might mean loss of reputation, loss of income, loss of office, sometimes rejection by family and friends, or at least misunderstanding. More's wife pleaded with him to obey the king and stay alive for his family. His daughter, Meg, was the only person who understood More's spiritual defiance of the king.

I was surprised to discover the teaching of Jesus reflected in Sufi spiritualism. Sufis are a devout branch of the Moslem faith. On two occasions I had the privilege of speaking at their international conventions. They have a high regard for the body, which is expressed in majestic dances. During the dances, hands are held with palms facing upward seeking God's Spirit. Later, the palms face down to remind the receivers to share with others the blessings received from God. They honor a former Sufi leader, Basmati, as a saint. He died in 874 AD. One of his religious transformations reminds me of that of Paul and the "pruning" described by Jesus. Basmati, who never wrote, said, "I have vanished (through ego annihilation). I glided out of my ego as a snake glides from a cast skin. And then I looked and what I saw was this; Lover and Beloved and Love are one." Elsewhere, he said in words reminiscent of those of Jesus, "I was the smith of my own self." He pruned himself — his ego, to grow in love.

The Sufis have a term for that pruning of self, under and by the hand of God, as "malamat." This means: blame, failure, discredit, disgrace and humiliation can lead to God. We Christians see that this was the road traveled by Jesus. It is difficult and most painful when we are asked by God to walk this road. One priest who had traveled this road of humiliation and failure in ministry told me he would have welcomed death instead. The greatest example of "malamat" in human history is that of Jesus in the Garden of Gethsemane. He was betrayed by a close friend. Religious leaders rejected him as a false prophet. He was aware of an approaching fate, familiar at the time when he would hang naked, nailed to a cross, humiliated and insulted, abandoned by those he called his friends, and called a blasphemer of the God he preached.

Yet, a Moslem story tells us that when people line up to enter heaven, the shortest line is the one under the sign that reads "Malamat." The person experiencing "malamat," even Jesus, needed friends in his loneliness, rejection, and sense of failure. To add to his "malamat," his friends slept after he asked them to stay awake with him.

Father Ronald Rolheiser, in a weekly column, outlined how to deal with "malamat," the "pruning" of the ego. He writes: "The discipline of the heart makes us stand in the presence of God with all we have and are; our fear and anxieties, our quiet and our shame, our sexual fantasies, our greed and anger, dreams and mental wanderings, and most of all our people, family, friends, and enemies — in short, all who make us who we are. We tend to present to God only those parts of ourselves with which we feel relatively comfortable and which we think will make a positive response. Thus our prayers become very selective, narrow, and unbalanced. And not just our prayer, but also our self knowledge, because by behaving as strangers before God, we become strangers to ourselves."

One of the greatest examples of a person who overcame ego and grew in love, who endured "malamat" in recent times, is Dr. Viktor Frankl, a Jewish psychiatrist in Vienna when the Nazis invaded Austria. He was contemplating coming to America but decided to remain with his wife and parents, and to face with them whatever ordeal lay ahead at the hands of the Nazis. He was arrested and sent to Auschwitz Concentration Camp.

His wife was in another concentration camp. He was not allowed to see her and at times was not sure if she was still alive. One icy morning while it was dark, he was stumbling to work with fellow prisoners driven by Nazi guards shouting and cursing at them. Suddenly his wife came to mind. Years later he wrote: "Real or not, her look was more luminous than the sun which was beginning to rise. A thought transfixed me: for the first time in my life I saw the truth as it is set into song by so many poets, proclaimed as the final wisdom of so many thinkers: that love is the ultimate and highest goal to which man can aspire. I grasped the meaning of the greatest secret that human poetry and human thought have to impart: the salvation of mankind is through love and in love."

St. Augustine echoes the message of Viktor Frankl when he preached, "The love with which God loves us is the same love with which we love one another." Paul in Romans, Chapter 8, is ecstatic about the love of Christ for us. He said, "I am convinced that nothing can separate us from his love. Death cannot. Life cannot. Our fears for today, our worries about tomorrow...nothing will be able to separate us from the love of God demonstrated by our Lord, Jesus Christ, who died for us."

An English priest and theologian, Father David O'Leary, gives us this reflection from many years as a pastor: "Older Catholics, especially, tend to haggle and bargain their prayers, penances, and good deeds so as to demand, deserve or barter for divine forgiveness, unconditional acceptance and ultimate salvation. It takes a special grace to undo the fear-filled damage to our bodies and souls arising from the instilled anxiety in childhood about judgment and punishment." I agree with Father O'Leary.

Chapter 9

My Two Mothers — Jewish and Irish

As a child in Ireland, my Irish mother, Mary Delaney Treacy, taught me to regard a Jewish mother, Mary, Mother of Jesus, to be my mother also. Some of the first words I learned to pronounce were, *"Holy Mary, Mother of God, pray for us sinners, now and at the hour of our death."* Every Sunday I attended Mass in the local church, which was dedicated to Mary. Over the altar there was a beautiful stained glass window of Mary, assumed body and soul into heaven. The Church was dedicated to Mary under the title of the "Assumption" when it was built in 1858. My maternal grandparents recited the rosary at 9:00 p.m. each evening. My mother kept up this tradition in our family.

Mary is honored especially in a small village, Knock, Co. Mayo, in West Ireland. Several people who survived the famine of 1847 witnessed the apparition of Mary in 1859. No words were spoken. But a powerful message was given to a dispirited and depressed people. It was a call to have faith in God who cared for them.

Another bonding with Mary took place through a classmate, William Meany. On one occasion, my father told me about the death of his father. My father was young at the time. He recalled the local pastor, a Father Meany, coming to the home and taking out his rosary beads and reciting the rosary. Years later, when I was on my way to the seminary, William Meany, a grand nephew of this Father Meany, was on the train with me. I recall saying to him with disappointment, "I forgot to bring my rosary beads!" He said, "I can help you because I have an extra one that belonged to my great uncle who was pastor in your home parish." I often wondered if this was the rosary that the parish priest, Father Patrick Meany, used as he prayed to Mary for my dying grandfather.

My attachment to Mary continued for the seven years in the major seminary. During those years my spiritual mentor was a Cistercian priest, Father Eugene Boylan, who lived in a monastery near my home. He was a brilliant scholar who was a pioneer in the study of nuclear science at the University of Vienna prior to World War II. Later he decided to be a priest. He was also a brilliant organist.

After ordination, I spent a few days with him before leaving for America. He asked me to promise him that I would be faithful to my daily rosary to Mary and that if the opportunity arose I would work with the Legion of Mary. This organization was founded in Dublin in 1921 by Frank Duff, an unmarried civil servant. Both men and women were members who pledged themselves to two hours of a particular ministry each week and to attend a weekly meeting.

Their first assignment was ministry to prostitutes in Dublin following the departure of British troops in 1921 after centuries of occupation. Individuals were contacted personally. Homes were found for some. Others were united with families, etc. All were treated with kindness and compassion.

Members also called on the sick, either in their homes or in hospitals. Though the seminary was only fifteen miles from Dublin, we were not introduced to the Legion of Mary. For seminarians, the policy about organizations was one of neutrality. As priests, we should examine organizations, evaluate them, and be guided by senior priests in whatever country we were called to served.

Consequently, I knew nothing about this great organization when I left Ireland. A year after arriving in Seattle, I was assigned to St James Cathedral, and among my assignments was that of chaplain, or spiritual director, of the Legion of Mary. It had been introduced to Seattle around 1936 by the then Bishop Gerald Shaughnessy. The ten members of the organization in the cathedral parish were excited to have a priest from Ireland to assist them, thinking that, coming from Ireland, I would be well versed in the organization. I was embarrassed to tell them I knew nothing about it. But remembering my promise to Father Boylan I decided to find out as much as I could about it.

In 1947, there was an international congress of members of the Legion of Mary in Ottawa, Canada. I attended and learned a great deal about its vision and the variety of ministries carried out by the members. Then in 1950, after an absence of almost six years, I returned to Ireland to visit my family. Once a month there was a meeting in Dublin with the founder, Frank Duff, and members from all over the world. I was amazed at the knowledge of Frank Duff about the Church in Seattle, in Africa, China, Europe, and the Philippines, as he received regular reports from these countries.

In 1934, a young Irish woman, Edel Quinn, who had contracted TB, volunteered to go to Africa to introduce the Legion of Mary. In spite of objections from many who were concerned about her health, Frank Duff approved her going to Africa. Devoted to Mary, the mother of Jesus, she crisscrossed central Africa for seven years, fostering the development of the Legion of Mary with its unique and special devotion to Mary. It had strong roots in Africa at the time she died in Nairobi, Kenya in 1944. A priest, a recent visitor to Seattle from Nairobi, told me the Legion of Mary is flourishing in Kenya today.

As the papal representative to Africa in the 1940's, Archbishop Anthony Riberi, watched with interest the development of this new organization rooted in Ireland. Prior to his assignment in Africa, he served as nuncio in Ireland during the early formation of the Legion of Mary. He was impressed by it then and more so as he observed it taking root in Africa and developing the faith of its members.

In 1946, Archbishop Riberi was sent to China as nuncio. One of his first decisions was to introduce Mary to China through the Legion of Mary. He selected an Irish missionary priest, Aidan McGrath of the Columban Missionaries, to head this work. He was to return to Ireland first to study the spirit and structure of the Legion of Mary and then would go and introduce it in China. Again it took root among Chinese Catholics, especially the youth. Father McGrath became a good friend of mine, sharing a special devotion to Mary. The very name of the organization "Legion of Mary" disturbed the Communists, who thought it was an underground military organization.

Realizing Father McGrath was responsible for its development in China, they arrested him and put him in a small cell in Ward Road Jail in Shanghai for 2 1/2 years before expelling him. Members in China were imprisoned and some executed simply for being active members of the Legion of Mary. With the expulsion of all priests and nuns in the early fifties, the next chapter of the Legion in China needs to be written.

In 1948, Archbishop Thomas Connolly appointed me Archdiocesan Director of the Legion of Mary, an assignment that lasted thirty years. This meant weekly meetings with parish organizations and monthly meetings with officers from Seattle and Tacoma. From Seattle it was introduced to the Yakima diocese and later to Anchorage, Alaska. On several occasions I visited Alaska to oversee its development. My right-hand helper was Joe Rindal who set aside his work on oil wells to attend Legion of Mary meetings.

Frank Duff was especially happy and interested in the Legion's growth in Alaska. He hoped that from Alaska we might quietly take the Legion into Mogadan, Russia during the Cold War. Though Frank died a few years ago, the Legion still counts on its dedicated ministers in Seattle and around the world. Rome is considering the canonization of Frank Duff and Edel Quinn.

My Seattle mentor, the late Father Joseph Fulton, encouraged me to honor Mary under the title of "Our Lady of Sion." He did this because of my weekly TV programs with Rabbi Levine, to foster better relations between Jews and Christians. Then Rabbi Levine and I founded Camp Brotherhood in 1966. It was to be a home for people of all faiths to ponder, pray, and discover what they had in common and to grow in respect for each other's convictions. Mary, mother of the human family, inspires me in this ministry of bringing people together.

It has been a long journey for a young Irish boy kneeling beside his Irish mother at the family rosary as we both requested the help of a Jewish mother. My Irish mother came to America in 1962, and watched me tape a TV program with Rabbi Levine who also joined us for lunch. It was a highlight of her life to see her son, a priest, become close friends with a rabbi. My beloved Irish mother died in 1966. My beloved Jewish mother has become dearer to me over the years.

I can say of Mary what St. Bernard said one thousand years ago: "Never was it known that any one who fled to her protection or sought her help was left unaided."

Chapter 10

Muslims, Jews, and Christians on a Common Journey

On September 28, 2005, Fr. Thomas Michel, S.J., director of the Jesuit Secretariat for Interreligious Dialogue, spoke at the Gregorian University in Rome at a conference marking the fortieth anniversary of "Nostra Aetate," the Second Vatican Council's document on interreligious dialogue. He is quoted in press releases as follows: "All religious believers try to answer the question, 'Does God have something to say to us?' "Muslims," he said, "believe the answer is found in the Quran, while Catholics believe the answer is found in Church. In dialogue all can find better ways to fulfill their religious quest."

Mona Siddiqui, a Muslim and head of the department of theology and religious studies at the University of Glasgow, Scotland, said the danger of believers focusing on who will or will not be saved "is that this will always lead to conditional and qualified acceptance of each other."

Christians and Muslims "claim to be the final repositories of the full truth, recognizing only partial truth in the other," she said. But dialogue is not about trying to convert the other or convince the other of the errors of their ways, Siddiqui said. "Dialogue is not about selling our respective theologies; it is about exploring our respective theologies through a common journey," she said. "Dialogue has been a process of learning and accepting, of questioning and appreciating, of self-doubt and humility," she said. "Most importantly, it has been to understand that talking about a common humanity demands much generosity in the face of practical differences." She said interreligious dialogue has helped her to see that "God is most present in us when we have the courage to open ourselves to each other in (the) search for Him."

Bishop Tod D. Brown of Orange, California, chairman of the U.S. Bishops' subcommittee on Interreligious Dialogue, said, "By means of the dialogue with religions, I have come to a better understanding and appreciation of my own religious faith and deepened my realization that

God in the Holy Spirit is at work leading these other people — along various paths — closer to God."

The following are some personal memories of my experience in about 60 years of interreligious dialoque.

1960

Beginning in the Fall of 1960 the Interfaith Program "Challenge" was aired for a half hour on Sunday evenings with the support of the station manager of KOMO, William Warren. Rabbi Levine and I were anchors for fourteen years with various Protestant ministers. The fourth Protestant panelist on the "Challenge" program was Dr. Robert Fine, Pastor of the Free Methodist Church attached to Seattle Pacific University. He served from 1972-1974. In 1973 his thirteen-year old daughter, Dolly, died suddenly from a brain aneurysm. He was heartbroken. Our producer, Marty Wilson, impressed by the faith of Dr. Fine in the midst of his sorrow, asked him if he would discuss on TV how he tried to cope with his sorrow. He willingly agreed and gave us a title for the program: "Stand up and drink to God." It was taken from the writings of a Catholic scholar in England, Gilbert Keith Chesterton. He had experienced great sorrow but it did not destroy his faith in God. At a meeting with friends, Chesterton showed his faith in God in spite of his sorrow by saying, "Let us stand up and drink to God." It was one of the most moving programs we ever did in my fourteen years on TV. Jesus said, "Let your light shine before others." Faith in a loving God in spite of darkness and sorrow shone from the heart of Dr. Fine as he recalled the passing of his beloved Dolly. Rabbi Levine and I attended her funeral service. The next year, due to complications from diabetes, he died. I visited him in the hospital where we recalled our TV days and a visit we made together with KOMO to Israel, where he, Rabbi Levine and I did two TV programs. After praying with him in his hospital room he turned to me and said, "Our bonding in faith is a great blessing to me and now our prayer together is a great consolation." He died a few days later. In the eighties, I was pastor in Stanwood, Washington, and found that his parents were nearby at Warm Beach Camp. I visited them regularly in appreciation of the friendship I had with their son.

Rabbi Levine was my mentor and guide during the twenty-five years of our friendship. On one occasion we visited New York together. He had some correspondence with the famed anthropologist, Margaret Meade. She invited us to her New York apartment and listened with great interest as Rabbi Levine explained our interfaith ministry and the founding of Camp Brotherhood where people of all faiths could feel at home. As we were leaving, she hugged me and the Rabbi and thanked us for our efforts to promote "true anthropology — unity among all people." She impressed me as a very kind, compassionate person.

JANUARY 1965

For months I had worked with representatives of the Council of Churches of Greater Seattle in planning for a city-wide Prayer Service for Christian Unity at the Opera House, Seattle, to be held during the week of prayer for Christian unity. To the great joy of all of us who planned for it, five thousand people attended this first all-city prayer service.

A straw can show how the wind is blowing, and I recall one small detail that hopefully spoke to many. We had agreed that my co-chairman, Pastor Oscar Rolander, Lutheran, would read the first scripture passage and I would follow. Before the service began he asked me if I would bring a "Catholic" Bible. I said to him, "When you finish reading from your Bible, please walk across the stage to me and hand me your Bible." For four centuries, Catholics and Protestants had been quoting scripture against each other. By the gesture of reading together from the same Bible, I intended to show we both accepted the Bible as God's Word calling us to unity, and not as a book to provide ammunition to attack each other, or as a book over which we fought concerning translations, phrases and words.

1966

In February, 1966, Rabbi Levine invited me to speak at a Temple Service in Temple De Hirsch Sinai, Seattle. This is how he subsequently described the event: "It was our regular Sabbath service which was not altered one iota from our normal Sabbath worship except that Father Treacy's sermon came at the end instead of in the middle of the service as was my normal practice. The large sanctuary was almost full with nearly 900 worshipers of all faiths. Father spoke about some of the far-reaching implications for ecumenism of Vatican Council II and that as a Christian he believed in the incarnation of God in Jesus who in a personal way manifested God's love and concern for human beings. For this reason, he said, he believed that it was in the person-to-person contact that we must come to know each other and love each other. After the service many worshipers, both Christians and Jews, told me they never had felt the presence of God so overwhelmingly as in the spirit of true brotherhood which radiated throughout the service that night. Mrs. Isaac Brown, who was niney-two and has since passed away, a founding member of our congregation, told Father Treacy with tears of joy that she thanked God she was privileged to live to see this day."

1972

In February, 1972, I walked with Rabbi Levine in the footsteps of Jesus on his way to Calvary, which is called the Via Dolorosa. Rabbi described his feelings that day: "As I was thinking of this man Jesus walking up these steps to his death at the hands of Roman executioners, I thought also of how every prophet — both among the ancient Hebrews and among all peoples even to our own day — was misunderstood and rejected by the people of his day. Throughout history this has always been so with far-visioned trailblazers in the spiritual life of mankind who have been done to death by those who could not understand the insights which made these martyrs for God the kind of men and women they were.

On that day I saw a baptism of love — a washing away of some of the terrible sins of anti-Semitism and religious bigotry through the centuries and a pledge of a new and better life when members of the human family can stand together in love with arms out-stretched to embrace one another and bridge the gaps between them."

On one occasion I attended a lecture in Seattle by a Jewish scholar, Itzhak Itzhaki. Elie Wiesel, in a letter I read, called Itzhaki one of the greatest historians in his time in Judaism. Born in Jerusalem in 1922, Itzhak fought in the Jewish War of Independence and later became

Director of Education for the Israeli Army. Many Jews came to Israel from countries with little knowledge of Jewish history. Itzhak designed programs of continuing education for them. Charlotte Spitzer, a travel agent and a Jewish member of Temple De Hirsch Sinai, had arranged a visit to Jerusalem for the "Challenge" panelists and was well-known to me. She introduced me to Itzhak and we became friends.

1978

I took several groups to Israel and Itzhak joined me as a guide and shared his remarkable knowledge of Jewish history with us. He and his wife had three boys. The oldest was killed when Egyptians, in 1973, attacked Israel. In September, 1978, I was visiting Itzhak and his wife. They invited me to join them in a small cemetery in Ramle near Tel Aviv for a memorial service for their son who was buried there. About a dozen other parents attended the service led by a Jewish military chaplain. Itzhak was on my right and his wife on my left. In the middle of the service she began to sob and weep for her firstborn child. She put her arms around me and rested her head on my shoulder. Tears came to my eyes. Whatever our faith differences, I experienced God's presence in that cemetery. Here was an Irish priest weeping with a Jewish mother, their arms around each other. This was interfaith sharing at the deepest level.

NOVEMBER 1978

A major ecumenical event took place in Seattle in 1978. A group of businessmen had been seeking suitable property for a downtown chapel for prayer and Mass. Realizing opportunity had passed them because of property cost, they approached Rev. David Colwell, Pastor of Plymouth Church at Sixth and University in Seattle, for permission to use their chapel for weekday Mass. He agreed, and Archbishop Hunthausen agreed. Fr. Michael Ryan, the busy pastor of St. James Cathedral, tried to help when his schedule permitted. At the time, I was pastor of St. Michael's Parish, Olympia. The idea of having daily Mass on weedkays in a Protestant church appealed to me. I consulted Archbishop Hunthausen and he approved of my assignment to this ministry. When

I consulted Pastor Colwell, I found a man with a strong commitment to interfaith cooperation. He said to me, "People come in to talk over their problems. You can have an office next to mine and consider yourself a staff person!" I accepted the office but not the staff position! I spent a year celebrating Mass each day, Monday through Friday, and then turned it over to the dedicated people who attended as I went back to an assignment as pastor. Since then, volunteer priests come to offer mass daily on weekdays at 12:10 and the attendance is at least thirty each day and sometimes double that amount. Visitors to Seattle are surprised when they see the Reader Board prominently on Sixth Avenue announcing, "Catholic Mass, Monday thru Friday at 12:10."

1982

Another interfaith event that touched my heart and left an indelible memory took place when the forty-five-year old daughter of Rabbi Levine died — the mother of three children. Her family requested me to take part in the service with her father. He asked me to drive him to the memorial service. On the way he was feeling sad and told me he might not be able to conduct the service. But when he began to speak, the fire of love energized him and he spoke with great faith and wisdom. My contribution was brief, and following the service the Rabbi requested me to drive him home. He was silent and I did not try to make conversation. I did reflect that if the Inquisition leaders of the Middle Ages heard it that a priest took part in a Jewish memorial service, I would be considered a renegade and subject to severe punishment. But I saw no denial of my Christian faith in what I did. Then, as if on a screen, I saw these words written by a Jewish man to Christians in Galatia in Turkey: "Bear one anther's burdens and so you fulfill the law of Christ." St. Paul, Gals. 6:2. In helping to show compassion to a Jewish father grieving for his daughter, I felt close to Jesus, who met a funeral procession of the only son of a widow and was moved with compassion. The story is in the 7th chapter of St. Luke.

I am very aware of the presence of the Holy Spirit in reaching out to others of different faiths, remembering the words of Malachi, written around 445 B.C., which Rabbi Levine frequently quoted. The prophet said in Chapter 2, verse 10, "Have we not all one Father? Has not the one God created us? Why then do we break faith with each other violating the covenant of our fathers?" This to me is a call to work for interfaith harmony and understanding.

Chapter 11

Rocks, Slides on the Road

Fifteen years as Assistant Chancellor of the Seattle Archdiocese were difficult years. Responsibility was limited. Archbishop Thomas Connolly, a good, able administrator, kept the reins in his own hands. During these years, priests had to obtain permission of the archbishop for the marriage of a Catholic and a non-Catholic. Pre-nuptial affidavits, proof of baptism and proof of freedom to marry had to be mailed to the chancery. We averaged about six requests each day. It was my assignment to check each request and prepare a document giving approval to be signed by the archbishop. In the case of a person previously married, a more thorough investigation had to be made. For validity, a Catholic should be married in the presence of a priest and two witnesses. Today a deacon can also serve as a church official. With proof of baptism, a civil record of marriage, and a divorce certificate, a Catholic could obtain a decree of nullity. Such marriages were regarded as invalid for what was called "lack of form." For example, making a will needed two witnesses for validity. Marriages in the Church called for an official witness. Suppose the person who made the will in the presence of two witnesses was of doubtful mental capacity; a difficult legal case to determine mental competence might result. Church courts now deal with many cases where one claims the partner suffered psychological and emotional weakness making them unfit to carry out a lifelong commitment which leads to a difficult legal case. Each year, I helped to process about 150 cases of defect of form for Catholics seeking to remarry.

When I left the Chancery in 1963, Archbishop Connolly wrote me a very comforting letter thanking me for the hundreds and hundreds of people I had helped with their marriage problems during the years at the chancery. To be honest, I found the work discouraging, dealing mostly with divorce. To counteract my negative feelings, I began a preparation program for couples contemplating marriage in the hope it would help them to avoid divorce. I assembled a team of Dr. Ray Clark, a Seattle obstetrician; Dr. James Riley, a Seattle psychologist; Luvern Rieke, Professor of Family Law at the University of Washington; a fellow priest and Franciscan, Fr. Barry Brunsman; and some three couples selected by Fr. Barry. We held these programs twice a year — spring and fall. Sometimes we had as many as ninety couples and never less than fifty. I still remember the shock I experienced when Fr. Barry introduced one member of the team, a young woman. She began by saying, "I am a mother of three, a single mother, in a situation where I hope none of you will ever be — divorced." Her message about what led to her divorce had a powerful impact on the young couples.

While at the chancery, I celebrated Mass on Sundays at Holy Names Academy at 7:00 a.m. Later, at 9:00 a.m., I celebrated a children's Mass in the "old" St. Anne's Church basement. For a while I wondered why couples would be waiting for me outside church to discuss marriage problems. One couple in their late seventies I shall never forget. He was a non-Catholic, married twice and divorced, and now wished to marry a woman somewhat younger than he from Australia. He would say to me, "Fr. Thomas Quain said we could get married if you say so." Later I found out that because I worked in the chancery, Fr. Thomas Quain, the pastor of St. Anne's, referred divorced couples to me for assistance. In the case of this gentleman who wished to marry the Australian, we needed a death certificate for his former wife. All efforts to obtain it failed. As his intended bride (not willing to be married just civilly) was about to return to Australia, we found the needed document and I officiated at their wedding. They had many happy years together. Because I held out for the necessary legal papers, he would jokingly say to me, "You were a hard man on me." But we remained good friends until his death, and then his widow returned to Australia.

For the past ten years, I have, with the help of two other couples, assisted married teams who conduct weekends for engaged couples at Camp Brotherhood. These begin on Friday night and end with Mass at 2:00 p.m. on Sunday. There is almost a sullen attitude when the couples arrive on a Friday evening. They feel this is an extra hoop they have to face because of Church law. By Saturday they begin to relax, and following mass on Sunday, they leave much, much happier than when they arrived. We host four to six weekends a year at Camp Brotherhood. Others are held at Palisades Retreat House in Federal Way. I estimate that in the past ten years I have spoken to two thousand couples, prayed with them, laughed with them, shared hopes and joys with them.

My heart always desired a personal ministry with people. In the chancery I did have a ministry for people, but it was from behind a desk and consisted of paperwork. On a day I was feeling far from enthusiastic about this ministry, a white haired gentleman came into my office. Without giving his name, he stated he had defrauded an insurance company in Seattle years ago. Now before he died he wished to make restitution. He gave me the name of the company, and then he counted out ten one thousand dollar bills. "See that the company I told you about gets this money." Then he walked out.

I seldom entered the office of Archbishop Connolly without an appointment. Carrying the ten thousand dollars, knowing he was alone, I knocked and entered. Placing one of the thousand dollar bills on his desk I said, "Archbishop, I wish to purchase my freedom from here." He looked at the money and looked at me in amazement. "If it costs more, here is another thousand," I added, as I placed a second thousand dollar bill on his desk. By this time he was smiling and said to me, "The only way you will get out of here is in a box!"

Archbishop Connolly's confidence in allowing me to be part of his staff for fifteen years is something for which I am most grateful. Some called him a "brick & mortar" bishop, since he supervised the building of many schools and parish churches and St. Thomas Seminary. But behind a somewhat stern exterior there was a humble, caring priest. On one occasion I caught a glimpse of his soul. A priest died who had some personal problems. Before arranging a date for the priest's funeral, I consulted the archbishop so as to fit it into his schedule. In the meantime, the archbishop, who at that time was fairly new to the archdiocese, looked at the history of the newly deceased priest. He turned to me and with great sincerity and humility gave me a glimpse of his soul by saying, "Bill, there but for the grace of God am I." Blessed be his memory.

Chapter 12

It Is Not the Luck of the Irish; It's God's Will

Much of the theology I received in childhood gave the impression we had to "earn " God's love. The Bible was regarded as a book with rules and moral guidance. It was not sufficiently emphasized that grace is a gift. It cannot be earned; love is not deserved, especially God's love.

I was ordained for several years before I heard of Julian of Norwich and her spirituality. Julian of Norwich, a 13th century mystic in England, had a vision of God one night that left her with a great feeling of optimism about the universe. She lived at the time of the Black Death when millions died in Europe. She asked God why this happened. She was told, "Wait, I will make all things new."

The Nazi concentration camps reveal the darkness and evil in human nature. But, they also reveal the strengthening of the human spirit. I have met several survivors who endeavored to make all things new. Dr. Elizabeth Kubler-Ross visited Dachau concentration camp as a young teenager after the war and was sickened by what she saw. She came out of Dachau and sat down in the sunshine, crying. A young woman sat beside her and began a conversation with Elizabeth. This young woman spoke gently saying, "Look at the chimney of the camp. May parents were part of the smoke in that chimney. I survived and promised myself to tell the world about the Nazi monsters. Then one day I realized I was planting seeds of resentment and hatred. In Berlin I discovered many innocent people, including children, who were severely injured by Allied bombings. Now I dedicate my life to nursing them." I heard this story in a conversation with Dr. Ross when she appeared with me on the TV program, "Challenge." We learn from the prayer of St. Francis of Assisi that our goal should be "Where there is hatred, let me sow love. Where there is injury, pardon. Where there is doubt, faith. Where there is despair, hope. Where there is darkness, light, and where there is sadness, joy." This is God's call to make all things new. We find

God through the lives of those who love others — such as the survivor of Dachau nursing wounded Germans.

A look at early religious education may indicate how we are influenced even about God through defective theology or bad art. I recall in grade school an illustrated Bible of a white haired father holding a knife to kill his son at the order of God. A face of another elderly man is in the background of the picture — God. At the last moment God cancels the order to Abraham. The father with the knife spares the son. This picture made me fearful of God. Later, in Medieval art, I came across hell visualized with devils poking unfortunate victims in fire, condemned there forever by God because of one mortal sin. I grew more afraid of this God, and fearful of being guilty of mortal sin by wrong doings and going to hell forever.

The story of Adam and Eve in Genesis indicated what could happen for disobeying God. Many saw their act of disobedience as a sexual sin, but there is no proof of this. We read in Genesis 3:8: "When they heard the sound of the Lord God moving about in the garden at the breezy time of the day, the man and his wife hid themselves from the Lord God among the trees of the garden. The Lord God then called to the man and asked him, 'Where are you?' He answered, 'I heard you in the garden; but I was afraid, because I was naked, so I hid myself.' Then he asked, 'Who told you that you were naked?'" This does not appear to be a judgment by God. In fact, in verse 21, we find an indication of God's compassion for the wrongdoers: "For the man and his wife the Lord God made leather garments, with which he clothed them." This is the first biblical insight into God's relationship with humanity. It is a sign of compassion and tenderness and seldom interpreted in this way. Chapter 3 of Genesis concludes with God banishing Adam (as well as Eve) forever from the Garden of Eden. My early religious training informed me that this expulsion meant heaven was closed to Adam and Eve and their descendents until Jesus suffered a most painful death and died for us and God changed his mind. Nobody explained to me that love is unconditional, and that God never ceases to love us. In fact, psychologists tell us God cannot forgive because God never condemns.

Jesus told one of his greatest stories to confirm this theology about God's compassion for us in Luke 15. A young man, presumably Jewish, leaves his home and religious training to live what we may call an irreligious life. Hungry, homeless, he decides to go back, planning to be a hired servant for his father. There was no condemnation, but, "the father was filled with loving pity and ran and embraced his son" as soon as he saw him.

This message about God's love was not as emphasized (even in the sermons I heard as an adult) as was the judgment of God. Many people ask, "Will wrongdoers go to hell?" For the answer in the spirit of Luke 15, I turn to mothers. I have met mothers whose children strayed from the faith and ideals they were taught by their mothers. To my question, "Is there anything your children could do that would make you reject them forever?" The answer invariably was, "No, nothing." We are then left with another question. Is the love of a mother greater than God's love? Isn't God the source of the mother's love and of all love?

Today, a new fear of God, the Judge, is fostered by those who are preoccupied with the end of the world and what they call the "Rapture." Then the "just" will be taken to heaven at once and the rest of the human race consigned to live in fear of a terrible end to come. This teaching crowds out the love of God.

The concept of the Bible as a book about laws and rules to be carried out to please God and avoid hell is contrary to its fundamental message about God's grace and love. Love is not merited. God loves us unconditionally. Shakespeare gives us an insight into our relationship with God when we disobey. He said, "Proud man dressed in a little brief authority plays such fantastic tricks before high heaven as makes the angels weep." I have witnessed many parents weeping over the wrongdoing of their children, but still their love for the errant one remained firm. This helps me to see God weeping at our sins because God knows that deep down we are not happy when we act like the younger son who left home, and in a sense left God, and ended up sad, lonely, heartbroken over his foolish decision.

Flashes of human love and forgiveness can give us an insight into God's love. Here is an example from a letter of an Irish priest involved in Christian-Moslem ministry in the Philippines:

"For me, this missionary call has brought me to live among people with a language, faith and way of life so different from my native Ireland. I find the sheer dedication and commitment shown by many of my friends during the Ramadan fast awe-inspiring.

I am reminded of the all-embracing presence of God during the morning Call to Prayer, followed by the sound of running water as the faithful wash their hands, feet and faces in preparation for dawn prayers at the mosque.

God's spirit blows wherever God wills and to hearts open to receive it; God's grace is abundant. A friend of mine, Sultan Maguid, recently shared that his nephew was brutally killed about ten years ago by a member of a rival political family. The cultural expectation was for Maguid's family to take revenge on the killer's family. He prayed long and hard about this and reflected deeply on the words of the Holy Qur'an.

"It may well be that God will restore the love between you and those of them who are now your enemies. God is All-Powerful. God is Ever-Forgiving, Most Merciful." (Surat al-Mumtabana: 7).

These words inspired him to pray for the grace to forgive his nephew's murderer. Two years later, Anwar, the brother of this murdered nephew, partook in the Holy Hajj *(pilgrimage) to Mecca.*

Amidst the millions of pilgrims from all over the world, the most unexpected thing happened. As Anwar approached the Kab'ah *(sacred black stone), the focal point of the* Hajj, *he was drawn to stand next to a man whose face seemed familiar to him, but whom he didn't recognize.*

Only when they looked each other in the eye did Anwar realize that the man was his brother's murderer. Maguid said a force like a magnet drew the two men to embrace each other and offer each other the kiss of peace.

For Maguid, this magnetic force was surely the grace of God calling both families to forgiveness and a change of heart. Maguid told me with a calm conviction, "Paul, I can now forgive the man who killed my nephew."

I am forever grateful to God for inviting me to be a missionary and giving me the privilege to experience His spirit at work among so many diverse peoples and places in ways I never dreamt possible."
(Fr. Paul Glynn — *Columban Mission Magazine)*

Because we overlooked God's Unconditional Love for all, I had two of the saddest experiences of my life in my early years as a priest. First, I had to go to Calvary Cemetery, Seattle, for the burial of an infant who died without baptism and who was regarded as not going to heaven. There was a certain corner of the cemetery reserved for such burials. Today I wish I could meet that grieving mother and assure her that even without baptism, God loved her baby. It is contrary to all our basic ideas of justice to believe — as was then the belief — that sins may have been committed before we were born, the nature of which we could not even grasp and which separated us from God.

My second experience of the lack of God's compassion in ministry I had to follow was withholding Christian burial to someone who committed suicide, or who died not married according to the laws of the church. On Easter Sunday evening, Jesus appeared to the frightened apostles who were behind "closed doors." Whatever the reasons why a person closes the doors on loved ones in fear and commits suicide, Jesus can enter those closed doors as he did on Easter Sunday evening.

A devotion common in Ireland when I was growing up, as in different countries, was known as "Nine First Fridays." If you assisted at Mass and received Communion on nine First Fridays you were told you could be sure of heaven. But an underlying principle of this devotion was the idea we could manipulate God into accepting us when God's love needs no persuasion. If we love God, we will respond by loving others.

A priest who inspired me by his ministry was the late Fr. William Dooley, O.P., who served as chaplain to students at the Newman Center for the University of Washington. One summer he was assisting in a parish near the docks in San Francisco. He received a sick call to a retired Irish Catholic seaman who had given up the practice of his faith. Fr. Dooley administered the sacraments of Reconciliation, Eucharist, and Anointing. At the door as he was leaving, the recently returned Catholic said to Fr. Dooley, "Father, do you really think God can forgive all my sins during my sailing years so easily?" Fr. Dooley replied, "Pat, you were forgiven. But I am bothered about the whopper you just committed." "What was that, Father?" he asked in amazement. Fr. Dooley replied, "Pat, when you went to Mass as a young man you heard the priest say three times at Mass, 'Lamb of God who takes away the sins of the world, have mercy on us.'" Pat remembered. Then Fr. Dooley added, "Pat, Jesus can take away the sins of everyone in the world by love. You committed some shenanigans as a sailor for a few years and you think they were so great that God cannot forgive you? Pat, that is a terrible sin of pride!" Pat thought for a moment then his face lit up and he said, "Father I understand. I have the luck of the Irish." Fr. Dooley said, "Pat, it is not the luck of the Irish, but God loves you unconditionally."

Much misunderstanding of a biblical text obscures our understanding of God. In Matthew 5:48, Jesus said, "In a word, you must be made perfect as your heavenly Father is perfect." Spiritual writers looked on this perfection like acquiring mathematical perfection, or the perfection of a good golf game. We were encouraged to examine ourselves thoroughly to see if we were making progress in the spiritual journey. Jesus spoke these words after giving us the greatest challenge in his teaching. In 5:44, Jesus said, "LOVE YOUR ENEMIES." While setting us an example of forgiveness on the cross, Jesus knew His followers would find this a difficult ideal that could only be accomplished with God's help. Actually, it is not when we think we are growing in perfection that we draw closer to God. This happens mostly in our failures. St. Augustine said, "My greatest wound is my greatest jewel." The call of Jesus to be perfect is a call to be conscious of God, the Perfect one, present in us. But the ideal is forgiveness.

Jesus left us a sign of how to find God. On the walls of the catacombs in Rome, on tombs of Christians in the first centuries, this sign was prominently displayed. It was the sign of Jonah and the whale. In Matthew 12:40 Jesus said, "Only an evil faithless generation would ask for further proof (in reply to those who asked Jesus for a miracle) and none will be given except what happened to Jonah, the prophet." Jonah wanted to follow his own agenda and tried to avoid God's will. Finally, he found himself in the belly of the whale and he was helpless, no longer in control of his life. God was patient with this reluctant prophet in spite of his imperfect record of obedience to God, and reached out to help him in various ways to grow in knowledge of God's love for Jews and non-Jews.

The pursuit of perfection can be a pursuit of our agenda, allowing us to be always in charge. One of the greatest spiritual books is *Abandonment to Divine Providence* by Jean DeCaussade. He warned against the "dreadful idea of perfection." More often our drawing close to God is from failures, our reluctance to follow what we believe is God's will. St. Francis prayed for humiliations. These were his stepping-stones to God.

St. Paul, in II Corinthians 11:30 wrote, "If I must boast, I will make a point of my weaknesses." Chapter 12, "Each time Jesus said to me, 'I am with you. That is all you need' my power shows best in weak people. Now I am glad to boast how weak I am. I am glad to be a living demonstration of God's power instead of showing off my own power, for when I am weak then I am strong, the less I have the more I depend on him."

Paul began life as a very zealous Jew persecuting the followers of Jesus. He discovered by a miraculous meeting Jesus how wrong he was, and like Jesus, he grew in wisdom, age and grace, by realizing God, through Jesus, is the giver of all good gifts we may have. Because of growth in love, the mature Paul wrote: "Love is very patient and kind, never jealous or envious, never boastful or proud, never haughty or selfish or rude. Love does not demand its own way. It is not irritable or touchy. It does not hold grudges, will hardly ever notice when others do it wrong. It is never glad about injustice but rejoices when truth wins out." What wonderful marriages would follow, the living of this ideal. What great neighbors. And war would be no more, if we kept our eyes on the peak, on God.

Chapter 13

"Your TV Partners Are Such Nice Gentlemen"

Ordained in 1944 to be a priest to serve in my native Ireland, I never heard at that time the word "ecumenism" and certainly nothing about inter-religious dialogue. Following the division in the Church at the time of Martin Luther, we Catholics (to use a Western term) "circled the wagons" and dialogue with other Christians was not entertained. Catholics were not to take part in YMCA activities. Marriage between Catholics and non-Catholics was discouraged. When they did take place, they were not held in the Catholic Church, but in church offices, without music, flowers, etc.

I spent fifteen years in Seattle where there were thousands of Jews. Yet, I never spoke to a Jewish person until Archbishop Thomas Connolly directed me to go to Temple De Hirsch Sinai in 1960 to discuss a proposed inter-faith program for TV with Rabbi Levine. We went on the air in late September 1960 with a Protestant panelist, Rev. Martin Goslin, Pastor of Plymouth Congregational Church, Seattle. Our first program discussed "Religious Freedom." At that time I was unaware of the importance of dialogue between Christians and other religions.

This form of face-to-face dialogue was a difficult challenge for a Catholic priest in 1960.

The Catholic attitude toward the Jewish people had been downright negative and hostile for centuries. Catholics and Protestants fought a bitter war between 1618-1648, ending with a negative solution. It was summed up in the principle *"Cuius regio eius religio."* The ruler of a country determined the religion of his subjects. Raised in Ireland, my people experienced horrendous sufferings from a Protestant government in England. Looking back I can see how ill-prepared I was for religious dialogue, but welcomed the opportunity when it came.

My fellow panelists, both about twenty years my senior, were extremely kind and understanding. No attempt was made to probe the weakness in the faith of the other, but every effort was made to discover what we had in common. Two years after we were on the air, the Knights of Columbus flew my mother to Seattle and later she was honored as "World's Fair Mother." KOMO TV invited her to the studio to watch the taping of two programs. Later, they hosted a lunch for me with her and my colleagues. That evening she indicated that she had the ecumenical spirit when she said, "Your TV partners are such nice gentlemen." While I never heard her say anything negative about Jews or Protestants, she did have some reservations when I told her in 1960 that I was gong to be on TV with a rabbi and a Protestant minister. She wrote to me and said, "About the TV program. I suppose if the archbishop approves, it must be all right!"

Rev. Goslin was a great mentor for me in regard to Protestants. He was succeeded by Dr. Lynn Corson, a Methodist, who spent six years with the program. We became good friends and participated in a People to People tour to Russia and Israel. He and I were roommates. Before turning off our lights at night, I read a chapter of St. John's gospel to him and he read from the writings of John Wesley, founder of the Methodist Church.

Rabbi Levine, raised in Czarist Russia until he was seven and then educated in this country, was interested in inter-faith relations all his life. Following ordination as a rabbi in 1932, he spent ten years in England and carried on a dialogue with several Protestant ministers. Gradually I realized that Jews did not need Christianity for their identity but Christians were rooted in Judaism. He helped me to better understand my Christian faith and inspired me to follow in his footsteps in fostering interfaith relations.

Encouraged by the Rabbi, I pursued my study of inter-faith dialogue. I found leadership in this field in a French priest and geologist, Teilhard de Chardin, who died in 1955. I adopted as my motto his words: "The cry I hear, O Lord, in all of creation is *Make us one!*" He saw our unity in the human family and the need for us to realize our unity and dependence on each other, and on the earth, its soil and water.

Teilhard de Chardin was born in France in 1881, ordained a priest in 1911, and served as a chaplain in the French army, (1914-1918), staying with troops during the major battles of that war. At the Sorboune in Paris in 1922, he obtained a doctorate in geology. In 1931 he took part in a scientific expedition through the Gobi Desert in China sponsored by the Citroen Automobile Company, to test a car in heat and cold. During the expedition he stayed in all Moslem villages and came to understand their piety. He is one of my heroes.

At the Vatican Council (1962-1963), Pope Paul VI said, "Promoting the restoration of unity among all Christians is one of the chief concerns of the Second Sacred Ecumenical Council." In January 1965, I was the Catholic representative coordinating the first Ecumenical Prayer Meeting in Seattle. The Seattle Council of Churches also co-sponsored it. Reverend William Baum, who later became Cardinal, was the speaker. He was in charge of Ecumenical Programs for the U. S. Bishops. Five thousand people attended. Another program was held in January 1966 at the Opera House, and Professor Brown of Stanford University was the speaker. Afterward, it was decided to have regional meetings in Seattle.

The Vatican Council, on October 28, 1965, issued the following statements, which are revolutionary for our time:

> *"The Church rejects as foreign to the mind of Christ any discrimination against men or harassment of them because of their race, color, condition of life, or religion."*

On the same day, the Council made this statement about Moslems:

> *"All through the course of the centuries many quarrels and hostilities have arisen between Moslems and Christians. This most sacred Synod urges all to forget the past and to strive sincerely for mutual understanding on behalf of all mankind. Let them make common the cause of safeguarding social justice, moral values, peace and freedom."*

The Council also acknowledged that Moslems, *"strive to submit whole-heartedly even to his inscrutable decrees, just as did Elijah, with whom the Islamic faith is pleased to associate itself. Though they do not acknowledge Jesus as God, they revere him as a prophet. They also honor Mary, his virgin mother."*

The Council also spoke of Hinduism, *"which contemplates the divine mystery and expresses it through an unspent fruitfulness of myths and their searching, philosophical imagery. They seek release from the anguish of our condition through recited practices, or deep meditation, or a loving trusting flight to God."*

It also spoke of Buddhism, *"which teaches a path by which men in a devout and confident spirit can either reach a stage of absolute freedom or attain supreme enlightenment by their own efforts or by higher assistance."*

Furthermore, the Council stated:

> *"Likewise, the religions to be found everywhere strive variously to answer the restless searching of the human heart by proposing 'ways' which consist of teachings, rules of Life, and sacred ceremonies. The Catholic Church rejects nothing which is true and holy in these religions. She looks with sincere respect upon those ways of conduct and life, those rules and teachings, which — though differing in many particulars from what she holds and sets forth — nonetheless often reflect a ray of that Truth which enlightens all people."*

These later statements can well be called revolutionary. As co-founder of Camp Brotherhood, I have assured members of these religions in the human family to regard Camp Brotherhood as their home.

The Vatican has also set up a Secretariat for non-Christian religions. Its members are bishops from all over the world and lay people. The aim of the Secretariat is to create a climate of cordiality between Christians and followers of other religions; to dissipate prejudice and ignorance — especially among Catholics; and to establish fruitful contact with members of other religions concerning questions of common interest.

December 7, 1965, saw the enactment of the *"Document on Religious Freedom"* by the Vatican Council. It stated:

> *"All nations are coming into even closer unity. Men of different cultures and religions are being brought together in closer relationships. Consequently, in order that relationships of peace and harmony may*

be established and maintained within the whole of mankind, it is necessary that religious freedom everywhere be provided with an effective constitutional guarantee and that respect be shown for the high duty and right of man freely to lead his religious life in society."

Now that the Church has begun a revolution in its theology and its vision for relations with other religions, we Catholics must carry on the revolution.

When a Pope Asks Forgiveness was written by the Italian journalist Luigi Accatoli.

It was published in 1998, seven years before the death of Pope John Paul II. It is a collection of ninety-six quotations from Pope John Paul II in which he admitted the past faults of the Church and frequently asks pardon for them. There are statements about women, Jews, Galileo, the Indians, the Inquisition, Israel, Luther, racism, Africans, Rwanda, and the division among churches.

Chapter 14

A Rabbi Makes a Church Altar

In 1964, I left Holy Names Academy, Seattle, after almost thirteen years to become the fourth pastor of St. Patrick's Parish, Seattle. The former beloved pastor, Michael Murtagh, resided with me until his death in 1965. He had been pastor for twenty-two years. I assisted him on weekends from 1955 to 1960 and celebrated the last Mass in the first St. Patrick Church on Harvard Street on August 15, 1960. It was then demolished with the small attached school to make room for the new freeway. During my years at St. Patrick's, we went through unprecedented church changes and turmoil. Vatican Council II was in progress in Rome between 1962 and 1965. While at St. Patrick's, centuries of the use of Latin at mass gave way to English. From the Middle Ages, the priest celebrated mass with his back to the people. Now altars were changed so the celebrant faced the people. This was intended to emphasize the Eucharist as a meal, with priest and congregation gathered around a table.

The altar in St. Patrick's Church, like most altars at the time, was fixed to the wall. To meet the new liturgical requirements, I needed at least a temporary altar. My friend and TV colleague, Rabbi Levine, liked to work with wood. I asked him to make an altar for me. In our first book, *Wild Branch on the Olive Tree,* he commented on my request: "One day Father Treacy came to me and said, 'Rabbi, you once promised to make me something if I ever had a parish of my own.' My hobby, as he knew, was working in wood and mosaic in the basement of my home. I had made a number of tables, mostly with a chessboard center, on which I had carved some of my favorite quotations. When he asked me to make him something, I thought it was something like a plaque for his study. He reminded me that Mass was now to be celebrated with the priest facing the people. And then he said, 'The altar at St. Patrick's is of marble and attached to the wall. It can't be moved. I need a new altar and I must have it within ten days.' I was flabbergasted. I knew that the altar was the focal point of Catholic worship, the holiest object in the church, and that he should ask me, a Jew and a rabbi, to make an altar for him touched me deeply. I went to work doing some research on what an altar was and discovered that the least one could use in a church the size of St. Patrick's was a six-foot table.

"I worked day and night. The result was an altar of mahogany, birch and walnut. With the help of Reeva [wife], I put on the altar all the symbols that Father Treacy wanted and which meant so much to him — the Chi-Rho in mosaic tile on the center front, and on an ornamental façade at the top, lilies and fish which are ancient Christian symbols.

"The altar was completed on the day before it was to be used. Members of his parish carted it to the church and put it in place. A newspaperman from The Seattle Times heard about the altar and decided to do a feature story for the Sunday edition on the day it was to be dedicated and the first Mass in the new form celebrated. The wire news services picked up the story and it was carried in newspapers throughout the United States and beyond. We began to receive letters from all over the world. The response to our simple expression of respect and love was heart-warming and indicated release of something also very deep in other hearts.

"It appeared that the impact of this incident touched the lives of many and awakened a hope and a faith that at long last religion which had divided our human family into mutually exclusive and so often antagonistic sectarian groups might bring them together to a spiritual unity as children of God. For had not the Hebrew Prophet Malachi said, perhaps 2500 years ago, 'Have we not all one Father? Hath not one God created us all? Why then do we deal treacherously, brother against brother?' (Malachi 2:15) And did not Jesus quote the injunctions from the Old Testament books of Leviticus and Deuteronomy when he said, 'You shall love the Lord your God with all your heart, with all your soul, with all your strength and with all your mind, and your neighbor as yourself.' (Luke 10:27) And Paul added: 'The whole law has found its fulfillment in one saying, you shall love your neighbor as yourself.' (Galatians 5:14) How can we show our love of God except as we show love for our neighbor?

"I tell the story of the altar to demonstrate the closeness of the relationship which Father Treacy and I had established so that he would not hesitate to ask his friend, the Rabbi, to make for him the holiest religious object in the Roman Catholic Church. On my part there was no hesitation to do this for him, even though some of my colleagues in the rabbinate thought that it was not the kind of object a rabbi should make even for his dearest Catholic friend."

I welcomed the change to English from Latin though my University degree was in Latin and Greek. Similarly, inviting lay people to read the scripture was welcome, as was the more popular music with guitar accompaniment. At St. Patrick's, we embraced the movement that drew churches together — ecumenism.

We also established a Parish Council with the Federal Judge William Lindberg as the first president. He was a saint in my book who attended Mass every day. After retirement, he came to noon Mass at Plymouth Congregational Church in Seattle; one day, he went back to his office and died.

During Lent, parishioners, on a Wednesday evening, joined for supper with members of the University Methodist Church and services. They joined us the following Wednesday for supper and service. The seven churches on Capitol Hill united to address the needs of the area calling ourselves CHOICE, Churches Organized in Common Efforts.

We had a Hindu Vendata Center in the next block to the church, and I invited the Swami, the leader of the small band of monks there, to speak at St. Patrick's. There was a full church to hear him speak. He spoke of Hindu monasticism and spiritual life. At the time there were young Hindu monks on Seattle streets dressed in sandals and saffron robes. At the question and answer time a parishioner asked the elderly swami why he did not wear his saffron robes but came dressed in a black suit and clerical collar. He paused for a moment before replying to the question. Then he said, "When Fr. Treacy asked me to speak, I pondered what I should wear. So I decided when in Rome, do what Rome does." The question and answer time was in the parish hall and he received prolonged applause for his remark. A few years later he died and I was honored by his community to be one of the speakers at his memorial service.

Problems arose concerning the school. When the property was sold for the freeway, the 200 students in the parish school were taken by bus to Sacred Heart School, Seattle. This area lost many families with children due to the World's Fair development around the church. The church is adjacent to the Seattle Center. Then Sacred Heart school closed and half the children from St. Patrick's went to St. Joseph's, Seattle, and half to Blessed Sacrament. Now parents transported the children and there was pressure on me to build a new school. But I decided that with declining families we would not be able to support a school. With more and more condos and apartments in the area today there is less need for a school.

I had three young priests during my seven years at St. Patrick's. Fr. Lester McCloskey (1964-1967), Fr. Thomas Vandenberg (1967-1968), and Fr. Marlin Connole (1968-1971). All were different and had their own special gifts, which they shared generously with parishioners. During these years, I also had a weekly TV program and many meetings to attend, so I depended a great deal on these dedicated young priests.

During those seven years as pastor of St. Patrick's, I experienced something of what another priest with a busy schedule as chaplain to Harvard University described. Fr. Henri Nouwen wrote in one of his last books: "There was a time when I got so immersed in problems of church and society that my whole life had become a sort of drawn out wearisome discussion. Jesus had been pushed into the background or had himself just become another problem. Fortunately it hasn't stayed that way. Jesus has stepped out again."

I will conclude with an example of one of the tensions added to coping with radical changes in the Church while I was pastor at St. Patrick's. The Vietnam War was at its height. The assistant pastor of St. Mark's Episcopal Cathedral in Seattle, and a dear friend, was devastated when his son was killed in Vietnam. Young men went to Canada to avoid the draft and were living in need of shelter and clothing during winter. A church group in Seattle decided to gather clothes for them and invited Dr. Robert McAfee Brown of Stanford University to be a speaker. He had spoken at my invitation to an ecumenical meeting in 1966. I agreed to host Dr. Brown in St. Patrick's Parish Hall. Dr. Brown spoke on compassion for those in need as the test of our faith in Jesus. The local papers covered the meeting. The next morning, a prominent politician and Catholic in Seattle, with whom I was acquainted, called me. He was very, very angry after reading the newspaper. He said, "If I could, I would strip you of your citizenship for trying to help those cowardly yellow bellies in Canada."

Fr. Nouwen helped me to cope with the above when he wrote: "Jesus stepped out in front again, so to speak, and asked me, 'And you, who do you say that I am?'" Fr. Nouwen admitted that events like the above could lead us to live in fear and become deaf to the voice of Jesus: "Do not be afraid." He added, "This reassuring voice which repeats over and over again, 'Do not be afraid, have no fear' is the voice we most need to hear." With this I fully agree. I still needed to hear that voice as much if not more so as a first-time pastor.

[illegible] the [illegible] conference [illegible]. The local paper [illegible] the evening. The next morning [illegible] and Canad[illegible] [illegible] was unqualified [illegible] [illegible] the [illegible] way [illegible] [illegible] of your citizenship for [illegible] have [illegible].

[illegible] with the [illegible] changed [illegible] and [illegible] that [illegible] above [illegible] [illegible] so as [illegible]

Chapter 15

A Camp for Healing, Understanding, Peace

America has experienced religion being used as a divisive weapon over the centuries. Historians tell us that anti-Catholic prejudice in America is older than racial prejudice. The Pilgrims brought this prejudice from England. It surfaced until well into the last century in blatant forms. Ads in newspapers in the Boston area for the most menial job would add, "No Catholic need apply."

A vigorous attempt was made to use religion for political purpose in 1960 when John F. Kennedy was seeking the presidency. Constant mailings warned Americans of the danger to the country if a Catholic was elected president. Then, it was claimed, he would take orders from the Pope, limit support for public education, etc. Similar charges were voiced in 1928 when Al Smith was seeking the presidency. Catholics accepted it as we accept the weather! But a Seattle leader took issue with those who tried to use religion for political purposes. He was Rabbi Raphael Levine of Temple De Hirsch Sinai Synagogue in Seattle.

The Rabbi discussed his concerns at a Rotary Club luncheon with William Warren, manager of KOMO TV in Seattle, the ABC outlet. As a public service, Mr. Warren agreed to give Rabbi a half-hour of prime TV time to discuss the religious issues dividing Americans. The program time was offered by Mr. Warren provided that the Rabbi could obtain a Catholic and Protestant panelist. Rabbi approached the Catholic Archbishop to discuss the program. At first he hesitated to take part in it, thinking it would lead to more duress. After a second visit by the Rabbi, the Archbishop delegated me to be the Catholic representative. Dr. Martin Goslin, Pastor of Plymouth Church, Seattle, was the Protestant panelist. The program began in the fall of 1960 and soon had an audience of between 300,000-400,000 people in Washington state and British Columbia on Sunday evenings from 6:00 to 6:30pm.

After six years on the air, the Rabbi approached me to discuss a project he had in mind. A firm believer in the value of camping for young people, he asked to establish a camp where young people of different faiths could have an opportunity to meet, get acquainted, and discover how to get on in business, in politics, at work, and as neighbors with respect for different races and religions. I agreed and pledged my support. With the help of generous friends we purchased a 300-acre farm in Skagit County for the sum of $85,000 in the fall of 1966. Our intention was to invite churches and synagogues to erect their own buildings on this spacious property, conduct their own programs, but have some common programs in sports, music, plays, and in lectures that would lead to greater understanding of the religion of the other. The land would be free for these buildings with only a small monthly charge to help with administration. We were shocked to find that churches *did not* accept our invitation!

Faced with the loss of the property due to taxes, Mrs. Levine remembered a young architect at the University of Washington, Lee Copeland, a professor who had worked with her in camping projects in California. She wanted him and another professor, Ralph Joyce, to visit the camp. They saw great possibilities in the camp. At their invitation, the senior class of the University of Washington School of Architecture offered to design and build with their own hands a lodge for us. It was to be their class project for graduation. They would donate their labor. For six months beginning in January 1968, fourteen of these students spent four days each week at the camp and two days at the university. They slept in the old farmhouse on the grounds and ate whatever food they pooled among themselves. They continued the work during the summer and on October 6, 1968, Governor Dan Evans dedicated the three-story building as the "Fisher Lodge" for the generous support of the Fisher family in Seattle. Since then, more than 100,000 people of all ages, from different churches and organizations, have used this lodge. Other buildings have been added as well: a ball field, a pavilion, lodges, a two million dollar dining hall, and kitchen, thanks to the generous support of the William Warren family. A retired Seattle school teacher gave us a quarter-million dollars for a beautiful chapel.

Rabbi died in 1985, and I promised him on his deathbed to continue to support the camp. Thanks to a good Board, a good CEO in

Randy Stime, a dedicated staff, and generous benefactors, we are about to give thanks for forty years of a unique project.

In the summer of 2005, some teenagers from Communist China visited the camp. They were raised to believe religion had no relevancy for daily life. They were amazed to find a beautiful camp with spacious grounds and buildings made possible by a priest and a rabbi.

Inter-religious dialogue is not about selling our respective theologies, but a process of learning and accepting, of questioning and appreciating the core belief of the other. One Moslem scholar has said, "God is most present in us when we have the courage to open ourselves to each other in our search for God." Mona Siddiqui is head of the Department of Religious Studies at the University of Glasgow, Scotland. She also points out the danger of believers focusing on who will or will not be saved, because, "...this will always lead to conditional and qualified acceptance of each other. In fact, dialogue is a religious act, an act of searching for the presence of God in the other. Conversion may happen, but conversion is not leaving behind previous religious belief and affiliation, but rather, undergoing a significant change of heart and mind because of what one has experienced through dialogue."

The hesitancy of churches to come together in dialogue has not disappeared in the past forty years. In fact, it is more necessary today than when John Kennedy was seeking the presidency. Camp Brotherhood is now poised with beautiful buildings and grounds to promote its original purpose of inter-faith dialogue with new energy.

Next year, we are expecting to have Protestant and Catholic families coming from the Belfast area to enter into dialogue and sharing with each other the peace of God's beautiful creation at Camp Brotherhood. We also have two programs of Elderhostel for Moslems in the Puget Sound area. During that week they will enter into dialogue with members of the Jewish and Christian faiths. To facilitate inter-faith programs, we hope to employ a program director with a degree in ecumenical theology who can facilitate church, synagogue, and Islamic dialogue.

Remembering the prejudice against Jews during his life in Czarist Russia and when he was a rabbi in London during World War II, and the many victims of Nazi persecution that he met afterward, Rabbi Levine often said to me, "We must promote dialogue or we will all perish."

There was no dialogue between Catholic priests and Lutheran pastors in Germany before Hitler came to power. Then on one occasion, hundreds of them sat down to a meal together. It was in Dachau Concentration Camp. One of them remarked, "If we had dinners and dialogue in the past, we might not be here in Dachau today."

The vision of Rabbi Levine for Camp Brotherhood and its future reminds me of the words in Genesis 9:13 which recall the reconciliation of God with the human family after the flood. God said, "I set my bow in the cloud and it shall be a sign of the covenant between me and the earth." Camp Brotherhood is another sign of God's love for a divided human family as it seeks to promote healing of relationships leading to understanding and peace.

Chapter 16

Soul and Body as Partners in Life

When beginning my pastoral ministry following seven years of seminary training, I was very concerned about theological correctness. Sacraments had to be administered according to the prescribed rules. This was the major concern of my ministry, rather than a caring personal approach to the victim of illness, sorrow or loneliness.

In my third year as a priest, I met a dear old man who was brought to the county hospital in Seattle from some impoverished area of Seattle. The hospital called the cathedral for a priest to minister to him, as he was on their critical list. I went over about 8:00 p.m. on a warm summer evening. His room on a top floor faced west, and with no window shade it was like a furnace. I gave him the sacraments of reconciliation, communion and anointing. Feeling I had adequately ministered to him, I was preparing to leave his furnace-like room. He turned to me and said, "I can hardly breathe." I can only attribute an insight from the Holy Spirit that moved me to pick up two pages of an old newspaper lying on a table and begin to fan him. He seemed to relax, even smile, and kept saying, "Don't leave me." I stayed a couple of hours and he fell asleep. While I was trying to exit quietly, he awoke and scared me with the energy he displayed by sitting up in bed. Then he said, "Wait, I have had few friends during my life, but no one has ever done more for me than you did tonight."

A man in need, a brother in faith, a cast off newspaper, a simple effort, a caring presence, and acceptance — those constituted the great gift in this man's life. And ever since, he has been giving to me — for he keeps before me the essence of giving, the utter simplicity of a gift, the barred uncluttered relationship of brother to brother. Unfortunately, I do not recall his name but his face lying in bed and his animated face as I left has indelibly impressed in my memory the message he taught a young priest.

Recently I read a story by a fellow priest in England, Fr. Daniel O'Leary, who also was called to a hospital where a baby had just died.

When he walked into the room an angry father said, "Where is this living God of yours now?" The priest recalled: "I remember mumbling words about the fact that God was probably crying with the parents." The English priest added, "What has stayed with me is that, ignoring me then, the father took his wife in his arms and said, 'You know I love you.'" The priest chaplain felt it was such a privilege to be present at a sudden, shy and emotionally charged moment, when a husband, following the loss of his child, spoke words of trust, words of love to his wife. He noted that in his priestly experience it is also God's joy, "to be worshipped in the way we touch and look at each other, in the way we listen and talk to each other, in the way we forgive and promise to start all over again." With this I fully agree.

This English confrere concluded his reflection on the death of the child and the reaction of the parents with these words: "We have forgotten that God can only love us through the human heart. Where else is there to experience the abundance of life promised by Jesus if not in the trust and encouragement of those who love us, in the almost impossible words of forgiveness from those we have hurt. Our senses and emotions, our most intimate feelings, our wildest aspirations and our deepest despair, our sins and our failures, such are the only moments in which our incarnate God can be intimate with us."

I have stood beside a wife of forty-two years as the doctor told her that her husband would live just forty-eight hours even with the help of a respirator. The husband was unconscious and the doctor did not expect him to regain consciousness. I told her I would stay with her if she gave permission to remove the machines that could keep him breathing for another two days. She said to me, "I need these two days to prepare myself to say farewell." God was in their human love through forty-two years and now was calling her to trust in a greater love when there would be new life and death would be no more.

Jesus, who embodied God and is called "true God of true God and true man," wept; He was moved with fear of death and apprehension such as to sweat blood, and He could sleep in a small boat during a violent storm. He healed illness of the soul and body, and, through His body nailed to a cross, gave us the supreme proof of His love for humanity. While I treasure the spark of divinity in every human being, life has taught me to honor, respect and cherish the body, my own and others. This is my faith as a believer in Jesus, a faith confirmed by sixty-three years of ministering as a priest to people. In the Irish tradition, we are told that when the soul leaves the body at death, its first act as a free spirit is to kiss the body and thank it for the partnership shared during the journey of life.

Chapter 17

TM, Centering, Contemplation

This chapter is intended to describe a stage in my spiritual journey in priesthood. It will indicate my discovery of Centering Prayer, or Meditation, indirectly through Transcendental Meditation. Centering Prayer was a casualty at the time of the Reformation due to the suppression of monasteries where this form of prayer had been cultivated from earliest times. The discovery has deepened my relationship with God. In describing it I do so to invite the reader to join me in the practice of Contemplative Prayer.

It was in 1973 that Rabbi Raphael Levine of Temple De Hirsch, Sinai, Seattle, returned from a vacation in California, excited, enthusiastic about a new discovery he made. While attending a course at Humboldt University, he also took a month's course on Transcendental Meditation. I recall his telling us how he found it a source of peace and tranquility. Every time he came to the studio to do a "Challenge" TV program he waxed eloquently about Transcendental Meditation.

Then our producer, Marty Wilson, said to him, "Rabbi, why don't you lead a discussion between the three of you on Transcendental Meditation." He agreed. My colleague, Dr. Robert Fine of the Free Methodist Church, Seattle, and I started to find out what we could about Transcendental Meditation. The leading exponent of Transcendental Meditation in America at the time was Maharishi Mahesh Yogi.

Because TM played a role in my spiritual journey, I will let the Rabbi tell how he discovered it, and how his discovery led to my finding Centering Prayer.

In his autobiography, Rabbi wrote: "Why then did I take TM? Not to take the place of my religion; TM is not a religious practice. As I see it, TM and religion confer entirely different benefits. From our religions, we learn the spiritual goals we are reaching for. The ancient prophets expressed it well; they told us we must live on a level of self-giving love in order to attain the abundant life promised by God." Centering Prayer helps us remove obstacles to the realization of God's love for us. In 1975 Rabbi flew to Switzerland and spent several days with Maharishi Mahesh Yogi. Rabbi wrote, "We filmed sixteen hours of dialogue on science, religion and TM." The tapes have been used worldwide to teach TM.

Moved by the Rabbi's enthusiasm and my own desire to become better informed, I attended a few sessions with a teacher of TM and watched about sixteen hours of videos by the Maharishi Mahesh Yogi. As a result, I began to spend fifteen minutes each morning and evening in silence, paying attention to breathing and endeavoring to put my mind on auto pilot with TM. I found the practice relaxing. Some compared it to time relaxing in a hot tub! I did not pay any attention to its Hindu source but could understand how Rabbi described it as "conducive to lessening stress and giving more energy and zest for life."

In the fall of 1975, I was given my first sabbatical for study and decided to take a three-month refresher course in theology and scripture given in the Old Mission in Santa Barbara, California. One day a Franciscan priest, Fr. Alan McCoy, OFM, told us about Centering Prayer or Meditation. In some ways he said it resembled Transcendental Meditation but had Christian roots. When Protestantism led to monasteries being suppressed, this form of prayer went into decline within the Church. He told us the best teacher on Centering Prayer was Abbot Thomas Keating, a monk in St. Joseph Abbey, Spencer, Massachusetts. I went to Spencer and spent several days with Fr. Keating and later made a ten-day retreat with him. He described Contemplative Prayer as, "a practice of interior transformation, of conversation initiated by God, and leading, if we consent, to divine union. It is not a rejection of other forms of prayer, but a further dimension, like a deep relationship between friends who can sit for a period of time just enjoying each other's presence." Fr. Keating is restoring to the church this treasure by his teaching and writings, making it better known. This form of prayer without words is known as Contemplative Prayer and is also called Centering Prayer as we endeavor to center our minds on God alone. Until I met Fr. Keating in 1975, my prayer life was based on intellectual reflection on scripture. This was the method taught to me in the seminary. Jesus, of course, held first place in my reflections, as well as everything God spoke to us in scripture. Centering Prayer brought about a revolution in my spiritual life. I realized with the help of Fr. Keating that intellectual reflection cannot comprehend God. This teaching of Fr. Keating and others in the area of contemplative prayer does not mean we downgrade (much less eliminate) the role of the intellect in prayer. To quote another great teacher, Fr. Stephen Rosetti: "In truth, the mystical way of knowledge does not contradict the intellect but builds upon it and finally transcends it. A properly guided intellect leads to the beginning of the mystical way."

Eckhart Tolle, in his best selling book, *The Power of Now* writes about the mystery of mind and intelligence:

> *"It wasn't through the mind, through thinking, that the miracle that is life on earth or your body were created and are being sustained. There is clearly an intelligence at work that is far greater than the mind. How can a single human cell measuring 1/1,000 of an inch across contain instructions within its DNA that would fill 1,000 books of 600 pages each? The more we learn about the workings of the body, the more we realize just how vast is the intelligence at work within it and how little we know. When the mind reconnects with that, it becomes a most wonderful tool. It then serves something greater than itself."*

To clarify the word "mystical" we must recall its use in the New Testament. A mystery is a truth we do not fully understand but approach with awe and wonder. The doctor who discovers that a young patient has malignant cancer faces a mystery, as does the patient. The cause is unknown.

Fr. Ron Rolheiser writes of the mystical imagination as, "the other half of the scientific imagination, and, like science, its purpose is to help us to see, imagine, understand, speak about, and relate to reality in a way beyond fantasy and imagination. But the mystical imagination can show us something that science, wonderful though it is, cannot — namely, it can show us the grace-drenched and spirit-laden layers of reality that are not perceived by our physical senses. The mystical imagination can show us how the Holy Spirit isn't just inside our churches but is also inside the law of gravity." Einstein said, "What is unseen is more important than what is seen." With this I fully agree.

In Celtic spirituality, as John O'Donohue points out in, *Anam Cara*, "Nature is the direct expression of the divine imagination. It is the most intimate reflection of God's sense of beauty. Nature is the mirror of the divine imagination and the mother of all sensuality; therefore, it is unorthodox to understand spirit in terms of the invisible alone...the imagination is the faculty that bridges, co-presents and co-articulates, the visible and invisible." Astronauts are discovering the mystery of God in outer space and scientists in laboratories. The mystery of God is also found in the music of Mozart and Beethoven.

At each Mass the celebrant intones after the Consecration, "Let us proclaim the mystery of faith." Several responses are suggested. The most common is "Christ has died, Christ is risen, Christ will come again." Mystery pertains more to the imagination than the intellect.

One of the great classical works on Contemplative Prayer is called, "The Cloud of Unknowing," which was written in the 13th century in England. This teaches us to trust God, and by sitting in silence we come to know God in a deeper way than we could by intellectualizing about God. When I was pastor of St. Michael's Parish in Olympia, I spent half an hour in contemplative prayer each morning with a local Presbyterian pastor, Jack Finney. When I left Olympia, he also left to obtain a degree in counseling, intending to teach and use Contemplative Prayer to heal, energize, and bring God's peace and joy to people.

On one occasion Jack shared with me an image that helped him with Contemplative Prayer. He compared it to drawing back the curtains in a room to allow the sunlight to enter — to allow God to be perceived by us. Jack had a son who was two years old when we began our morning prayer. He experienced God's love when he held his sleeping son in his arms. The experience revealed to Jack how God gazes at us with love.

Over the years, I devoted time to this form of prayer with faith and perseverance, just as I do physical exercise believing it is good for me.

But often I felt the absence of God — no great insights or consolations came to me. In fact, the opposite happened. I became more aware at times of my failures in life; aware of persons over the years I may have hurt, of love and compassion not given when needed by parishioners or friends. I wondered if I was a real failure as a priest in the eyes of God. Then I learned from a current master in the spiritual life who also has a doctorate in psychology that, "instead of fleeing all that is human, mystics necessarily enter more deeply into their own humanity and the human condition. Thus, they are allowed by God to experience their own sins and the sins of humanity in a more direct and intense way."

Fr. Stephen Rosetti, Ph.D., author of *When the Lion Roars* gave a retreat to the priests of Seattle in the summer of 2005. Letting go and letting God is the secret to happiness. As a seminarian I tried to achieve the best grades. In priesthood I was concerned about my accomplishments and status in the eyes of the Archbishop. As a pastor I wanted the approval of my parishioners, friends, etc. Like so many I pursued perfection.

The psalmist who gave us Psalm 23 describes God's loving care under the figure of a shepherd and his flock. He refers especially to trust in God when leading sheep "through a dark valley" where wild animals or robbers might attack. The dark valley can apply to any time of crisis in our lives. Another translation refers to the dark valley as "the valley of the shadow of death."

Then a few years ago, in a particularly dark valley, God led me to ask how I would face life without the approval of bishop, parishioners, even friends! Could I walk alone? It was a very painful time of spiritual evaluation for one who had been carried along by the approval of others in so many areas of ministry. Some have asked me what the dark valley I traveled was? Was it a crisis of faith, a crisis in my vocation, etc.? A spiritual guide reminded me that a wound either physical or spiritual that has been healed should not be probed or reopened.

Corrie Ten Boom was a Dutch woman who was sent to a Nazi concentration camp in WWII for aiding Jews. She was released by mistake on Christmas Day, 1944. After the war, she traveled the world preaching on forgiveness, on self-acceptance in spite of sins and failures because of God's love for us that heals us. She regularly quoted Micah 7:19. "God you will cast into the depths of the sea all our sins."

Then Corrie Ten Boom added: "Because I grew up next to the sea I believed that when God casts our sins into the depth of the sea; he then puts a sign which reads, "No fishing allowed here!" But after the dark valley I was able to say, "God, you love me. That is all that matters." With this came great peace and joy. The "dark valley" varies from person to person and varies with age. Youth has its dark valleys, and scripture refers to the "noonday devil," the loss of energy and enthusiasm in middle life. Gray's poem, *Elegy in a Country Churchyard,* sums up the final years and our attitude to saying "Farewell:"

"Whoever left the warm precincts of the parting day
And cast not one long lingering look behind."

With age comes a sense of loneliness as we face good-bye to all we cherished.

Now in my 63rd year as a priest, I have become more aware of God's love and try to reflect on this as often as I can each day. A mother expecting the birth of a child is aware of a plan unfolding in her body, a divine blueprint coming to life. Jesus assures that not even a sparrow falls to the ground without God's awareness and therefore God has a blueprint for my personal life and for my relationship with others.

St. Therese tells us, "Everything is a grace, everything is the direct effect of our Father's love — difficulties, contradictions, humiliations, all the soul's miseries, her burdens, her needs — everything, because through them, she learns humility, realizes her weakness. Everything is a grace because everything is God's gift. Whatever be the character of life or its unexpected events — to the heart that loves, all is well."

The fruit of Contemplative Prayer, of endeavoring to live in the constant awareness of God's love for us and discovering God's will is beautifully expressed by the 16th century saint, Francis de Sales in his book, *Introduction to the Devote Live:* "Do not look forward to what might happen tomorrow; the same Everlasting Father who cares for you today will take care of you tomorrow and everyday. Either he will shield you from suffering or he will give you unfailing strength to bear it. Be at peace, then, and put aside all anxious thoughts and imaginings." This I try to do each day unburdened by past failures or present weakness because I am conscious by faith of God's power to heal my past and to sustain me today.

In 2002 I made a week's retreat with John O'Donohue, a fellow Irishman and best selling author of *Anam Cara* and *Divine Beauty*. It was a grace-filled time, and I will conclude this section with a paragraph from *Divine Beauty* that sums up much of what he shared with me in his retreat. My own experiences as a priest have confirmed what he says about compassion:

> *"Compassion is one of the most beautiful presences a person can bring to the world and most compassion is born from one's own woundedness. When you have felt deep emotional pain and hurt, you are able to imagine what the pain of the other is like; their suffering touches you. This is the most decisive and vital threshold in human experience and behaviour. The greatest evil and destruction arises when people are unable to feel compassion. The beauty of compassion continues to shelter and save our world. If that beauty were quenched, there would be nothing between us and the end-darkness which would pour in torrents over us."*

The great sixteenth century Teresa of Avila wrote words that sum up where I am on my spiritual journey: "I know that the Lord constantly looks at me and that His gaze is loaded with Love, this suffices to me."

Because I believe that I am loved unconditionally by God, I recall the words of Paul in Romans 8:28: "We know that God makes all things work for the good of those who love him, who have been called according to his decree." Something can come from apparent failure, the injustice and pain caused by others. This is the lesson of Jesus, a victim of intrigue and murder who triumphs in death.

Chapter 18

Saying "Thanks" Often

"Blow, Blow Thou Winter Wind"
Thou Art Not As Half As Unkind
"As Man's Ingratitude to Man"
— Shakespeare

Brother David Steindl-Rast, O.S.B., is a Catholic monk who has written a book entitled *Gratefulness*. Born in Vienna, he studied art, anthropology and psychology there, holding degrees from the Vienna Academy of Fine Arts and the University of Vienna. His sense of gratitude for life came to him in Nazi-occupied Vienna during WWII. An Allied air attack on the city sent him hurrying into a nearby church for shelter. As the bombs fell around him he thought each moment would be the last. When the bombing ended he emerged from the church. He noticed a small courtyard with spring grass and some flowers in bloom. He was filled with gratitude for life and for the beauty of creation. Rainbows took on a new meaning for him. He was in tune with the poet W.H. Auden who tells us:

Weather, is what nasty people are
Nasty about, and the nice
Show a common joy in observing

WHY GIVE THANKS?

An agnostic Jew is quoted in an article on Judaism in the *Seattle Post-Intelligencer,* October 3, 2005, as saying he does express thanks at meals for the ability to buy bread, for the nature that gives rain, for the guy who drove the combine, etc. I also hope it is an expression of humility.

I agree with him that gratitude is an acknowledgment of our dependence on others and, for believers, a dependence on God and all God created and creates, from the most distant star to the newborn baby. A story is told about two English philosophers, G. K. Chesterton, a strong believer in God, and Professor T. M. Joad, an agnostic, who held a debate on free will. Joad held that there is no real free will on the part of people. They are motivated by greed, or selfishness in some form. Chesterton believed human beings could overcome selfish urges in sacrifice and love for others. Finally both philosophers sat down to dinner together. Chesterton said a prayer of thanks for the food while Joad remained silent. After the blessing Joad said to his partner, "Would you please pass the salt?" Chesterton did and Joad thanked him. Chesterton asked Joad why he said thank you. "Was I compelled to pass you the salt?" he asked. "Wasn't your thank you an acknowledgment? I exercised my free will on your behalf." I agree with Chesterton that a thank you to someone is an acknowledgment that they exercised their free will on my behalf.

There are numerous references to gratitude in the Bible. Psalm 109: "I will speak my thanks earnestly to the Lord and in the midst of the throng I will praise Him." Psalm 100:47: "Save us O Lord our God and gather us from among the nations that we may give thanks to your holy name and glory in praising you." It seems to me that the psalmist saw the purpose of life as giving thanks to God.

The Moslem concept of thanks is told by Jamal Rahman in his book, *The Fragrance of Faith,* Page 9:

> *"One morning, the Mullah discovered, to his dismay, that his donkey had disappeared. His helper, companion, and source of livelihood had vanished! Frantically, he began to search. His neighbors joined in looking in the hills and valleys, far and wide, but to no avail. The donkey was missing. At dusk, the neighbors turned back to give the Mullah the sad news. They found him in the town square on his knees, hands stretched out, praising Allah and exclaiming, "Thank you Allah! Thank you, Allah!" Puzzled, the townsfolk asked the Mullah if he knew that his donkey was lost, maybe forever. "I know, I know," beamed the Mullah. "But I have so much to be thankful for. Imagine what could have happened to me if I was on the donkey!"*

The poet Rainer Maria Rilke writes of gratitude as follows:
"Oh, if for once all were completely still!
If all mere happenstance and chance
Were silenced, and the laughter next door, too;
If all that droning of my senses
Did not prevent my being wide awake —
Then, with one thousand fold thought,
I would reach your horizon
And, for the span of a smile, hold you
To give you away to all life
As thanksgiving."

Katrina and Rita, the recent hurricanes that brought much destruction to the Gulf States, also saw people reach out with great compassion and generosity to meet human needs. Catholics in the Seattle area contributed between one and two million dollars. Others did likewise.

Rabbi Levine described Jewish gratitude to me. At the Sabbath service there was a seat in the synagogue in Russia where a stranger or very poor person could sit. The first person to leave the synagogue had to take the stranger home for dinner in gratitude to God for the food and shelter they enjoyed.

Rumi, the Moslem poet, wrote of gratitude: "For sixty years I have been forgetful every minute, but not for a second has this flowing toward me stopped." In other words God loved him every moment of his life.

In our Catholic prayer, at the Mass, we say, "It is right and proper at all times and places to give praise and thanks to God." We recall at Mass the last meal Jesus had with His followers. Thanks was expressed several times by Him. This sense of gratitude for life was reflected among the people with whom I grew up in Ireland. A greeting on a sunny day went like this: "Fine sunny day." Reply, 'Tis indeed, thank God." When it was bitterly cold and freezing you said, "It is a fine hardy day." The reply was, 'Tis indeed, thank God." "Welcome be the will of God' was another frequent prayer in joy and sorrow. Giving thanks in time of pain and suffering calls for a special vision of life.

GRATITUDE IN DIFFICULTIES

Jamal Rahman in his book, *The Fragrance of Faith,* gives us some practices to deal with pain in our lives and to move to greater awareness of God, as expressed by Rumi. "Don't run toward pain and just don't run away from it. The dark thought, the shame, the malice meets them at the door laughing, and invites them in. Be grateful for whoever comes because each has been sent as a guide from beyond." Jamal Rahman continues: "Angels have no physical bodies and so do not suffer the anguish of painful sensations. They are in awe of humans who receive the sensations with awareness and who with compassion, little by little, metamorphize their beings."

There is a Jewish story which says that when you are about to be born God takes you to a field covered with bundles. Each bundle represents a particular set of troubles. You can choose any bundle, but the one you choose you have to take to earth with you. The rabbis say that if at the moment of death God were to take you back to that field and let you choose another bundle you would always pick the same.

Christians see in the death of Jesus a miscarriage of justice but one accepted with such love that it can give meaning to all our pain. Pain ushers in life and love. The death of Jesus calls on us to reject violence in our lives.

CONCLUSION

Meister Eckhart, a great Medieval theologian said, "If the only prayer you ever said was, 'Thank You' it would be enough." Pain and gratitude are woven into our lives at birth. We enter this world through the pain of another, but that other, our mother, is grateful she was the giver of life. To all mothers who gave life, our thanks. Dag Hammersold, at the United Nations, said, "For all that has been thanks, for all that will be, Yes."

Archbishop Thomas Murphy of Seattle was diagnosed with leukemia in May 1997 and was confined to Providence Hospital in Seattle. He later recalled an experience he had in the hospital. "Of the people that shared my floor at Providence Hospital on December first, there are probably about three of us still alive. My next door neighbor was a young 21-year-old man who had no faith tradition. He started with a growth on his leg — a rare form of cancer. He was told he would have maybe eighteen months to live. I arrived when he re-entered the hospital, and at that time he was told he had only two weeks to live. We became friends. He didn't know what an archbishop was, which made it easier perhaps. He told me when he saw all those priests in black coming into my room he thought, 'either you are very sick or very bad.' Talking to him one day, I asked him if he felt angry because he would probably have such a short life. He said, 'No, I've had a good life.' I was surprised by that. 'Do you have any regrets?' I asked. He said, 'Let me think about one.' And I remember coming back that night and he said, 'Let me tell you the answer to your question. Yes, I have regrets,' he said. 'I regret that I didn't take time to say "Thank you" *enough.'*

"How often do we say thank you to each other?" the Archbishop continued. "My mother worked as a maid in a hotel to make ends meet. We always knew when someone left her a tip because she would bring home candy. That's why I can't stay in a hotel today without leaving a tip. Because that simple tip is a sign of appreciation for the work of another human being. And, too often, it's the simple things we forget. Things as simple as saying, 'Thank You.'

"How often do we thank others for their unexpected gifts? The horror in the hospital is not the sound of the needle entering your bones for the bone marrow in your chest. The horror is the cries of lonely people that break the endless night.

"Next Tuesday I will go to Providence Hospital — as I do every three weeks — for a blood transfusion because I can't generate enough blood to keep me going. If you have given blood recently you know it's not like the past. In the past you would be able to have blood designated for you. But now when you go and give blood the nurse brings in a pint and you don't know who has given it. I don't know if it's a man or woman, tall or short, fat or skinny, Native American, Asian, Hispanic, or White. But someone anonymously, and with no strings attached, has given me a gift that keeps me alive.

"How many gifts do we give without condition? That pint of blood is a symbol of people sharing the gift of life. I pray for each of them when I receive their gift, and I say thank you.

"That's why I call those thirty-nine days in the hospital a grace and a blessing. I learned more fully the preciousness of life. I learned that the quality of your relationships will determine the quality of your journey to death. And, I've learned to say, 'Thank you.'"

(Archbishop Murphy died June 26, 1997).

Chapter 19

Welcome Be the Will of God

The word "passion" comes from the Latin word "pati" meaning, "to endure," "to accept." A patient is one who accepts care as given by another. We refer to passion when enduring strong emotions. We speak of being passionately moved by music, anger, sexual feelings, passionate in regard to patriotism, etc.

Fr. Richard Rohr speaks of Jesus as accomplishing more by acceptance, by passion more than by action. At the moment of conception, the mother of Jesus commits herself to acceptance of God's will with the words to the heavenly messenger, "Be it done unto me according to thy Word." She places no conditions, asks no questions, but humbly and obediently accepts the role given to her. With her deep understanding of the Jewish scripture, she must have known in her heart that to be the mother of the Messiah would mean great suffering and heartache.

As I look back at my life, I see the greatest moments, the most crucial, were those where I accepted new invitations to follow a particular road in life with no map. When these situations occurred, all I could do was repeat the words of Mary, "Be it done unto me according to thy Word."

As soon as my ministry in Seattle began, I learned how much of life is acceptance. A young mother came to me for counseling. Her husband, an Air Force pilot, was shot down and killed on one of the last days of battle in the Philippines. Six years later I officiated at her second marriage, but she lived with the constant memory of her deceased husband. Another widow came to me with a similar story. Her husband was missing in action. After waiting for almost a year, the Navy declared him officially dead and again I officiated at her second marriage, after she endured a year or more of waiting and grieving.

Jesus is our great example of acceptance. He did not deliberately seek death and suffering. He did seek to help the poor and abandoned in society. He had a special compassion for those who were ill. About twelve times in the Gospels he took meals regarded by some of his contemporaries as with the wrong people, at the wrong time, or in the wrong manner, not clean enough. Jesus knew some of the religious leaders and politicians were bitterly opposed to him because of his teaching and lifestyle. But he did not compromise in these areas though he must have known the consequences, especially when his cousin and prophet, John the Baptist, was beheaded.

As the shadow of the cross drew closer, Jesus prayed in Gethsemane: "Father, if it is your will take this cup from me. Yet not my will but yours be done." Luke 22:42. There is a fascinating story in the 12th chapter of St. John, which some scholars see as an opportunity offered to Jesus to take action to avoid accepting crucifixion.

John tells us that some Greeks who had come to Jerusalem to attend the Passover paid a visit to Philip who presumably spoke Greek. "Sir," they said, "we want to see Jesus." What did they say to him? St. John does not tell us. Some say they invited Jesus to move to Greece from the threatening atmosphere of Jerusalem. This is deduced from the words of Jesus to those Greeks: "Unless the grain of wheat falls to the earth and dies it remains just a grain of wheat. But if it dies it produces much fruit." By these words, Jesus committed himself to full acceptance of what lay ahead and made no effort to escape with those well-meaning Jews from Greece.

Being born is to accept life, as male or female, as well as the family, the country, the religion, and the culture into which we are born. Shakespeare wrote of the seven stages of life to be accepted. The seventh was old age with its infirmities and weaknesses leading to death. Our culture tries to ignore this important stage in life either by warehousing the elderly with others, or by trying to hide age and its effects on us with the help of beauty parlors, medications, etc.

Growing up in Ireland and learning facts about Irish history, I have had a growing appreciation and admiration for the courage and faith of my ancestors in accepting suffering and deprivation. In the midst of the Great Famine, 1846-1848, endured by my grandparents, they survived in Ireland, yet, to preserve life, many others decided to accept the challenges and chances of getting to America. In a town near me a resident left this account of the Famine Years: "Well, I remember the long procession of country carts lent by kind neighbors to carry the poor emigrant and his baggage to the railway station. These flittings usually took place at night and I was often awakened by the wails and cries of those who were leaving all that was dear to them in their native land. One night I counted a hundred carts pass my father's door. The wailing and cries of the poor people was heart wrenching to listen to."

This acceptance of suffering of the unexpected as was the potato famine, was expressed in a Gaelic phrase I heard over and over again as I grew up. It was spoken in time of illness, accidents, death — *Failte le toil De.* "Welcome be the will of God." Not just a reluctant acceptance out of necessity but a welcome was given.

The English poet William Wordsworth captured this dimension of a faith-filled life when he wrote, "Thousands at His bidding speed and post o'er land and sea without rest. They also serve, who only stand and wait." These words apply to the sick, the prisoners, the poor, the unemployed, the elderly, and the dying. Many are broken-hearted by their condition of life and find acceptance of their life situations very difficult. To them I repeat the words of Psalm 147:3, "God heals the brokenhearted, binding up their wounds." Then as a reminder we are remembered by God. The psalmist adds, "God determines the number of the stars and calls each by name." When acceptance is most difficult, I recall the words of Jesus in the Sermon on the Mount — Matthew 6:26, "Look at the birds in the sky. They do not sow or reap, they gather nothing into barns; yet your heavenly Father feeds them. Are not you more important than they?"

Chapter 20

Justice and Love Related

Jewish and Christian theologians are studying the relationship of love and justice in God. Shakespeare, a shrewd observer of human nature, told us, "According to the strict letter of justice, none of us would see salvation." The problem is stated simply by people who feel somewhat uncomfortable with sermons about God's unconditional love. They ask, "Can an evil tyrant like Hitler go to heaven?"

Let me share with you the insight of a man who knew Hitler. His name is Martin Niemoller, a Lutheran pastor in Germany. He was a submarine commander in World War I and was decorated for his naval skill. Following the war, he was ordained a Lutheran pastor and is one of the few who confronted Hitler when Hitler began the persecution of the Jews in the mid-thirties. Niemoller went to see Hitler, in 1937, possibly because he was a war hero. He told Hitler that his anti-Jewish policy was losing world respect for Germany and that Jews could be a strong support for Germany, both economically and militarily. Hitler responded to Niemoller by sending him to Dachau concentration camp.

In Dachau, Neimoller had a severe heart attack and became unconscious. Guards carried him out of the cell and left him to be collected with the dead in the morning and then taken to the crematorium. Before the vehicle arrived he regained consciousness and walked back to his cell.

In a lecture he gave in Seattle, while on a world tour after the war, he told of his release following the Allied capture of Dachau. He returned to his wife and family. Sleep was difficult, but one night while asleep, he had a vivid dream. He was very familiar with Hitler's voice. In his dream Hitler was screaming at him, "You never told me the real reason."

After much reflection, Niemoller recalled that he had hesitated to tell Hitler that he was violating the Law of God, because he thought his argument of a social and political nature would be more powerful. He regretted not reminding Hitler of God's compassion for Jews persecuted in Egypt who were rescued by God. His lecture tour was intended to remind people that political decisions must not ignore the Laws of God.

I give these facts about Hitler to indicate where people failed Hitler. Others have told me that Hitler was brutalized by a father who beat him with a leather strap when he was a child. In other words, there is much we do not know about what warped the mind of Hitler, or that of others like him. But God knows how minds are warped. And here I should point out that while acts may be evil this does not mean that those who do these acts are evil.

In 1902 Alessandro Serenelli, a young Italian, tried to rape a young neighbor girl, Maria Goretti. She resisted and he killed her. For his crime he received a life sentence in jail. He was released thirty-five years later, shortly before Christmas, 1937. At Christmas midnight Mass, he came to the church in the small town of Nettuno, Italy, and stood at the back. After everyone received Holy Communion, he proceeded to approach the altar, but not alone. A woman dressed in black walked forward to receive Communion with him. It was Assunta Goretti, the elderly mother of Maria, showing her forgiveness for the man who murdered her daughter.

Investigation of Serenelli revealed a terrible relationship between him and his mother, who was mentally ill. To get rid of him at age three, she threw him in a well from which he was rescued by a neighbor. The mother was unable to care for her son and the same was true of the father who was an alcoholic. While not justifying what Alessandro did, I feel confident God had compassion for him as did Assunta, the mother of the murdered girl who reveals the power of love.

We find an interesting blend of justice and love in the life of Moses. He was a victim of discrimination by Egyptians. His mother should have killed him at birth by Egyptian law. But her love made her disobey as she placed her newborn son in a basket and let him float down the Nile, hoping, I expect, that an Egyptian mother would rescue him. Actually, that is what happened. He was discovered by an Egyptian Princess and raised as an Egyptian prince. Later he was to discover his true identity. While living as an Egyptian with royal status, he observed an Egyptian cruelly mistreating an Israelite. In his anger, Moses struck the Egyptian, who died. Because of this, Moses, regarded as a murderer, had to flee Egypt for his life. This was the man God called to lead the Israelites en masse from Egypt. God did not charge him with murder.

Psalm 86:15 emphasizes God's compassion: "But you, O God, are merciful and gentle, slow in getting angry, full of constant loving kindness and of truth." St. Luke gives Jesus the title "Lord" for the first time in Chapter 7 when Jesus revealed his compassion — the quality and essence of God. We read Jesus "...met a funeral procession as he approached the village gate of Naim. The boy who had died was the only son of his widowed mother. When the "Lord" saw her, his heart overflowed with sympathy." Jesus restored the young man to life.

Jesus gave us an insight into the harmonizing of love and justice in one of the most beautiful stories he told. It is the story of a father's heartache and sorrow when his son took a considerable sum of money from the father's generosity and left home to squander it in a selfish lavish lifestyle. Finally, when penniless and with no friends, he decided to go home. From his father he expected justice for what he had done. Not presuming to be accepted as a son, he had made up his mind to be accepted as a hired servant. This meant his status was beneath that of a slave. A slave in a Jewish home had to be fed and housed and released to freedom after seven years. The hired servant was only called when needed and paid by the hour. But the father's love brushed aside all condemnation and pain the son had caused. Instead, he ran to the son as he saw him coming, kissed him lovingly, and invited him into the family as the son he was.

I do not claim to fully understand how God can be just and can love with unconditional love. There are many indications in scripture that invite us to trust in love. One of my favorites is Psalm 62:8, "O my people, trust him all the time. Pour out your longings before him for he can help." Then the psalmist reminds us there is a narrow line between "the highest and the lowest." In verse 9, we read, "The greatest of men and the lowest, both alike, are nothing in his sight. They weigh less than air on scales."

Lastly, one of the greatest statements in religion was spoken by Jesus in Matthew 5:44, "Love your enemies. Pray for your persecutors."

Granted, some people die defiant of God, enemies of God, yet God loves them in spite of themselves. So it would appear that God's love transforms those individuals, like silver purified by fire. What emerges from the flames of love is the image of God in every soul, which, I believe, is the relation of justice to love.

Chapter 21

Start Your Engines

Mass is the term used for the celebration of the Eucharist in the Latin rites of the Roman Catholic Church. The word itself is derived from the phrase with which the liturgical celebration concludes in Latin, *Ite, missa est,* meaning, "You may go, this is the dismissal." This ceremony is now more commonly called Eucharist, in which we recall that Jesus offered bread and wine to God as he did on his last night on earth. It has developed into a ritual with prayers and ceremonial. Raymond Brown, a leading Catholic scripture scholar, concludes that the Last Supper of Jesus, "was not a Passover in the strict sense, but a meal that had 'Passover characteristics'."

Let us look at the Passover for Jews that may help us to a better understanding of Eucharist. This feast in the spring of each year is one of the most sacred in Judaism. Father Raymond Moloney, S.J. writes: "The Exodus (deliverance of the Jews from Egypt) could claim to be the foundational event of the Jewish nation, containing within itself the sign and promise of redemption. Liberation is central to its spirit and remains one of the central themes of the Passover. This idea is expressed in Deuteronomy 6:21, "Once we were Pharaoh's slaves in Egypt and the Lord brought us out of Egypt by his mighty hand."

One of the key words in the Passover celebration is the word 'memory'. It is not used to recall a historical event but an event which has a key role in the life of the person recalling the past event. This is evident in the current Passover text of the feast which I celebrated for twenty-five years with Rabbi Levine. The text of the service reads: "In every generation each one is bound to consider himself as though he himself had come out of Egypt. God, the Holy One, blessed be He, redeemed not only our fathers but he also redeemed us with them."

Since the first Christians who celebrated the Eucharist were Jews this must have been their understanding of the words of Jesus, "Do this in memory of me." Then the idea of the Eucharist, or Mass, was one of liberation. No matter what happened to us, even a death with cruelty by Romans or others, it did not mean our destruction. We were liberated from the fear of death by our faith in the Resurrection of Jesus. In fact, the Jewish Passover led the Jews to a new land "flowing with milk and honey." Christians were called to live a life of love liberating others from hunger, suffering, loneliness, etc. Pagans who observed these Christians in daily life remarked, "See how these Christians love each other. Christians refused to take part in war. Hundreds of members of a Roman legion (called the Theban legion) were killed for their refusal to take part in battle."

A gradual change in this understanding of the death of Jesus began to creep in during the 4th century after Constantine became Emperor and a Christian. Then, military service and killing were accepted when ordered by a Christian emperor. Rome in the West collapsed in 476 and Germanic tribes wiped out much of Christianity. Now an interesting development takes place. Monks from Ireland went to Europe to introduce the invaders to Christianity. I suspect that these ancestors of mine (as well described by Thomas Cahill in his book, *How the Irish Saved Civilization)* had a difficult time communicating the Jewish understanding of Passover and Eucharist as liberation to this warlike people.

A very decisive understanding of the Eucharist (Mass) took place in 1097 when Anselm, a leading theologian, explained the Eucharist as a literal re-enactment of the death of Jesus. Emphasis was placed on the suffering of Jesus reflected in crucifixes with all the gory details of crucifixion. This was a marked difference from the picture of Christ in the 6th century magnificent Cathedral in Ravenna, Italy. There, the picture of Christ is over the high altar. He is not on the cross but is surrounded by saints. About the time of Anselm, with the new emphasis on the suffering of Jesus to win God's favor for us, Pope Urban in 1095 blessed the Crusaders who set out to attack Moslems in what were called the "holy places" associated with Jesus. At the same time, antagonism and downright persecution of Jews became a factor in society.

Other deviations from the first understanding of the death of Jesus followed. In the early church it was a call to usher in an era when the followers of Jesus would be known by their love for one another. Now in the Middle Ages, wars became common. Later, torture, the Inquisition, the burning alive of heretics, became common. Countries tried to surpass each other in cruelties. The Irish Archbishop, Oliver Plunkett, was hanged, his intestines cut out and thrown in a fire, by a Protestant government in England in 1681. From 1618 to 1648 there was a war between Lutherans and Catholics, all professing faith in Jesus, who died to liberate us from the sins of murder, violence, greed, and cruelty to each other. At this time great emphasis was placed on Purgatory, a place of suffering for purification to enter heaven. Many, like Tetzel, who preached against Luther, preached on the flames of Purgatory from which liberation came by indulgences, gained by prayers, donations, pilgrimages, etc. Emphasis on Purgatory has faded due to an acceptance of the mystery of what happens after death.

Pope Paul VI in his encyclical, *Mysterium Fidei,* summarizes our new understanding of the Mass as a growing awareness of the presence of Christ. He is present in the people who gather in his name, and also in the reading and preaching of the word. Because of the Sacrament of Ordination, he is present in the priest and then in the central action of the Eucharist, "by the power of the Holy Spirit." He is also present in the tabernacle and in the people who have received communion and leave to make him present in our world.

But while we reflect on Christ's vision from the Cross, a world where all human beings can be free and enjoy the banquet of life, we must also remember that sin and selfishness keep most people from the banquet of life. Fr. Moloney S.J., reminds us, "There is no community without self-denial. There is no resurrection without the cross. There is no banquet without sacrifice. The bread of life is a bread broken for a broken world." He reminds us that, "The Eucharist is fundamentally an image of the great feast of the blessed in the kingdom of God with which salvation will reach its consummation…that the Eucharist is the image of this future life is a way of saying that this is the destiny to which the sacrament gives us access."

Recently I attended a lecture on the Eucharist by two women scholars in the Baptist Church, Seattle. They spoke of eucharistic life on earth as a beginning of what we call paradise. This had been regarded as life with God after death. Through scripture and tradition they stated that living by faith with Jesus on our earthly journey is living in paradise. Moloney concludes his study of the Eucharist with this inspiring message: "Similarly, the Eucharist looks forward to the great banquet of the kingdom at the end of time. Again, on the level of external form, it can scarcely be considered a banquet. Where do a piece of wafer and a sip of a cup constitute a banquet? But because it is the sacramental sign of that future banquet, it really is a banquet and really contains an anticipation of those exalted events of the end of time. The Eucharist, then, is the supreme gesture of Our Lord's love in the life of the Church, summoning us to immerse ourselves every so often in the reality and in the graces of our origin and our goal."

Lastly, the Vatican Council in *The Document on the Church in the Modern World,* reminded us that, "The joys and hopes, the griefs and anxieties of men of this age, especially those who are poor or in any way afflicted, these are the joys and hopes, the griefs and anxieties of the followers of Christ." Then it adds, "The world fallen indeed into the bondage of sin yet emancipated now by Christ. He was crucified and rose again to break the strangle hold of personified evil, so that this world might be fashioned anew according to God's design and reach its fulfillment."

In parts of Africa, the presentation of the gifts at the Offertory is not just the carrying forward of the bread and wine as we do in the West. Each person presents himself or herself as a gift to God. They do this at the Offertory by joining the celebrant in a joyful dance to and around the altar. The prayer that follows, listed as a "Prayer over the Gifts," is a prayer over the people gathered as gifts to God. To me this attitude seems to be an expression of the faith of the congregation in the words of Jesus in the 17th chapter of St. John's Gospel. Jesus, in His farewell the night before His death, said, "Just Father, the world has not known you, but I have known you; and these men have known that you sent me. To them I have revealed your name, and I will continue to reveal it so that your love for me may live in them, and I may live in them." (verses 25-26) A joyful African dance at the Offertory of the Mass expresses who the people believe they are — other Christs, filled with the Father's love, which makes them truly gifts to God.

The Mass is a call to live with faith in the Resurrection of Jesus and with love for others as we go out from its celebration. A church in Indianapolis, near where the auto races take place, recalls a moment before the race begins. There is a shout — "Start the engines!" As the people prepare to leave the church, a pastor aware of the call of the Mass to serve and love others would say, "Start the engines!" And the congregation joyfully responded, "Start the engines!" I believe Jesus would be pleased with this understanding of the Mass, which we generally refer to now as the celebration of Eucharist (Thanksgiving).

Chapter 22

Joyful Hope

Christmas is first of all a fantastic discovery for the human race. We all feel so vulnerable in life. We are born with no blueprints that tell us why we were sent here. We observe the world around us, beautiful and mysterious. There are beautiful sunrises and sunsets, moonlight and starry nights, birds of various kinds, animals, and, of course, lots of people and languages. There is also sickness, violence and death. But the big question we all confront is — Who began this universe? What does the future eventually hold for us? The answer to these questions is given by an infant. For centuries before he was born, great thinkers gave us insights into the origin and purpose of life. An unknown author wrote a book about the start of the universe and called it Genesis. Names such as Abraham, Moses, Jeremiah, Isaiah and the Psalmist gave us some great insights about life and our relationship to the Giver of Life — God.

But the greatest insight about God is given by the infant in Bethlehem. This infant tells us God really cares about everyone, about every infant who is born, whether here in a hospital or in a slum in Calcutta. That is why Mother Teresa is a saint. She understood the message of Bethlehem so well that she picked up the infant sick and abandoned and lovingly cared for it.

This baby born to heavenly music is not born in a palace but in a broken down shelter for animals. Shepherds who seldom had an opportunity to attend religious services heard the music and left everything to visit the newborn. As they returned home, they told all the people they met about the child in the straw.

Now we turn to a great Christian artist for his insight about Bethlehem. Tintoretto painted the Nativity with the child lying on straw watched over by Joseph and Mary. But around them are lots of people, poor people who heard about the impoverished family and brought food and clothes to the family. Tintoretto saw the message of

Bethlehem, which called people to care for others, especially the poor. Every child born in the world reveals God and comes to us made in the image and likeness of God. We are all loved unconditionally by God.

The true Christmas spirit would make us free at last from a constant barrage of advertisements trying to tell us there is something wrong if we don't have the perfect tree well decorated and the right gifts for the right person. The holidays do not eliminate illness or grief. Sometimes they can magnify it, but Christmas brings us magic and mystery. Take time to be alone and hear the music of heaven from the hills of Bethlehem, so that our Advent prayer is realized, that our hearts are filled with wonder and praise.

The Christmas spirit in some mysterious but real way is found in those not formally Christian. Fr. Ron Rolheiser writes in a recent column in the Catholic press about those he calls his pagan friends: "They rarely go to church, mostly disregard the church's teaching on sex, pray only when in a crisis and are basically too immersed in life here and now to think much about God and eternity. But even so, they radiate life sometimes in ways that shame me." He continues: "I look at some of my pagan friends, at their energy, their generosity, their warmth, what they bring into a room, and I believe in God more deeply. They don't go to church and that isn't good, but they are on the side of life."

That means in their own way they believe in Christmas, because with joy they celebrate the gift of their own lives and can reach out to celebrate the gift of life joyfully with others. That is the true Christmas spirit.

Pope Benedict, in his 2005 Christmas message, urged people to spread joy through smiles and acts of kindness. He said this was an antidote to the ills of society. "Joy" he said, "is the true gift of Christmas, not expensive toys that cost time and money. Give true joy instead."

Chapter 23

Forgiveness — Seventy Times Seven

Former President Jimmy Carter and Archbishop Desmond Tutu direct a ten million-dollar "Campaign For Forgiveness Research." The subjects to be covered are forgiveness in family relationships, secular and spiritual forgiveness, the effects of forgiveness on political relationships, and the relations of forgiveness on health.

We hear much about the social causes of violence and crime, about the need for punishment, for three strikes and you are out, but seldom do we hear discussions about forgiveness in society. Robert Enright from the University of Wisconsin in 1984 co-authored a book with Joanna North, *Exploring Forgiveness*. Enright grew up a Roman Catholic, later became a Methodist, and is now back to Catholicism. With a Biblical outlook on life, he wondered why the social sciences that are supposed to help people did not study the healing effects of forgiveness, since the Bible clearly teaches the importance of forgiveness. When he started a pioneer academic study of forgiveness he observed that, "Academic eyes would glaze over 90 percent of the time. Nine percent had hate filled eyes, one percent was delighted."

Much has been written from a theological viewpoint about how God forgives. As Catholics, we have studied contrition and purpose of amendment as necessary, with the sacrament of reconciliation to be assured of God's forgiveness, as only God can forgive sins. The necessity to forgive other people was not studied with the same intensity. Today the Pope has asked forgiveness for the wrongs committed by Christians against Jews, Muslims, women, other Christians, and Native Peoples around the world. As individuals, we need to pray for those we have injured so that they may turn the hurt to strength by granting forgiveness.

Cathy Noble, an Episcopalian from Texas, set out with a group of fellow Christians in 1996, the anniversary of the First Crusade to walk from Cologne, Germany to Jerusalem in the footsteps of the Crusaders. Interest in their plea for forgiveness led to discussions in high schools and colleges in the towns they visited concerning the true nature of Christianity. They reached Jerusalem in December 1999, the thousandth anniversary of the arrival of the Crusaders, and had a meeting with Yasser Arafat and the Chief Rabbi of Jerusalem. Both complimented them for their heroic three-year project seeking religious harmony, understanding and true forgiveness.

New research is revealing the benefit that forgiveness brings to the one who forgives. Forgiveness does not mean that you forego justice. People must take responsibility for their actions. Forgiveness can take time. “When trust is shattered between persons where there is a significant relationship (between spouses, parents and children, or pastors and parishioners) forgiveness can be very difficult to attain,” writes Robert Enright. It may be a gradual growth in grace until we reach the ideal of Jesus to forgive from our hearts when there is a total cessation of negative feelings towards the offender, and the relationship is restored and grows. This calls for constant prayers.

The most difficult challenge of forgiveness is when we experience the loss of a loved one through violence. Many feel that the only way to obtain peace of mind is to have the murderer executed. Gary Zukav in his best selling book, *The Seat of the Soul*, tells us “When you refuse to forgive it is like agreeing to wear dark gruesome sun glasses that distort everything, hatred of evil does not diminish it, but increases it.” Zukav also recalls how Gandhi was so severely beaten on two occasions that he nearly died. He forgave his assailants and did not seek prosecution believing forgiveness would heal them and society.

Archbishop Nguyen Van Thuan spent twenty years as a prisoner in a Communist jail in his native Vietnam, nine of these years he spent in solitary confinement. The guards often asked him if he hated them or if he would try to kill them when he was released. He replied, “I love you, because Jesus Christ has taught me to love everyone, even my enemies. If I don’t do this I am not worthy to bear the name Christian. Jesus said, ‘Love your enemies and pray for those who persecute you.’”

In the Sermon on the Mount, Jesus said: “Don’t resist violence. If you are slapped on one cheek, turn the other.” (Matt. 5:19) Last fall I heard a radio commentator in Seattle admit he could not obey these words of Jesus and believed even most Christians could not or would not obey them either.

A few weeks later, the Amish people suffered a great tragedy when several grade school children were shot in school. The killer who took his own life was not Amish. Seventy-five people attended the funeral of the killer. Half of them were Amish. Later they took up a collection to aid the wife of the killer of their children. The Amish revealed to the world that they followed the teaching of Jesus concerning forgiveness.

Chapter 24

Doom and Gloom No! — Good News Yes!

In recent years I have been amazed at the interest of young and old in regard to the final end of our universe. Some trace this interest to William Miller, the founder of the American Adventist Movement. He predicted that the end of the world would come between March 21, 1843 and March 21, 1844. When the end did not come, the speculation continued. A new date was set for October 22, 1844. Still, predictions of the end are frequent and taken seriously, as by the Branch Davidian sect in Waco, Texas in 1993, where members paid with their lives in a confrontation that should not have taken place.

In 1969, Hal Lindsay published, *The Late Great Planet Earth*. It sold 34 million copies in 54 languages. He gives a timetable for the end of the world. First, the Jewish Temple in Jerusalem will be rebuilt. Sacrifices discontinued in 70 AD will be restored. The Anti-Christ will attack the new Jewish State and destroy Jerusalem. But the final battle between good and evil will culminate in what is called "ARMAGEDDON." Jesus will intervene and destroy the Anti-Christ and the Jews will recognize Jesus as Messiah. Wars, earthquakes, and natural disasters will indicate the end time is near. Then will come the final judgment and the end time for our world and all in it.

How do people find any support for such a far-fetched theory? Harvey Cox of Harvard Divinity School tells us, "One of its most curious features is that sometime before the end — no one claims to know exactly when — all true Christian believers will be snatched away from this troubled earth into the Savior's arms. This is called 'RAPTURE.'"

Proof that this is not a theory held by just a few are the eleven novels under the title *Left Behind.* This refers to the unfortunate people who are left behind when the "Rapture" takes place. I again quote Harvey Cox: "The sheer bulk and technical urgency of the end time advocates have all but drowned out alternative Christian views of the future." It is a theology in contrast to the teaching of Jesus and is certainly bad news for Jews. Some of these believers in ARMAGEDDON assign Jews to another type of holocaust to introduce the end time.

A word about "ARMAGEDDON": Megaddo is a town in Northern Israel — a place where invading armies fought many battles. When speaking of any great conflict, people speak of it as "Megaddo" or "Armageddon." Some, of course, speak about a final battle called the real "Armageddon" between the forces of good and evil, to take place before the end of the world.

As a Catholic, I ask you to join me in reflecting on how the Bible treats the end of the world. From about 200 BC to 200 AD there was a form of writing called "apocalyptic," which literally means, "drawing back the veil." It appealed to people in times of persecution and suffering, calling them to look ahead to the distant future when God would change sadness and suffering into victorious peace. The writers used standard images to indicate the VICTORY ahead. Stars would fall from the sky, the sun and moon would be darkened, plagues would take place. Our language also has a strange way of expressing the universe. We speak of it "raining cats and dogs." He "hit the roof." He or she is "on cloud nine," et cetera.

The Bible is not a book with coded messages, but is primarily a book with good news.

When I read apocalyptic language, I am reminded of a form of Irish literature in the 18th century called the "AISLEANG." The Irish people, dispossessed from their land, forbidden to practice the Catholic Faith, lived under oppressive rule called the Penal Laws. Poets tried to communicate hope for an end to British exploitation and oppression without being accused of treason. So they wrote the "AISLEANG." Each poem had a basic outline. The poet met a woman in rags, with no shoes, no jewelry, but he could perceive a great hidden beauty and dignity in her. Moved with compassion, the poet resolved to find robes to befit her dignity and beauty, with golden slippers for her feet and diamonds on her fingers, thus restoring to her the dignity she once enjoyed before famine reduced her to poverty. The reader knew underneath that the poet was referring to Ireland. This poetry saved the poet from being classified as a revolutionary. In a sense, the "Aisleang" used apocalyptic language.

Jesus used apocalyptic language, especially in Luke 21:11-23. But the language actually refers to the destruction of Jerusalem, and this language is wrongly applied to the end of the world. But also in Matthew 26:29 Jesus does speak about the end of the world. Actually, we find the same language in the 13th chapter of Isaiah. He wrote: "The stars and constellations of the heavens send forth no light, the sun is dark when it rose, and the light of the moon does not shine...the heavens tremble and the earth shall be shaken from its place." But the prophet is telling about the fall of Babylon six centuries before the time of Jesus.

Is the sun cooling? Is the universe expanding or contracting? Will a nuclear war destroy life? The end of the world will come for each of us at our death, and how death will come to us is unknown. But Jesus is our assurance by his resurrection that "the best is yet to be, the last for which the first was made."

We say in the Nicene Creed, "Jesus will come again in glory to judge the living and the dead." We believe the presence of Jesus will be fully revealed at the end of the ages. The priest scientist Teilhard de Chardin called this the "OMEGA" point of history. The image of Jesus in the Creed "seated at the right hand of the Father" expresses honor, not a geographic place. We don't know what this coming will be like. Catholics generally are not preoccupied with doom and gloom scenarios for the end of the universe. We try to remember the words of Jesus in Matthew 28:20: "Behold, I am with you always until the end of time." Harvey Cox teaches a course at Harvard, summed up in his book, *When Jesus Comes to Harvard.* He concludes his chapter on the end times as follows: "Follow the advice of Jesus. Avoid speculating about the *when* or *how.*" In the meantime, it is best to follow the counsel of the Hasidic rabbi who was interrupted by one of his followers while he was tending his garden. "What would you do, Rabbi," the student asked, "if you knew the messiah was coming today?" The rabbi replied, "Well, I would continue to water my garden." With this I fully agree. Catholics call it, "living the sacrament of the present moment."

Chapter 25

"Vocation" Misunderstood

The word "vocation" comes from the Latin "vocare" — to call. For centuries, Catholics regarded a vocation as a call to religious life, as a priest, sister, or brother. In Ireland, if you left the seminary, the learning center for priesthood, you were regarded as a "spoiled priest." Respect for the call to be a priest was strong in the faith of Irish parents who considered a son who became a priest a special blessing for the family.

This faith was based on the dedication and love of priests for their people during the centuries of persecution beginning with Henry VIII in the 16th century. The British Parliament officially repealed anti-Catholic legislation in a law known as "The Act of Emancipation" in 1829. For some years prior to 1829, Catholics were permitted to practice their faith in matters such as attendance at Mass, etc., but suffered discrimination in numerous other areas of life.

During the centuries of persecution, priests in both England and Ireland paid with their lives for their devotion and commitment to ministering to their people. Christmas, 2004, I was in the Irish College in Rome where, because of persecution in Ireland, many priests, like Oliver Plunkett, were smuggled out of Ireland to be ordained here. After ordination, some were tempted to avoid Ireland and the persecution there by accepting ministry in a European country. To prevent this, seminarians were asked to sign a pledge to return to Ireland after ordination. Oliver Plunkett returned to Ireland around 1650. After years of ministry, while hiding out in isolated areas in all kinds of weather as he pursued his priestly vocation, he was captured and taken to the Tower of London. Condemned to death, he was dragged behind a horse to his place of execution. There at a London suburb called Tyburn, in 1681, he was "hanged, drawn, and quartered." Since then, because of his commitment to his priestly vocation, he has been officially declared a saint and loved in Ireland. Supposedly a bystander took his severed head, which is venerated today in Ireland.

The love and respect of Irish parents for a priestly vocation in the family had its negative as well as its positive effects. A priest who attended the same seminary as I did came to America following his ordination. A few years after he arrived he was taken to a hospital very seriously ill with appendicitis. A young Catholic nurse cared for him and a friendship developed. He resigned from the priesthood. They married but had no children. After about ten years they divorced.

He obtained a high paying job in industry. But in spite of his success in the business world, he kept thinking of priesthood. Each summer he would vacation with some priests he knew. Finally, a bishop who heard his story decided to accept him back in priestly ministry. In the meantime, this priest had reflected a great deal on what he considered his vocation and the nature of priesthood. He recalled his mother died after she gave birth to him, her eighth child. The devout grieving husband used to say to his youngest son as he grew up, "Remember, son, your mother is praying for you. Maybe she wants you to be a priest." He concluded that he followed his father's desire rather than a real vocation. In his later years after a business career, he experienced a personal call to priestly ministry and was an outstanding priest. A picture of him beside Pope John XXIII spoke eloquently to me about religious vocation. The Pope commended him for his ministry to priests with special needs.

In my family, my mother had three first cousins who were priests and a sister who was a nun. I admired them and the local priest who gathered his flock around him on Sundays, comforted them in death, and visited with them in their homes. In high school I thought of priesthood from time to time. On graduating from high school at age eighteen, I applied to be admitted to a seminary. If accepted, I could have been sent to Rome, Spain, Paris, or the National Irish Seminary. I was nominated for the latter, received a scholarship, and also was accepted to be a priest in my home diocese in Ireland. I was very blessed with this call to serve with the Irish people I loved and never intended to leave Ireland.

It was very common to enter a seminary in Ireland after graduation from high school. Many young women in pursuit of a religious vocation also entered religious communities about the same time. Today many who pursue a vocation to priesthood or religious life already had a vocation in business, in teaching, in the military, or the academic world.

For example, my former pastor at St. Thomas More Parish, Lynnwood, is the Rev. Robert Camuso. Following high school, he spent three years in the Navy and then attended college, which led to a career in advertising. He spent several years with a large company in New York. He moved to Seattle and had his own business. From time to time, he thought of a vocation to the priesthood. He became acquainted with some Seattle priests and decided to apply for a seminary in his late thirties. The archdiocese of Seattle accepted his offer of priesthood, and in his forties he was ordained a priest. He is a dedicated, talented, pastor, but also uses his experience in communication. He has a weekly radio program entitled "Conversations with Father Bob" in which he interviews local church and community leaders about their work. It is broadcast on eight stations in the United States and Canada.

Personally, I feel that narrowing the word vocation to apply only to the religious vocation of priest, nun, or brother is a misunderstanding of vocation. The call I received was more or less like a whisper, causing me to reflect on the work of Jesus. The desire to minister to people was the main attraction of priesthood for me, leading me to be ordained a priest at age twenty-five. But a vocation is true of all professions.

St. Bernard in the 12th century was speaking to his monks in the Cistercian Order about their religious vocation. They owned a large farm and grew food to feed their monks and local people. He said to them, "Those farm implements you use to grow food for God's people make those instruments as sacred as the vessels I use in the worship at the altar."

It is my personal conviction that God calls all kinds of people to ministry on behalf of the human family. The doctor in medicine, the dentist, the lawyer, the electrician, the policeman, the fireman, the carpenter, the sales person, the farmer, the automobile mechanic, and so many other professions all have a vocation to provide a needed service for people. The voice that calls to that profession may be very soft and gentle. A woman doctor told me she found a small bird when she was in grade school. Evidently the mother had died or was killed. She took the small animal into her home, fed it and then released it. In this experience she felt a vocation to minister to the physical needs of people as a doctor. The example of a parent may lead to a vocation. Recently, I met a man who owns a dental lab in Seattle. His father founded it. The son, as often happens, followed his father, and together they worked side-by-side for twenty-five years in the same vocation. A mother told me her vocation was working for the State of Washington. She had six children and to me she was a stay-at-home mom. "What do you do for the State of Washington?" I asked her. She replied, "I am concentrating, with my husband, on raising our children by staying at home. In this way the State will not have to house and feed them in jail or in juvenile detention." She had a good concept of her vocation as a mother.

There should be respect for every genuine vocation that serves the human family. This recognition should not be based on the financial remuneration of the work but on its essential ministry to the human family. One of the strangest vocations, with tragic overtones, was described in the Seattle PI newspaper on January 26, 2006. The title of the story read, "It's a dirty job — but." It is that of crime scene cleaners. Whatever the needed service. I feel the call comes from the Holy Spirit.

Vocations are subject to change. A well-known doctor in Seattle spent his first ten years supporting his family as an electrician. A doctor in a big city may feel the call to serve the poor or AIDS victims overseas.

A vocation that is subject to change at present — which seldom happened in the past — is priesthood. A hundred years ago, a young man in Italy was engaged to a young woman who contracted illness and died. He decided to enter a seminary. He was sent to Seattle as a missionary. One day he met a woman with a remarkable likeness to the girl he had intended to marry. As he pondered his vocation and his emotional state when he entered the seminary, he decided to leave priesthood and to marry the woman he met here in Seattle. Headlines in the local paper read "Woman Takes Priest From Church of Rome." Because of the publicity, he could not get a job. I read a very sad comment about his problems in a Seattle court document. He told the court that, "Because I was a Catholic priest, I cannot obtain a job with my own name." The court changed his name. He died later and was buried in Calvary Cemetery,

Seattle, under his court name. In 1945 I officiated at the wedding of his daughter. Sixty years after the court had agreed to change his name, his granddaughter and I had his real name placed on his grave. This was done out of respect for her grandfather and to eradicate the rejection he had experienced.

One most remarkable insight about a vocation is given to us by Jesus on his last night on earth. He foresaw the terrible death ahead in the pursuit of his vocation and prayed, "Father, if it is possible, let it pass." In other words, "Don't ask me to face crucifixion as part of my vocation." As a priest who faced loneliness and separation from country, family, and classmates, I can relate to the prayer of Jesus, as I too prayed to be spared from difficulties and trials while living my vocation.

In living out my vocation as a priest I have had two goals. The first is to assure everyone of God's unconditional love. Even when in the seminary I had a great devotion to St. Therese, the French Carmelite nun who was born in 1873, died in 1897, and was declared a saint in 1925. She is also recognized by the Church as a Doctor in Theology. In her theology she inspired me to personally believe in God's unconditional love. "Whatever my sins and failures in living my vocation," St. Therese writes in her autobiography, "I am certain that if I had on my conscience every imaginable crime, I should lose nothing of my confidence, but would throw myself with sorrow into the arms of the Savior. I remember His love for the Prodigal Son. I have heard his words to Mary Magdalene, for the woman taken in adultery and to the woman of Samaria. No — there is no one who could frighten me for I know too well what to believe concerning His Mercy and His Love."

My second goal is to work for understanding and respect among different religions. Vatican II, in speaking of other religions, reminded us that, "The Catholic Church rejects nothing which is true and holy in these religions. She looks with sincere respect upon those ways of conduct and of life, those rites and teaching, which though differing in many particulars from what she holds and teaches, nevertheless often reflect a ray of that Truth which enlightens all people."

Each day, I pray as a friend long deceased taught me. I begin each day with the words, "Father, I come to this day unburdened by past failure or present weakness because I am conscious of your power to heal my past and to sustain me today. Let me feel the power of your Spirit of Love in me so that guilt, regret, or shame will have no power of their own, but be lovingly redeemed by you and become an essential part of the newness and strength I feel today."

At each Mass as the years of ministry move on I am becoming more sensitive to the prayer before communion which reads: "Deliver us, O Lord, from every evil and grant us peace in our day. In your mercy keep us free from sin. And protect us from all anxiety as we wait in joyful hope for the coming of our Savior, Jesus Christ." By the power of the Spirit in me I seek to live each day in joyful hope.

My vocation as a priest has been strongly influenced by St. Therese. There were times when she wished that she could become a priest. But then she was moved by the spirit of St. Francis of Assisi who declined the honor of priesthood and became a deacon in complete humble service.

St. Therese never left her Carmelite convent in Lisieux, France. She had desired to go as a missionary to Hanoi but her health would not allow it. Yet, she is called the Patroness of Missions. She wrote: "Beyond all doubt it is by prayer and sacrifice we can help our missionaries, but sometimes when God is pleased to unite two souls for His glory, He permits them to exchange their thoughts and to rouse one another to a greater love for God."

Year after year in celebrating Sunday Mass I have been inspired by the opening prayers. My favorite that speaks to my heart is the one for the third Sunday of the year.

"Almighty Father,
the love you offer
always exceeds the furthest expression of our human longing,
for you are greater than the human heart.
Direct each thought, each effort of our life,
so that the limits of our faults and weaknesses
may not obscure the vision of your glory
or keep us from the peace you have promised.
We ask this through Christ our Lord. Amen"

Chapter 26

The Pains and Joys of the Priest

Pope John Paul II, prior to the year 2000, publicly admitted Church culpability for events in the first 2000 years of the Church. On ninety-four occasions he apologized for Church attitudes toward the Crusades, the treatment of women, Jews, the Inquisition, Luther, Racism, Division among the Churches, Native People, Slavery and Islam, etc. On some occasions he personally asked for forgiveness. In his Encyclical Ut Unum Sint (May 1995) he said, "To the extent that we are responsible for these, I join my predecessor Paul VI in asking for forgiveness." On October 21, 1992, speaking to native peoples of South America, he said, "As Pastor of the Church I ask you in the name of Jesus Christ to pardon those who have caused pain to you and your ancestors during these 500 years." He also said, "At the end of this second millennium we must make an examination of conscience, where we are, where Christ has brought us, where we have deviated from the Gospel." It is an examination we all need to do from time to time. I look back over sixty-three years as a priest and see the need for forgiveness from parishioners and friends, from Church members and non-Church members, where I may have failed them in time of need.

As a member of the Catholic Church, I apologize to the Jewish people for my lack of understanding and concern about the harsh treatment they received from the Church over the centuries. There were a few thousand Jews in Dublin, Ireland, but I grew up with little knowledge of what the Church did to the Jews, and Rabbi Levine who came into my life in 1960, helped me discover my lack of knowledge. One day he said to me, "There are many pages missing from Catholic histories about the persecution of the Jews." From him I learned that Crusaders in 1095, before leaving Germany, killed thousands of Jews. We know little in the Catholic Church of the suffering of the Jews expelled from Spain and England or details of pogroms and persecutions of Jews confined to ghettos by the Church. I learned from him that Jews were forbidden to appear on the streets of the city during Holy Week. They were excluded from many professions and social clubs, and they were denied promotion in the academic and business worlds.

Rabbi Levine came to America from Czarist Russia when he was eight years old and began his education in a public school in Duluth, Minn. His teacher was a Miss Calverly, a Christian. She had a remarkable influence on his life that he described in his book, *Wild Branch on The Olive Tree:* "All through grammar school, Miss Calverly was my staunch friend and confidant. Through her I learned to love America and Americans and the fear of Christians that I brought with me from the Russian ghetto gradually disappeared. I even got to the point of becoming Miss Calverly's personal messenger delivering her Christmas cards and presents to her friends without feeling that I was betraying my own Jewish faith. During my grammar school years I made a number of Christian friends who also helped me overcome my fears. I began to learn that there were all kinds of Christians, that while there were still boys who taunted me as "Sheeny" there were others who were ready to defend me even to the point of fighting with others. I was in America now and this awareness was reassuring and heart-warming."

As a priest I regret my blind acceptance of total separation from other Christians during my seminary years and my first sixteen years in the priesthood until I started in 1960 a career on TV with Rabbi Levine and Protestant ministers. A partial explanation for my failure to relate to other Christians was due to the almost military-style obedience that Catholics gave to Church leaders. Unless bishops gave leadership we accepted the status quo. In Ireland, Catholics have experienced centuries of persecution and confiscation of their land together with the prohibition of the exercise of the Catholic Faith by a Protestant English government. Catholic emancipation was only granted to Ireland by the British Parliament in 1829. A wooded area in a field owned by my family was a place where in secret Mass was celebrated in the 18th century. I grew up in Ireland that after a thousand years obtained its freedom from England. Catholics and Protestants attended the same school with me, with much more tolerance for each other than in Northern Ireland. There, Protestants are in the majority. A sign of the division between

Catholics and Protestants in Southern Ireland, where Catholics are in the majority, can be seen in the following. My parish church in Ireland was built in 1858. Out of a hundred students who attended grade school with me about fifteen were Protestant. Both Catholics and Protestants followed a policy of "circle the wagons," and did not mingle with each other. The first interfaith marriage, between a Catholic and a Protestant, took place in my parish church in Ireland in 2005. I am told it has led to warmer relations between Protestants and Catholics.

New winds of change have been blowing in the Catholic Church since Pope John XXIII "opened the windows" during his brief reign, 1958 to 1963. This new openness is taking hold in spite of the fact that many theologians in the past forty years have been disciplined for views considered not in harmony with official teaching. Father Hans Kung, professor of Catholic theology at Tubingen University in Germany, was forbidden to teach as a Catholic scholar, because some of his views were critical of traditional teaching. He was a leading theologian at Vatican Council and afterwards was invited to speak in many countries. He came to give a lecture at Seattle University in 1962. I had the privilege of spending a day with him, but also I had the sad duty to inform him of a message received from the office of Cardinal McIntyre, Los Angeles. Father Kung was scheduled to speak there following his lecture in Seattle, but Cardinal McIntyre sent word that Father Kung was not welcome to speak in the Los Angeles Archdiocese.

On that occasion, I saw the soul and spirit of Father Kung. On hearing the news he laughed and showed no resentment. He told me that, as a seminarian, he questioned the views of his teachers and received poor grades. An elderly priest who was his counselor said to him, "Hans, always say it as you see it, but be prepared for rejection and pain." He proved to me that evening what St. Paul said, "Love is patient, kind, without envy, and does not act perversely." When he was a professor at Tubingen, he hired the present pope (Benedict XVI).

In spite of serious differences in theology between them in later years, I was pleased to read that Hans Kung and Pope Benedict had a long visit together after he became Pope. The press termed it "cordial." Hopefully it will be true of others also disciplined since Vatican II.

Examples of new insights can be found in three key areas in the Church with regard to Poverty, Celibacy, and Obedience. **Poverty** is being faced in a new way by the Church today. It can be summed up in the phrase, "Live simply so that others can simply live." As a seminarian, my funds were so limited that it was not possible to contribute to other human needs. I am indebted to a Seattle priest, the late Fr. Howard Lavelle, for inspiration in regard to the spirit of poverty. Every Lent he donated all the money he received to the Missions. We both worked side-by-side in the Chancery that was next door to the Blood Bank. He encouraged me to join him in donating blood at the end of Lent on Good Friday each year.

I have grieved at the poverty I read about in foreign countries and have been inspired by the priests and nuns like Mother Teresa who ministered to the poorest of the poor. In 1962, I met Bishop Anthony Padiyara in Seattle when he was on his way to the Vatican Council. While in the seminary in India, his expenses had been paid by a Father Corrigan from St. Paul, Minnesota. At the time that Bishop Padiyara came to Seattle, Father Corrigan had died. His niece lived in Seattle and she introduced me to the Bishop. He and I became good friends. He kept inviting me to visit his diocese of Ootacamund in India. I accepted in 1969, and, to celebrate my 25th ordination anniversary I visited him where he gave me the honor of baptizing twenty-five people who had been instructed in the faith. The poverty was heartbreaking. In his native city of Changanacherry he founded a home for children with polio, operated by an Indian community, the Sisters of the Destitute. With the help of parishioners over the years we sent about $100,000 to help the Mercy Home for Children and other charities in India. Bishop Padiyara came to St. Michael's Parish in Olympia in 1975, when I was pastor there, to celebrate the 100th anniversary of the parish. He also visited me at St. Cecilia Parish in Stanwood and at Sacred Heart Parish in Bellevue. Parishioners who met him donated small amounts of money each month to assist him. Together with some larger bequests we were able to assist him in his ministry to the poor until his death a few years ago. Bishop Padiyara became Cardinal Padiyara in 1988 in Cochin, India.

There are 3000 references in the Bible to the needs of the poor. Jesus spoke in Matthew 25 of service to the poor as service to Him. To live in the spirit of poverty calls for a new vision of service to neighbor such as Sr. Joan Chittister, a Benedictine sister, in her book, *Called to Question* describes: "To say that we can possibly minister to the poor and never read a single article on the national debt; to think that we can be moral parts of a global community and never study a thing about the Third World debt; to imagine that we can save the planet and never learn a thing about ecology; to infer that we work to promote the women's issue but never go to a women's conference, read a feminist theologian or spend a minute tracing the history of ideas about women; to say we care about the homeless dying and never say a thing about the evil of homelessness, or the lack of medical care for the indigent, smacks of pallid conviction at best. Simply to do things is not enough anymore. Professional education that fits us for particular skills but neglects to prepare a person for dealing with the great questions of human life is not enough anymore. The world needs thinkers who take thinking as a spiritual discipline. Anything else may well be denial practiced in the name of religion." This is a new approach in the Catholic Church about poverty, other than meeting the immediate need. It turns our attention to the causes of poverty.

Here is a view of poverty today in Calcutta as seen by a young volunteer from Seattle: "This is what I have been contemplating on my way to and from work this week. My scenery changes throughout the day...the early morning walk, when so many people are waking up on the streets and yawning and stretching and picking up their sheets or blankets...starting the day of continual noise and activity. After Mass, the pace is picking up on the streets...I walk (and dodge and weave) through the racing taxis, cars, buses, and rickshaws as I cross to the other side of the street and catch a bus to Kalighat. After work...the scenery changes again. I walk out of Kalighat, and it is lunchtime, with people streaming down the street, and children and adults filling in all of the surrounding areas and cracks around me...sitting, selling buying, talking, yelling, walking, riding bikes...they wind past me and around me as I head for the underground subway and home for lunch. I weave down Sudder Street where the street vendors and sidewalk food merchants are all calling out 'Sister' or 'Auntie'...'come and see!' My afternoon walk is a frenzy of vehicles as I take my life in my own hands crossing the streets...motorcycles and auto-rickshaws narrowly avoiding me as their mark...it is a crossing game. Finally, at the end of the day, I walk home in the twilight, where the hustle and bustle of the day starts to wind down...past the food stalls and houses of prayer, past the people lining up in 'their place' for the night, past people calling out to me...the cycle is complete.

"In all my daily wanderings...when should I stop? To stop, or to walk on by...that is the uncomfortable choice that I am faced with at all times. So sometimes I choose...I buy a protein drink for a small girl, a coconut for an older woman, a blanket for a man in the street, a kilo of rice and a kilo of dhal and some oil for two women, I share my lunch with one of the boys who is watching me eat on the street corner, or buy an injection at the pharmacy for a woman bitten by a dog who has a rabies prescription from a doctor...but no way of filling it. So sometimes I stop, and sometimes I don't...and it is difficult, random choice that I have been given.

"And so I ask myself...why me? Why was I, by chance of birth, given this choice 'power' to choose? However, no matter if I say yes, or if I say no...the choice is always uncomfortable...and perhaps THAT is the lesson...awareness.

As Mother Teresa said, "The whole work is only a drop in the ocean...so you begin, I begin...one, one, one..."

The Catholic Church in Western Washington addresses poverty by supporting eleven Family Centers that provide housing, medical care, mental health assistance, help for the elderly, and childcare. It is the largest provider of social services, next to the state; yet, we must not forget there are 8,000 homeless in the Seattle area each night. I was comforted to read that 400 college students from around the country met at Seattle University the second week of November 2005, to discuss how to deal with the roots of poverty and homelessness. The Church also needs to help people struggling to find a Christian perspective on daily work. In their book, *Your Work Matters to God,* the authors, Sherman and Hendricks, estimate that 90% of Christians have never heard a sermon that drew a connection between their religious beliefs and work life. In the past we did not pay enough attention to the enslavement of workers that gave rise to Communism. Today we need to be concerned about jails and work conditions where, for one reason or another, people are exploited, especially women and children. For example, a priest friend of mine in the Philippines, Father Shay Cullen, has discovered that there are about 20,000 children in adult jails, some as young as five years old. He has already secured the release of twenty, and is working to sensitize the country to the plight of the others.

Because of the above, some theologians today would shift the emphasis from a vow of poverty to a vow for stewardship, or better still, a vow for "mutual sustainability." Under God, all of creation is given to our care and none should die from starvation due to hoarding and manipulation of the resources of the world by a few. In the liturgy we are called "stewards of creation." Poor stewardship allows thousands of children to die of starvation each day. The organization "Bread for the World" helps me and thousands to carry out the call of God to good stewardship, to assist the poor here in America and wherever. In the year 2000, some 191 countries pledged to eliminate poverty by 2015. Bread for the World lists 8 areas to be addressed by 2015:

1. Eradicate extreme poverty and hunger.
2. Ensure that all boys and girls complete primary school.
3. Promote gender equality and empower women.
4. Reduce by two thirds the mortality rate among children under five.
5. Reduce by three quarters the ratio of women dying in childbirth.
6. Halt and begin to reverse the spread of HIV/AIDS and incidence of malaria and other major diseases.
7. Ensure environmental sustainability.
8. Develop a global partnership.

Members of Bread for the World communicate with legislators to encourage the achievement of the above.

OBEDIENCE

On June 18, 1944, at my ordination, I promised obedience to the bishop of Ossory, Ireland, and to his successors. He granted me permission for five to ten years to leave Ireland and answer the call of Bishop Gerald Shaughnessy of Seattle for priests to serve the great numbers that had come here to work during WWII. After a year in Seattle, Bishop Shaughnessy called me into his office and asked me if I would like to remain permanently in Seattle. At the time I was on his staff in the Chancery. Having reflected and discerned about the possibility of staying in Seattle, I replied, "Bishop I will stay if you want me, and if my bishop in Ireland agrees." Pleased with my answer he wrote to my bishop in Ireland. Due to the subsequent illness of Bishop Shaughnessy and the arrival of a new bishop, Bishop Thomas Connolly, my formal membership in the Seattle Diocese only took place on June 25, 1951 when I pledged allegiance to Archbishop Connolly and his successors. (He became Archbishop of Seattle shortly thereafter.) Archbishop Alex Brunett, currently the Archbishop of Seattle, is the ninth bishop of Seattle with whom I have served, beginning with Bishop Gerald Shaughnessy, Archbishop Thomas Connolly, Bishop Thomas Gill, Archbishop Raymond Hunthausen, Bishop Donald Wuerl, Archbishop Thomas Murphy, Archbishop Alex Brunett, and now his assistants, Bishop Joseph Tyson and Bishop Eusebio Elizondo. Obedience for a diocesan priest, as I am, is to the bishop who has ordained me or accepted me for service in his diocese. In the past this obedience had a military style flavor to it. It was unquestioning. Today it is more fatherly and compassionate on the part of bishops in their guidance of priests. My present bishop, Alexander Brunett, exemplifies for me this fatherly approach to his office.

Rosa Parks has much to say to us about obedience. It was her disobedience to an unjust law discriminating against black Americans that led to a massive rebellion against racial discrimination. Soldiers are sworn to obedience. But again they may find themselves in situations where they must disobey rather than to do something they consider immoral like the torture of prisoners in Iraq or elsewhere, or the shooting of prisoners and civilians.

Obedience is learned by life experiences. Jesus prayed to be delivered if possible from the horrible cruelty of crucifixion. But when deliverance was not granted he obediently accepted. This sense of obedience is expressed in the prayer so common in AA: "Lord grant me the serenity to accept what I cannot change, courage to change what I can and wisdom to know the difference." In Hebrews 5:8 we read, "Even though Jesus was God's son he had to learn from experience what it was like to obey, when obeying meant suffering." Thus, I would sum up obedience as listening actively to God, to self, to others, and all creation. Our final act of obedience is accepting death.

CELIBACY

Another requirement for priesthood today is for celibacy, the challenge to live a single life dedicating one's whole self, soul and body to the priestly ministry outside marriage. I took this vow a year before ordination at age twenty-four. With a student body of five hundred and a class of seventy-five, in which all shared a common vision and ideals, it seemed relatively easy to accept the challenge of celibacy.

Coming to America after ordination and having said good-bye to all seventy-five classmates who spent seven years with me, facing exams, sharing visions and hopes for priesthood and becoming like family to each other, I found myself suddenly with no family or relatives here. I began to experience loneliness, especially my first Christmas. No priest from Ireland had come to Seattle for fifteen years before my arrival. Loneliness has come and gone over the years. For the first Christmas, I collected all the mail from Ireland and opened it when alone on Christmas day. This is a tradition I still observe.

Most seminarians today enter the seminary later than I did at age eighteen. The present day seminarian may have a university degree or experience in another profession before entering a seminary, bringing with him a varied life experience.

Fr. Diarmuid O'Murchu wrote a book, *Poverty, Celibacy & Obedience*, published in 1999. He was raised in Ireland and now serves as a missionary priest in London helping the homeless and lecturing internationally. In the above-mentioned book he wrote: "However the tensions, the challenges and risks, the choice to have close human friendships and to devote time and energy to their development is non-negotiable."

O'Murchu, instead of speaking for a vow of celibacy, would speak for a "vow for relatedness." He writes, "Celibacy was perceived to require a special relationship to God, making human friendship largely unnecessary. This often produced a sour celibacy in people devoid of warmth and the capacity to express affection or tenderness, needs often met by celibates in charitable work."

St. John of the Cross tells us that in all our human searching for a love that fulfills our longings, we are actually searching for God, the Source of Love. Voluntary celibacy can be a gift and blessing for oneself and others whatever the struggle. There are many men and women who have to embrace involuntary celibacy due to the serious illness or death of a spouse. Climbing Mt. Rainier has its risks, and it claims lives in this process each year. Yet, it is an acceptable risk for mountain climbers. Celibacy has its challenges and its risks and failures which can be painful, but must also be regarded as an acceptable risk undertaken with God's help. Again, to quote my friend Fr. Diarmuid O'Murchu, "Personally and collectively we must outgrow the violent denial of the past, the pretense that we could live like some type of divine angelic creatures, devoid of all sexual thought or feeling. Our sexuality is at the very core of what it means to be human. We must learn afresh to befriend this divine gift with its volatile mixture of light and shadow. Aided by God's grace, we can then begin to come home to our true selves as sexual people." Lastly, one of the great priests in America, the late Fr. Henri Nouwen, a former chaplain at Harvard and Yale, a prolific writer and authority on spirituality, writes, "We need to bring our bodies home. Your body needs to be held and to hold, to be touched and to touch. But you have to keep searching for your body's deeper need. The need for love. The Spirit of God overshadowed Mary and in her all enmity between spirit and body was overcome."

In endeavoring to live as a celibate priest I find companionship and inspiration from fellow priests, but I also find inspiration in the lives of women who have embraced a religious vocation. I have been especially impressed by a cousin from Ireland who emigrated to San Francisco in her early twenties. Some years later she traveled around the world working for a time in Australia, Japan, and Hawaii. Then she devoted one year to a ministry for troubled youth at Covenant House, New York.

Returning to San Francisco, she acquired a job in real estate with a good salary. On weekends she visited the city jail and also ministered to victims of AIDS. In her mid-thirties she made a retreat with the Dominican nuns in San Jose, California. She decided to apply for membership, giving up the job, her apartment, her dating, her car, her desire to travel. Today, in the field of education and youth ministry she is committed to her vows of poverty, chastity, and obedience. The light of her faith shines on the paths of many to give guidance and encouragement. I am one of those especially inspired by her faith and commitment to bring God's love to others.

I believe there is a bond that connects the vow of poverty with the vow of celibacy. St. Paul experienced poverty and at times abundance as he tells us in Philippians 4:12, "I have learned how to cope with every circumstance — how to eat well or go hungry, to be well prvided for or do without." Paul trusted God to care for his needs.

In Chapter 16 of Romans, Paul lists scores of friends who helped him in his ministry such as the husband and wife, Prisca and Aquila, "who risked their lives for me" and Lydia who welcomed Paul to Europe in her hometown of Philippi. Due to his ministry and travels, Paul's time was limited with his friends, calling for many tears of farewell in a spirit of detachment from those he loved, a poverty of spirit. I have served in twelve different parishes and made friends in each and then, due to new assignments, had to say farewell to them. Like Paul, priests suffer at times from misplaced trust in people as when he tells us, "Alexander the coppersmith did me a great deal of harm." (II Tim. 4.13.) At times, loneliness claimed Paul. Again in Chapter 4 of II Timothy, he writes to Timothy, "Do your best to join me soon for Demas enamored of the present world has left me. Cresius has gone and Titus. I have no one with me but Luke. Get Mark and bring him with you — get here before winter if you can." We are all human and fumble and stumble in our response to God's love. Francis of Assisi,

Clare, Therese, who cultivated friendships, and all the saints assure us that in spite of the fumbles and stumbles, God loves us unconditionally at all times.

The ideas expressed in this article find an echo in the statement of the Congress for Consecrated Life held in Rome in 2004. The Congress reflected on the spirit that should unite those who are pledged to a vow of celibacy. "Within the 'distortion of love' which is so evident in our times, our community life could be converted into a means of affective stability and living together inspired by faith and open to complete fulfillment. Relationships would be less rigid and impersonal than in the past. They would allow for adequate manifestations of affection and tenderness and give greater attention and care to physical and emotional well-being. An excessively erotic mentality and context would, however, be a danger for us. Let us admit that with the help of divine grace we can speak of our life as a reclaiming of the primeval project of God for humanity: 'in the beginning, it was not so' (Mt 19:8). From this perspective we have a new way of understanding celibacy as an evident consequence of the relationship between genders and a more integrated vision of sexuality."

During sixty-three years as a priest I have experienced incredible joy and consolation sharing the gift of faith with others, having been inspired by their faith and example following in the footsteps of Jesus. There have been moments of great spiritual and human sorrows as I shared in the pain and suffering of others, or experienced heart-breaking sorrow due to my own failures or due to misunderstanding by others. Yet, I thank God each day for the gift of priesthood.

On one occasion, I took part in Jewish services for Yom Kippur, the Day of Atonement, when Jews spend nine days of preparation in prayer and fasting to purify themselves before God. Rabbi Ted Falcon, a friend, said that when growing up he did not feel comfortable at the prospect of appearing before God the Judge. Now in his mature years, he does not see God as a judge but one who accepts him with infinite love, a love that is unconditional. Priesthood is helping people to know this love and to live lives of trust in love and to experience great joy.

On December 27, 2004, I was privileged to shake hands with a great priest, Pope John Paul II. In that handshake I affirmed his leadership and his understanding of priesthood, not realizing it was to end April 2, 2005. Here is one of his messages to priests needed today in our world, spoken by Pope John Paul:

"We need heralds of the Gospel
Who are experts in humanity,
Who know the depths of the human heart,
Who can share the joys,
The hopes, the agonies,
The distress of people today,
But who are at the same time,
Contemplatives who have fallen in love with God."

As priests, we are personally aware of our sinfulness, that we are loved and forgiven by God. Then we can enthusiastically speak about God's love for us. Nelson Mandela, in his inaugural speech as President of South Africa, revealed his own deep faith in God's love. He said:

"Our deepest fear is not that we are inadequate.
Our deepest fear is that we are powerful beyond all measure.
It is our light, not our darkness, that must frightens us.
We ask ourselves, who am I to be brilliant,
Gorgeous, talented, fabulous?
Actually, who are you not to be?
You are a child of God.
Your playing small does not serve the world.
There is nothing enlightened about shrinking so that
Other people won't feel insecure around you.
It is not just in some of us;
It is in everyone,
And we let our own lights shine,
We unconsciously give other people permission to do the same.
As we are liberated from our own fear,
Our presence automatically liberates others."

Nelson Mandela, Inaugural Address

Slowly, I believe I have come to this understanding of priesthood. Our retreat director this past summer, Fr. Stephen J. Rosetti, Ph.D., who has extensive experience in counseling priests, left us this message from a former president, Teddy Roosevelt, a message that is a challenge to all of us on the journey of life:

"It is not the critic who counts, not the man who points out how the strong man stumbled, or where the doer of deeds could have done them better. The credit belongs to the man who is actually in the arena; whose face is marred by dust and sweat and blood; who strives valiantly; who errs and comes short again and again; who knows the great enthusiasm, the great devotion, and spends himself in a worthy cause; who, at the best, knows in the end the triumph of high achievement; and who, at worst, if he fails, at least fails while daring greatly, so that his place shall never be with those cold and timid souls who know neither victory nor defeat."

I try to communicate this message to others as well as to try and live it myself. I agree with Emmet Fox and his description of the power of love, the presence of the Holy Spirit in and with people:

Love Will Conquer

There is no difficulty that enough love will not conquer;
no disease that enough love will not heal;
no door that enough love will not open;
no gulf that enough love will not bridge;
no wall that enough love will not throw down;
no sin that enough love will not redeem...
It makes no difference how deeply seated may be the trouble;
how hopeless the outlook;
how muddled the tangle;
how great the mistake.
A sufficient realization of love will dissolve it all.
If only you could love enough you would be the happiest and most powerful being in the world...

by Emmet Fox

Chapter 27

Nun Shares Friendship with a Priest, Pope

Pope Benedict XVI and Sister Emmanuel in 1998.

All who were watching for a significant clue to the reign of Pope Benedict XVI received it in his first official letter. He wrote about love — human and divine — stressing the importance of both. True love is caring for widows, orphans, the homeless, and the ill in body or soul. He added words that touched me in a special way having spent over fifty years in interfaith ministry. He said that those who minister to others must not seek to proselytize or engage in particular political programs. He reminds members of the human family that we can love one another without fear and without exploitation, believing in the greatness of God's love and that of human love which comes from God.

A friend saw a picture of Pope Benedict when he was Cardinal Ratzinger. In the picture he is standing outside his office in Rome beside a Carmelite nun and they are holding hands. I cannot recall ever seeing a picture of a Pope standing beside a woman and holding her hand. The friend who observed this picture of the Pope with a nun twenty years younger than himself, regards it as a picture worth ten thousand words. It reveals him as a warm, compassionate priest with the heart of Christ, with hands like Christ that held other hands of men and women with love and compassion.

Touch, like speech, is frequently abused, but when we turn to Jesus we observe how speech and touch can be integrated in loving service to another. One of the most human events in the life of Jesus is described by St. Mark in Chapter 8. He tells us that, "Some people brought Jesus a blind man and begged that he touch him." What other healing touches Jesus must have used are not told by Mark, but apparently, others knew about them.

Jesus took the blind man by the hand, and hand-in-hand they walked out of the village. Then in a secluded spot, Jesus touched the man's blind eyes with both of his hands, but for some mysterious reason sight did not return. "Then a second time Jesus laid hands on his eyes and he saw perfectly."

In the very first Chapter of his Gospel, Mark reveals the healing touch of Jesus when he entered the home of Peter and went over to the ill mother-in-law of Peter and "grasped her hand." With his other hand he helped her up and cured her fever. St. Thomas only came to faith in the Resurrection when he touched the body of Jesus. Hands touching another in the ordination ceremony, or in the anointing of the sick, at confirmation, or in a loving greeting, all can reflect the tender love of Jesus revealed by his life.

So back to the picture of Benedict with the Carmelite nun. I may have had a small part in this beautiful friendship between them. To put it in perspective, I must take you back to 1953. I was assisting the pastor in Enumclaw, Washington. One evening as I was leaving to return to Seattle he said to me, "I have two parishioners of German background with no children. They have a German cousin who is a teenager and they would like to bring her to America to reside with them and attend a Catholic high school. Could you help to bring her here?"

As I drove home I felt that I had been given an impossible task because so many were trying to come to America in these post-war years. I felt like declining, but the next day I began proceedings that led to the arrival of this fifteen-year-old teenager, Emma Hofbauer, to attend Holy Names High School in Seattle while living with her relatives in Enumclaw. I had no idea that my decision would affect a future pope!

I was in Ireland when she arrived in 1955, and I did not return until late September when she was already a boarder for a month at the school. That first morning when I approached the altar to celebrate Mass, she told me that a voice spoke to her in some mysterious way, conveying a message that she and I would be friends for life. When told about her by one of the nuns I asked to speak a word of welcome to this new student. Emma sent word, "I do not wish to meet him until I can speak English." We talked for the first time at Christmas, 1955, when I shook hands with her. Her "yes" meant "yes" and her "no" meant "no!" All through high school, though my days were spent at the Chancery, she and I became friends, as were her foster parents in Enumclaw.

In 1959, she graduated from Holy Names High School. She had a suitor very interested in marriage, but from her earliest years she wanted to become a Carmelite nun. She returned to Germany to say goodbye to her parents. They were so upset at her staying in America as a nun that they became lifelong Jehovah Witnesses. Emma returned to Seattle and immediately joined the Carmelite nuns in Seattle. I was celebrant of Mass at her entry. Mrs. Reeva Levine, a renowned Jewish artist, attended also and painted Emma, but left her face indistinct to signify she could be any woman making a total offering of her life to God.

After she entered the Carmelites, I was allowed to visit her about once a month since she had no family here. But I did not get to shake hands with her for thirty-five years. Then I was celebrant of a Mass at Carmel and it was now customary for the celebrant to give the greeting of peace to one of the nuns. As I walked over to the area reserved for the nuns, a smiling Emma extended her right hand which I first held forty years ago and now held again after thirty-five years.

In 1965, I was in Germany and spent time with her parents who were hospitable, and with her aunt, Teresa, who died recently. But who is Emma? She was born in the Sudetenland, which was a large German colony in Czechoslovakia. In 1938, Hitler invaded Czechoslovakia with the excuse that it was necessary to liberate the Germans in the Sudetenland. Emma's father was conscripted into the German army and was involved in the invasion of Russia and captured. Sent to Siberia, he escaped after seven years. When he came home, Emma was scared and hid. She was only a baby when he left and, of course, did not recognize him, having been born in 1940.

In 1945, as the Nazis were defeated, the Czechs took out their anger on the Sudetenland Germans. They treated them somewhat as the Germans treated the Jews. They put them in cattle cars on trains and sent them back to Germany. On Palm Sunday, 1945, Emma was locked in a cattle car with her mother, two brothers, her aunt Teresa and hundreds of other Germans. On Good Friday they were deposited in the Bavarian mountains with no food or accommodations. They lived in this area of Garmisch-Granau for several years. Emma slept on a table. Rats scurried around at night. The local bishop built housing for them. He had the services of a newly ordained priest, Josef Ratzinger. After a couple of years this priest went to graduate school and became a professor at Tubingen and other universities. He was one of the leading theologians at the Second Vatican Council. Appointed a Cardinal, he was called to the Vatican in 1981 and became Prefect of the Congregation for the Doctrine of the Faith, making him one of the two most important assistants to Pope Paul II.

While Cardinal Ratzinger was still a teenager in his native Germany, a Jewish woman who had become a Carmelite nun suffered the fate of millions of her people — death in a concentration camp. Edith Stein was born in Germany October 12, 1891. At age thirteen she shocked her devout Jewish parents by declaring herself an atheist. She attended the university and became an assistant to Edmund Husserl, a brilliant professor at the University of Freiburg. In 1921 she found the Autobiography of St. Teresa and spent the whole night reading it. This religious experience led her to be baptized a Catholic on January 1, 1922, having first spent a night in prayer in the synagogue. With the rise of the Nazis she was dismissed from her teaching position. In 1938 she joined the Carmelite sisters in Cologne. Later she agreed to be secretly transferred to Holland to avoid any special Nazi attention to her community. Then, in 1940, the Nazis invaded Holland. Edith continued her religious studies, reading the writings of St. John of the Cross. On July 26, 1942, the Dutch Bishops denounced the Nazi persecution of the Jews. In anger, all Jewish Catholics were arrested in retaliation.

On August 2, the Gestapo came to the convent for Edith where she had been joined by her sister, Rosa, also a convert. Rosa was distraught with fear of what might be ahead. Edith spoke to Rosa, "Come, Rosa, we are going for our people." She was always lovingly aware of her Jewish roots. She died in the gas chamber on August 9, 1942. In 1998 she was canonized by Pope John Paul II who recognized in her a solidarity with her Jewish people and went to her death as an atonement for the evil of the world.

The lives of Sister Emma and Cardinal Ratzinger converge in Rome in 1998. Sister was granted permission to visit her elderly parents and to attend the canonization of Edith Stein. She was also in communication with the Jewish niece of Edith who lives in California and planned to attend the canonization.

The Prioress of the Seattle Carmelites, knowing that Cardinal Ratzinger corresponded with Sister Emma, sent him an e-mail telling him she would be in Rome. He immediately replied and invited her to his residence for Mass and a visit. It was on that occasion that they were photographed standing side-by-side holding hands.

I do share a love for Pope Benedict as the leader of the Church. I have served as a priest for over sixty years. But we also share something unique. We share a special friendship with a German-born Carmelite nun who supports both of us by her prayers in the spirit of St. Therese.

Chapter 28

The Priest I Would Like to Be

Looking back to my first years as a pastor following Vatican II, I endeavored to incorporate new insights such as lay persons serving as lectors, eucharistic ministers and members of a parish council. Today I view the role as pastor as one I would approach with a whole different outlook than what I had fifty years ago.

A friend who recently went on a pilgrimage to the Holy Land with some non-Catholic Christians remarked on her return, "I was amazed at their misinformation about the Catholic Church." During my first twenty-five years as a priest, I helped to direct the Religious Advertising Program of the Knights of Columbus in the State of Washington. With the financial support of the Knights, ads were placed every week in some sixteen newspapers in the State. The thousands of replies we received from these ads revealed to me the centuries of false teaching about the Catholic Church that were held by the descendants of those who separated from us centuries ago. The separation was not a peaceful one at the time and one of the causalities was truthfulness about each other.

When we speak about evangelization, of bringing the message of Jesus to others, I see this as a challenge to bring truth to others. A truth to free us from fear and ignorance about each other due to false information. To meet this challenge to evangelize I would, as pastor, form a committee to explore financing to place a weekly ad in the local paper to explain Catholic teaching. In spite of TV and radio commercials, big companies still believe in the power of newspaper advertising. Parishioners could benefit from learning about the responses of their neighbors to Catholic teaching as the parish carried out the mandate of Jesus to promote unity among people by helping them to better know their neighbors.

I have been associated with Catholic schools as pastor, and for thirteen years, I resided as chaplain in a girl's high school. But while Catholic schools are important, I see the need in the future to regard the family as the best force for Christian education of youth.

Love is the greatest of the virtues. A student in a Catholic school may memorize the words of Paul on love in 1 Corinthians 13. But to see love in action he or she must observe how their parents speak to each other, how they speak to the children, how they respond to others, especially those in need. In other words, the parents put a human face on love for their children and model love in action.

Unfortunately, parents may fail in this responsibility. Due to their inadequacy to cope with problems as they arise, they exclude love by surrendering to anger, impatience, condemnation or the harboring of resentment.

Families have approached me with problems due to financial needs, needs for money to pay rent, fuel, school tuition, gasoline, etc. Thanks to organizations like St. Vincent de Paul, a parish could assist with such family crises of a financial nature.

But often the deeper problem, the failure of husband and wife to really communicate and make their home a place of love and not a place of tension, often was a greater problem than financial needs. In the parish of the future, I hope every pastor will have a pro-family committee. This committee should bring excellent family counselors from wherever available to spend evenings once a week during Lent or Advent helping families to find harmony in their relationships which would lead to happiness in their homes.

I would invite some families to a retreat at a place like Camp Brotherhood. As a pastor, I would challenge the Family Committee to help raise the funds for such a retreat. Often these families cannot afford a seaside vacation, or any vacation, even dining out. A weekend in a peaceful setting with others led by a counselor could contribute to healing relations and to happiness in the home.

The Church of the Middle Ages was Europe-centered, and communication was limited to the local community. The Christians in Ireland knew little about the Church in the rest of Europe and nothing was known about America, Africa, or the Far East. There was an emphasis on "saving one's soul" and avoiding personal sin. This attitude is slowly beginning to change as we absorb the idea of the human family. The Hindu, the Muslims, the person of no religious faith is my brother or sister. The hungry child dying in Darfur or Nepal is a family member given the gift of life by God as I was. To foster this idea as a pastor in this century, I would have the parish school adopt a school in a poor area of the world and help with textbooks and other needs. Here I would copy some Protestant churches who send members on missionary assignments overseas. They keep in touch with the sending church and members of the church who can afford it will visit the area the church has adopted. In this way the bonding is strengthened for the blessing of the giving and receiving church.

I would recommend to a future pastor to select a group of people who would make their priority a mission of prayer. In spite of priest and sister shortage, the Church allows those in contemplative prayer communities like the Carmelites, Poor Clares, the Cistercians, to continue their vocation and not abandon it for pastoral ministries. A group of parishioners willing to spend thirty minutes to an hour in contemplative prayer, each day if possible, would perform an essential mission of acknowledging the primacy of God and bring blessings on themselves and their parish.

St. Therese, known as the Little Flower, wrote in her autobiography that she would spend her heaven doing good on earth. With her love of priests, I trust she will obtain for me the grace to spend my heaven helping the priests of the future. I shall seek to obtain for them the gift of the Holy Spirit that will give them courage in the face of the unknown. And I shall also ask for them a full measure of compassion, that will enable them to be compassionate to themselves in times of human weakness, sins and failures.

The writer of the Letter to the Hebrews tells us that the priest, "is able to deal patiently with every sinner for he himself is beset by weakness, and so must make sin offerings for himself as well as his people." (Hebrews 5:2) Jesus, also "Son though he was he learned obedience from what he suffered." (Hebrews 5:8)

Father William Treacy's parents, John and Mary Delaney Treacy, in 1918.

Father William Treacy with his "World's Fair Mother" in Seattle in 1962.

Father William Treacy's university graduation in 1940, Maynooth, Ireland.

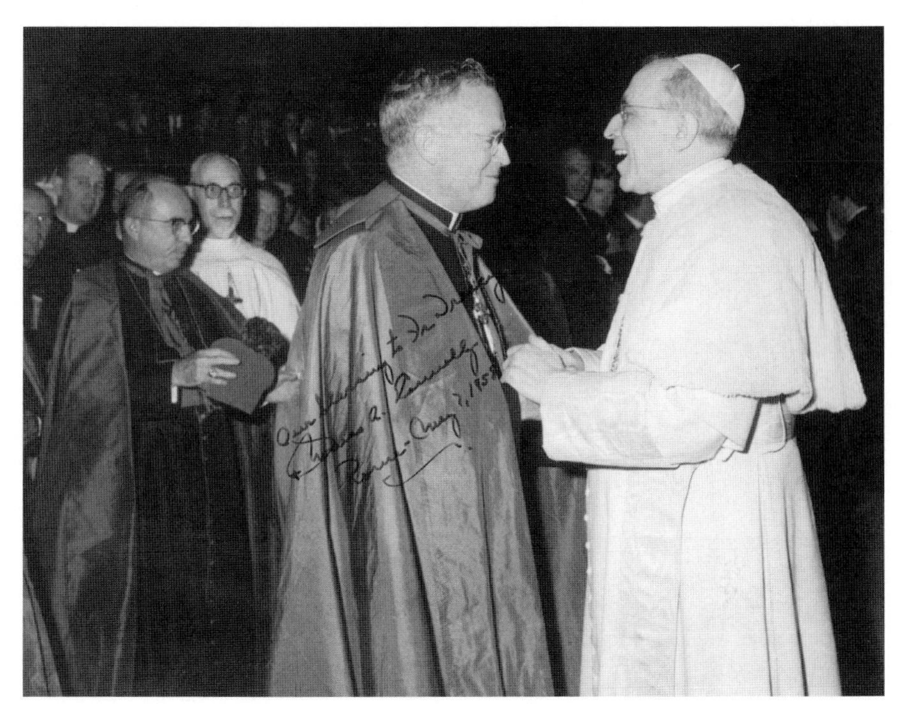

Pope Pius XII (the Pope when I was ordained) with Archbishop Thomas Connolly, who appointed Father William Treacy to the television program, "Challenge."

Leonard Bernstein and Felicia Monteleagre with their family. Leonard wrote and Felicia performed in the Kaddish Symphony, *which had its American debut in the Seattle Opera House in the 1960s. Further reference to the* Kaddish Symphony *is found in Chapter 6.*

"Challenge" TV show with panelists Father William Treacy, Dr. Martin Goslin (Congregationalist), and Rabbi Raphael Levine, 1960-1962.

"Challenge" TV show with panelists Father William Treacy, Rabbi Raphael Levine, and Dr. Oscar Rolander (Lutheran), 1969-1971

Father William Treacy with Rabbi Raphael Levine at the wedding of Jim and Helen Pilcher in 1978. Actors Dick Van Dyke and Kathleen Quinlan were the witnesses. Jim was the sound engineer of the movie, "The Runner Stumbles," which was filmed in Roslyn, Washington. Father Treacy was the assistant to Dick Van Dyke, who played the role of a priest.

Father William Treacy (third from left) with friends in the Philippines in 1986.

Father William Treacy visiting lepers (cared for by the Sisters of the Destitute) in Kerala, India.

Father William Treacy (on donkey) on Palm Sunday in Stanwood, Washington.
The children insisted Father Treacy ride the donkey. They had the animal waiting outside the church, without Father Treacy's knowledge. At first he hesitated, but saw the disappointment on the children's faces, and decided to go for it!

Father William Treacy with John and Marsha Baumann, who for years assisted with the Engaged Encounter program for those contemplating marriage.
Photo by Bruce Hudson, www.hudsonportraits.com

Father William Treacy at the wedding of Sonja Ronning and Daniel Belz on June 2, 2006.

Father William Treacy retires as a pastor in 1989.

Father William Treacy with Carol and Shirley Stipek in 2003. The Stipeks were introduced to each other 51 years ago by Father Treacy. They are the parents of eight children.

Father William Treacy on his 88th birthday, May 31, 2007.

Father William Treacy celebrating Mass at Camp Brotherhood with his friend and fellow board member, Father Jim Dalton.

Father William Treacy welcoming people at the door of the Interfaith Chapel at Camp Brotherhood. The door was donated to us by Sam Spading, a skilled carpenter who was on our staff for several years. He acquired the door many years ago when dismantling an old apartment house in Seattle.

Photo by Bruce Hudson, www.hudsonportraits.com

High school students from Sacred Heart Church in Bellevue pray over Father William Treacy at Camp Brotherhood in 2000.

Father William Treacy with altar servers, Jody and Benjamin Crosby, at the Immaculate Conception Church in Mount Vernon, Washington, in 2007.

Father William Treacy with friend Vilem Sokol, director of the Seattle Youth Symphony for many years.

Father William Treacy meditating at Camp Brotherhood.
Photo by Bruce Hudson, www.hudsonportraits.com

Father William Treacy with Christopher Abata, parish helper.

Father William Treacy shepherding a steer at Camp Brotherhood.

Father William Treacy met Earl Wymore after arriving in Seattle in 1945. They've remained good friends ever since.

Father William Treacy relaxing at Camp Brotherhood.

Father William Treacy with Christine and Randy Stime. Randy is the executive director of Camp Brotherhood.

Father William Treacy with Floyd Schmoe, an artist who carved a statue of St. Francis of Assisi. The statue was carved from a cedar tree and is at Camp Brotherhood. Floyd Schmoe lived in the spirit of St. Francis. He was a professor of forestry at the University of Washington. He and Rabbi Raphael Levine were good friends, and Rabbi introduced him to Father Treacy on Floyd's eightieth birthday. This picture of Floyd was taken shortly before his death at age 105.

Father William Treacy with the chalice given by Rabbi Raphael Levine. The chalice was made by a Moslem in Jerusalem and purchased by the Rabbi in 1972. It was first used at a Catholic Mass in Jerusalem in 1972, where 12 Jews, 12 Catholics, and 12 Protestants were present.

Photo by Bruce Hudson, www.hudsonportraits.com

Chapter 29

Crises

The word "crises" in the Chinese language is a combination of the words for "challenge" and "opportunity." A crisis in health, in a relationship, in our personal lives can be the source of much pain and anxiety. Yet, it has been said that we should thrive on crises. They can destroy our self-made idols and our pride in ourselves and our accomplishments.

Rabbi Levine reminded me of the many crises faced by the Jewish people beginning with slavery in Egypt. On their escape from Egypt they were pursued by an Egyptian army. During forty years of desert wandering they were attacked by local tribes and experienced lack of food and water. Eventually, they reach the Promised Land. They built a magnificent temple to God. It was destroyed by the Babylonians and the Jews were again enslaved. A new temple was destroyed in 70 A.D. and again the people were enslaved and scattered over the known world.

Christianity also had crises. The greatest was the crucifixion of Jesus. Following His resurrection, the first followers of Jesus faced a crisis over the admission of non-Jews to their ranks. Then the Roman Empire tried to destroy Christianity. Century after century seemed to bring a new crisis. But each new crisis brought some new blessing. Gentiles became the strength of the new followers of Jesus. Roman persecution ended with a Roman emperor who claimed to be Christian.

Today I feel pain experiencing a major crisis in the church due to pedophilia among my fellow priests. But my faith in the presence of the Holy Spirit with the Church in the past gives me assurance that the Church will emerge more humble and more aware of the need for prayer and for God's help as we endeavor to reveal God's love to young and old.

All of us have faced crises big and little in our lives. They may have happened in childhood, in less than perfect families, by negative religious experiences, by human weakness and sin. The latter may be due to failure in regard to moral regulations. John O'Donohue, in his best selling book, *Anam Cara,* tells us, "Moral rules encourage us to act with honor, compassion, and justice." Then he adds, "When we notice something immoral, we normally tend to be harsh with ourselves and employ moral surgery to remove it. In doing this we are only ensuring that it remains trapped within. We merely confirm our negative view of ourselves and ignore our potential for growth." This can cause a crisis in our self confidence. Another way of looking at our failures, our sins, our woundedness is to view them as enemies to our peace and joy. Jesus gave us the challenge to love our enemies. This gives us true freedom from enslavement to resentment and hatred. We have used crises well when we love them as a way to open our hearts and souls to receive the healing love of God. A French Dominican priest wrote a book many years ago. I do not recall his name, but his book is called *Les Cicatrices (The Scars).* It tells how he came to a better understanding of the love of God through the hurts and wounds of his life. Jesus faced the crisis of suffering and death. After His Resurrection His body revealed the wounds he suffered, signs of His love. What a challenge to give up a negative view of our wounds and failures and see them as signs of the presence of God's healing love in us. This can be a crisis of faith — a challenge, an opportunity.

Crises are called "trials" by St. Paul. In II Corinthians 1:4 he writes, "He comforts us in all our afflictions and thus enables us to comfort those who are in trouble."

He reminded them of the positive benefits possible from crises saying, "If we are afflicted for your sake it is for your comfort and salvation; and we also receive comfort for you that you may endure the same sufferings and experience the same comfort that is ours." He tells us also in Chapter 1 that due to the trials or crises he experiences in his work, "We were crushed. It was too much. It was more than we could bear. We had already lost all hope of coming through alive…but this happened that we might no longer rely on ourselves but on God. He freed us." Then he added a request that I make to all who read this, "You must help us with your prayers," and so, "there will be many to give thanks to God on our behalf for making crises draw us closer to God."

The Book of Sirach tells us in Chapter 2:5, "For as gold is tested by fire, so are worthy people in the crucible of humiliation."

Chapter 30

Ireland and Islam

Above is the title of an article in the November issue of *The Furrow* magazine, published by my Alma Mater and written by a Belfast priest, Owen O'Sullivan. I found it sad reading — disturbing and challenging. I was raised in the Irish Church which Fr. O'Sullivan describes in his opening sentence as a Church "built on a control system and underpinned by guilt and fear."

The challenge in Ireland is secularism, which is a practical denial of the relevance of God. It "looks down its nose at religion" seeing religion as divisive and seeks to exclude religion from daily life.

The author points out the obvious danger: "Secularism does not provide an adequate basis" for moral cohesion in society because experience teaches that, "law needs morals and morals need faith." I fully agree with the author that, "secularism is like the prodigal son living off the accumulated riches of the Christian past."

Many Catholics in Ireland feel ashamed of their faith and that of the Church due to the sex abuse crisis and its mishandling by Church authorities, teachings about contraception, the prohibition of condoms to diminish AIDS, and the exclusion of women from leadership in the Church. In Ireland, Vatican II (1962-65) "represented a hope, one that died the death of a thousand cuts through a failure of leadership at all levels." Fr. O'Sullivan concludes: "Is Ireland heading for Islam? It could be in the long run. People will opt for the real rather than the pretended, for certainties (I want to say truths) rather than drift, for the demanding rather than tokenism or playing games. The latter is what we are doing." All Europe seems to be going the same way.

Needless to say, the article made me sad. He does offer some hope saying, "There is still time, energy and goodwill in the local church to develop alternatives if we have the courage and imagination to use it." Since I was ordained to serve the church in Ireland, I've been left with a love and concern for the Irish church.

I find consolation in the fact that three hundred people — young and old — joined me last August to honor the Catholic faith of our ancestors by erecting an altar where, in time of persecution, the people secretly attended Mass.

The Church in Ireland and in America needs to recognize that the Spirit calls us as, Pope John XXIII pointed out, "to read the signs of our time." A few weeks ago, I heard a Catholic radio host speaking on KIRO radio about the Gospel he heard the previous Sunday. In the Gospel, Jesus said, "If your enemy strikes you on the right cheek, then turn the left." The host admitted he could not live the message and felt most American Christians who supported war in Afghanistan and Iraq did not believe it either.

Then the loud and clear sermon came that was preached by the Amish people concerning the man who murdered five of their children and took his own life. Not only were half of the attendees of the funeral Amish, but the Amish community took up a collection to help the widow of the man who murdered their children. This example is Jesus showing us that his call to faith and forgiveness is possible. Bill and Melinda Gates, Bono, and others call us to them in reaching out to help victims of poverty, illnesses like AIDS, malaria etc.

The national leader of the Evangelical Church in America has been disgraced for sexual misconduct, for what he called, "negative demons against which he struggled all his life." Is this a wake-up call for all of us? How should people of faith respond? We need to bring together the best doctors, psychiatrists, psychologists, sociologists, anthropologists and religious leaders to find out how sexual addictions are caused. The late Cardinal Suemens of Belgium planned to hold a similar symposium on sexuality at Louvain University. He insisted that God gave us sex and would give us the wisdom for its best use. He died before plans were completed. I hope Ireland will accept the challenge to bring together the best brains in the world to study sexuality, its aberrations and blessings.

This challenge reminds me of the years I served in the late fifties and sixties on the King County Committee on Alcoholism. At that time, public drunks just on the street and not endangering others in cars were sentenced to jail. We worked to get the medical profession to recognize alcoholism as an illness. The next step was to get insurance companies to pay for medical treatment of alcoholism. Then came our effort to provide housing and facilities to help those addicted — still a need today. I learned a great deal from the commitment of the twelve people on the committee to deal with one of the great problems of our time. Doctors, politicians, lawyers, a judge (later a Supreme Court Justice), and business people joined in what I now see as living the Gospel to help the needy. It has been said that the positive teaching of the Church on sexuality is unknown, while it is instead regarded as being anti-sexuality as was pointed out by Fr. O'Sullivan.

Fr. Thomas Casey is an Irish priest teaching in Rome. Writing in the Jesuit magazine, *America,* Nov. 27, 2006, he reminds us: "Of course, the news from Ireland is not all bad. There is still a deep spiritual hunger and openness in the Irish people, and epiphanies are unfolding before our eyes. I find tremendous hope for the Christian future of our country in the huge number of immigrants who have arrived on our shores in recent years. They are not as enslaved as we are to consumerism, and they are blessed with a much stronger sense of community — two key ingredients to an Irish future that is less pretentious, more authentic and receptive to a fully Christian vision. Indeed, the 160,000 Polish immigrants who form the largest single group of migrant workers in Ireland are astounding as with their faith commitment. St. Patrick was not born or raised in Ireland but brought the Catholic faith there. Today, immigrants from Poland and Africa are giving vitality to the faith Patrick brought sixteen centuries ago."

Chapter 31

A Rabbi Reflects on Mary

Rabbi Zalman Shlacter Shalomi is a Seattle rabbi interviewed some years ago by William Elliott for his book, *A Place at the Table.* He was asked to comment on the virgin birth of Jesus. The rabbi has 10 children and 22 grandchildren. Answering the question about the virgin birth, he said, "I was present at the birth and assisted at the labor of four of my children. There is such a holy silence in the room that if one were Catholic, one would make the sign of the cross. I was so full of awe that I wanted to kneel in front of that woman and say: Hail, Hail Mother full of grace, the Lord be with you, blessed are you, blessed is the fruit of thy womb."

"Then when I saw the labor, the agony of birth that is almost like dying, yet brings forth life, I have to say "Holy Mother, pray for us at the hour of our death." So the process that occurs when any woman gives birth evokes such a mystical feeling that I have to say, "I believe in the virgin birth."

St. Augustine commented on the motherhood of Mary and her conception of Jesus saying, "Prius concepit in mente quam in corpore." She conceived Jesus in her mind and soul before she conceived him in her body. As a devout young Jewish woman, blessed with a soul full of grace, she had a longing for this Savior foretold by Isaiah and other prophets. She must have understood the suffering and rejection to be faced by the promised one. Isaiah in Chapter 53 describes the messenger to be sent by God "as a man of suffering accustomed to infirmity, one of those from whom men hide their faces, spurned, and we held him in no esteem."

Yet when Mary realized that she was invited to be the mother of this suffering servant of God, she said to the angel Gabriel, "Be it done to me according to thy word." The French theologian, Father Marie-Dominique Chenu, used to speak of "constant incarnation and constant creation." In a sense every mother who conceives a child made in the image and likeness of God does so by the power of the Holy Spirit. A better understanding of this great mystery, the presence of the Holy Spirit as Giver of Life present at every conception would consider abortion a desecration of the divine fetus.

We have geese at Camp Brotherhood. This past summer we had a flock of goslings. A hawk circled overhead ready to snatch one. The older geese sensed the danger and crowded around the young ones. The caring mother instinct of every animal, and of every good mother, is a revelation of the maternal in God. I believe Mary as Mother of Jesus mediates the maternal love of God to us and especially close to those women who by conception have experienced within them an incarnation of God. By revealing motherly love to the fullest, Mary is what the poet Wordsworth called, "Our tainted nature's solitary boast."

Some years ago, Jewish parents took me with them to a small cemetery near Jerusalem. A rabbi conducted a memorial service for those killed in the war, including their son. In the middle of the service the mother was overcome with grief and wept as she put her head on my shoulder. This Jewish mother weeping for her son brought me closer in understanding to another Jewish mother, Mary. She weeps with every mother who suffers the loss of a child.

Following the devastating potato famine of 1847 in Ireland, Our Lady appeared to the forlorn survivors at a small village of Knock in 1879. She said nothing. Her appearance is interpreted as a motherly sign of her love and compassion. She makes real in our lives the words of the psalmist about God, "But you O Lord are a God merciful and gracious, slow to anger, abounding in kindness and fidelity." Ps. 86

Chapter 32

The Emperor Penguins

March of the Penguins is a video that might also be called "The Power of Love." It tells the story of penguins at the South Pole. When they are about six months old, they take their first plunge into the frigid Antarctic Ocean. Then after four years at sea, a secret call requires them to leave the ocean and walk seventy miles in a week — day and night — to a place where life began for them. There, male and female, after some preening and gentle touching of beaks, decide to become partners for new life. After about two months the egg arrives, and has to be protected immediately from the Arctic cold. Exposure for a minute could be fatal. The mothers transfer the eggs to the males who cushion them on their feet and keep the egg close to the skin of their bellies. Then the females, as if obeying a musical conductor, say good-bye to the males and the eggs to walk seventy miles to the ocean to obtain food for themselves and the chicks.

The males gather in a circle to protect the eggs. The temperature may be eighty degrees below zero with winds at 100 miles an hour. Those who are at the center of the circle are protected from the wind, but those on the outside are given some time in the shelter zone also.

For two months, the males shelter the eggs and then the hatched chicks await the return of the females who have to find their way back across seventy miles of snow in darkness. There is great excitement as the mothers return and find their mates and offspring, which they proceed to feed with the fish in their insides. Sometimes a chick dies and you can see the grief of the parents who may try to steal a live chick in sorrow.

There is much these penguins know about life. They know the urge for a partner as is evident from the signs of affection they give each other. They realize one has the special gift of producing the egg, but both contribute to the feeding and care of the offspring.

They seem to know that love calls for trust in the other. The males trust the females when, after leaving them with the newly laid eggs, they leave for the ocean. On the other hand, the departing females trust that the males will care for the eggs and await their return. This is the kind of love that takes away anxiety and worry and gives peace. Fr. Thomas Keating, the internationally known speaker on contemplative prayer, tells us, "Love of God is resting in peace, without fear."

Some in the animal world battle for partners in the mating season, but the male and female penguins show no such traits. They meet at the rendezvous location after their long journey, and treat each other with reverence and tenderness as if they knew they were about to be partners in a great undertaking. After the females return, the males set out for the ocean. First they tune into the unique call of their offspring which they will recognize on their return.

Penguins give us a wonderful example of an outside power guiding them and enabling them to survive in one of the harshest places on earth. For me as a Christian, they remind me of the words of the ancient creed, "We believe in the Holy Spirit, the Giver of Life." Penguins reveal to me the influence of the "Giver of Life," guiding them in Arctic waters, through long journeys to their mating area, to a partnership in giving and nourishing life that is truly extraordinary.

The penguins reveal another great spiritual truth to me. A lonesome penguin who sets out behind the main group to reach the ocean or the assembly location has little chance of survival. But there is a spirit of caring and support for each other. This to me is the vision Jesus Christ had for people — a spirit of compassion, encouragement and acceptance of each other. He called it the Kingdom of God. There was no fighting or selfishness. When those things did surface — as when a mother penguin, after losing a chick, tried to steal another chick — the community rallied to keep the chick with its mother.

There was an acceptance of mystery by the penguins as they responded to the hidden call to assemble for mating, and as the females then left the eggs with the males to be hatched under blizzard conditions. The young were protected and gradually directed to the ocean.

Penguins teach men and women to appreciate each other with a sense of mystery built into us by the Creator. Each helps the other to discover that mystery, that unique contribution each makes to the other and to the continuation of life on earth. The scripture reading on the day I watched the story of the penguins was from 1 Thessalonians 3:11, "May the Lord make you increase and abound in love for one another and for all." Love for one another was evident for the penguins. The tenderness of the penguins for each other and their reverence for life reveals the essence of love. I was surprised (and happily so) to read the following in the leading Catholic newspaper, *The Tablet,* in England on the love of man and woman:

> *Something to do with love... What has been happening in society is a gradual shift from emphasizing the contract of marriage to emphasizing the relationship within it, as being at the human heart of the marriage. This shift is not a radical rejection of a Christian understanding of marriage, though it may be a radical rejection of post-Tridentine Church legalism. Indeed, it may even be a step in the other direction, towards a more humanistic and fluid appreciation of what a marriage is. It would be ironic if those wishing to safeguard a Christian understanding of marriage dug their last ditch in defence of a contractual view of marriage which was all about inherited property, and rejected an emerging view of marriage that was trying tentatively to say that it had something to do with love.*
>
> — Clifford Longley

I sometimes wonder if penguins felt at times like the anonymous writer of *A Blessing in Dissatisfaction.*

> *Many a time I wish I were other than I am.*
> *I weary of the solemn tide; of little fields; of this brooding isle.*
> *I long to be rid of the weight of duty and to have my part in ampler life.*
> *O Thou who art wisdom and pity both, set me free from the lordship of desire.*
> *Help me to find my happiness in my acceptance of what is my purpose;*
> *In friendly eyes; in work well done; in quietness born of trust and most of all in the awareness of your presence in my spirit.*
>
> from *The Little Book of Celtic Blessings*

Chapter 33

God As A Friend

Fr. William Barry, S.J., a respected spiritual writer tells us in the *America* magazine of October 2, 2006 about a growing spiritual movement in spirituality to regard God as a Friend, rather than "Father." The spirituality of "Father and Mother" as terms for God regarded us as children in relation to God. "God holds us as a mother holds an infant in her arms." But how does a forty-five-year-old parent of children react to such images?

Fr. Barry writes: "I am concerned that adult members of our churches are not being encouraged to relate to God as adults, and I wonder if, as a result, they lose interest and stop participating in religious activities. This is a real concern because I believe that God is offering a different relationship to mature adults."

We continue to know our parents when we reach adulthood. But then we become more like equals. We become more sympathetic to them and realize some of their journey of raising children without maps. Fr. Barry adds, "We may even find we trust them as good friends in whom we can confide without expecting that they then shoulder the burdens we know we have to carry alone."

God wants our friendship. Indeed, God can be defined as: "The vulnerable one who saves us by offering us friendship." St. Thomas Aquinas defined love of God as friendship with God. Growth in friendship means developing from a child to an adult relationship. We realize that, "if God did not intervene to stop the crucifixion of Jesus or save the Jews from death in the gas chambers, then God cannot change human hearts unless those hearts agree to change."

"Our prayer for human needs of ourselves or others does not mean we expect God to intervene and change the circumstances to what we want, but we hope that expressing our concerns will have an effect on God's presence and action, " states Fr. Barry.

Another insight into our relationship with God at an adult level is what happens when parents and adult children engage in a cooperative business. "In the course of their common work, parents and adult children grow in mutuality, camaraderie, friendship, and cooperation."

The Book of Genesis pictures God walking in the Garden of Eden and conversing with Adam and Eve as friends, perhaps discussing how they were to cultivate the Garden, how it might need water, sunshine, etc. This took place in the cool of the evening. There is an implied insight that the conversation included the subject of shared work between God and the human family. This leads us to consider that whatever "garden" or work God has entrusted to us that God is interested in what we do and is available as a friend to help us. For example, we will not have peace on earth, as Pope John Paul reminded us many times, unless we work for justice so that no member of the human family in Africa or Asia will die of starvation or be homeless on our streets.

One of the great graces we can receive is to become aware of God's presence. "That sense of God waiting for my attention indicates God's willingness to be vulnerable. God can make all things work for good," Fr. Barry said. The war in Vietnam was wrong. It was cruel, but from it America has been enriched by thousands of Vietnamese, many of whom brought a strong Catholic faith purified during centuries of persecution. I feel sympathy for the suffering people of Vietnam, Darfur, Rwanda. But if I can feel sympathy what must be the reaction of God? A nun who is a friend of mine told me she weeps with God and for God when she reads about war, famine, and violence in society. She has developed a very mature adult-type friendship with God. This leads her to direct all her life's actions to revealing God to others in a prayer that says, "Let me, God, be your presence to others as a friend in a way no other person can." St. Ignatius tells us God wants our love as much as we want God's gifts and love. He adds, "Each shares with the other." Fr. Barry writes, "It may seem inconceivable that God would want something from me, but Ignatius came to this conclusion from his *experience* that God wants such mutuality."

Another author who has written about our relationship with God as one of friendship is Fr. Paul Hinnebusch, O.P., in his book, *Friendship in the Lord,* published in 1974. Another insight into our relationship with God was explained to me by Fr. Tom Gallagher, S.J., who spent almost fifty years in Alaska working with tribes in remote areas. They are not cerebral people, as are those of us raised in cultures with European roots. They communicate from the heart more than the head. They have a womb-sense of connection with life. The Divine Spirit, God, is always forming us toward a full life. This to me is an echo of the great medieval theologian Meister Eckhart. "God" he said, "is constantly on the birthing table." Fr. Hinnebusch writes the following passages about friendship:

"In friendship, not only must I live in expectation of greater things to come — I must also avoid fear. Fear prevents growth by keeping me from taking the risks which are involved in loving others. To allay this fear, I must be convinced that friendship does have its imperfect stages, and be willing to accept my imperfections without discouragement. The wonderful fullness of friendship to which I aspire in lively expectation can be reached only by steps.

The fact is, I cannot possibly be utterly giving and totally selfless in love until my needs are being cared for and I am receiving in love what I need. By its very nature as fostering growth, friendship cares for my needs, as well as enabling me to give to the other. Love knows how to give. And this is absolutely true of my love for God, which is forever receiving. I cannot be fully open to God's infinite love and generosity until I have accepted my neediness and lovablenesses.

Too often the very ability to grow in Christian love and friendship has been wounded or killed by excessive fear of the risks involved. If in a friendship each person has a profound reverence for the other as belonging to God, and if each is faithful both to God and to the friend, the seemingly excessive emotional captivation will pass, and a more selfless stage will evolve. Nothing that we are experiencing now is the ultimate. If we are faithful to God and to one another, then there is even more yet to come. This thought will allay paralyzing fears. Fear is an even bigger enemy of growth in friendship than is presumption.

I must have boundless faith in God's love. Faith is like getting a new set of eyes. The new set of eyes is this: to realize that in friendship with God, the best is always still to come; to put no limits on God's love and generosity; to always expect more."

Kahlil Gibran writes: "Your friend is your needs answered. He or she is your field which you sow with love and reap with thanksgiving. You come to each other with your hunger and you seek from each other peace. And let there be no purpose in friendship save the deepening of the spirit."

The "Song of Songs" tells of the great love of a man and woman that can lead to marriage. But Ch 5:16 has the woman exclaim about the man she loves: "Such is my friend and lover." Jesus spelled out the qualification for friendship with Him. He said in John 15:14: "You are my friends if you do what I command you." And Jesus left us one commandment: "Love one another."

Jesus, in his farewell to the Apostles, said in John 15:15: "I no longer call you slaves, for a master does not confide in his slaves. But you are my friends, proved by the fact that I have told you everything the Father has told me." We have too few paintings of Jesus with arms outstretched in greeting like a beloved friend greeting a friend. Shakespeare, with his usual insight into human nature, has Polonius (in *Hamlet*) speak words of advice to his son Laertes: "The friends thou hast and their adoption tried grapple them to thy soul with hoops of steel." Friends adopt each other! Genesis gives us a beautiful picture of Adam and Eve and their relationship to God before sin entered their lives. "God walked with them in the cool of evening," like friends.

There are many quotations from the Bible in regard to friendship. Jesus himself followed that great ideal of friendship, "laying down one's life for one's friend" (John 15:13). Jesus had a special friendship with Lazarus. On learning of the death of Lazarus, Jesus said in John 11:11: "Lazarus, our friend, sleepeth." Jesus wept at the tomb of Lazarus with such emotion that the bystanders said, "How much Jesus loved Lazarus." Proverbs 17:17 reads: "A friend loveth at all times." Psalm 126:2 states: "God provides for his loved ones even when they sleep."

Father Bob McCahill has been a priest in Bangladesh for twenty years and never baptized a man, woman, or child. Bangladesh is 98% Moslem. He rents a small house in a village and moves in with all his belongings — principally, a bicycle! The local people ask him, "Who are you? Why are you here?" He replies: "My name is Brother Bob. I go around looking for sick people — that is, persons who are so poor that they do not even think of professional treatment and who lack the courage to go to government facilities. I offer to help them by accompanying them to the hospital — sometimes carrying them in my arms or on my bicycle." He tells them, "Jesus is my model in life. Personal service to people in need is an important part of my religion." They ask, "Do you want us to be Christian?" He replies: "I do not. I want you to be the very best person God wishes you to be." Moslems first thought his love was tainted — an attempt to change their faith. His life of service is based on the belief that people need to experience pure love that has no strings attached. This seems to take about three years in a village. When he begins his stay in a village, the people are suspicious of his motives. The second year, trust grows, especially by those he has helped. By the third year, there is increased affection for him. He is "Uncle" or "Abba." He is a friend they trust. In him, the people of Bangladesh meet Jesus.

Jesus was invited as a friend, by a young groom, to celebrate his wedding in Cana. Perhaps because Jesus brought some of his friends to the wedding, the wine was in short supply. Jesus changed the water into wine for his friend the groom, but the miracle was not just for the groom, but for you and me and all who try to follow Jesus. The miracle tells us that above all, Jesus wishes to bring joy to life. Through our contact with others, some joy should enter their lives. Jesus, our friend, in his farewell to us said: "You have sorrow now, but I will see you again and then you will rejoice and no one can rob you of that joy." (John 16:22)

God is a friend to all of us and, when we attend church, it should be with an acceptance of our affirmation of friendship. An appropriate sign for a church could be, "No perfect people need apply. Those with failures, regrets, sadness, frustrations and sin, are welcome." With this spirit of acceptance, we should listen to others patiently and without judgment. I have learned over the years that what people most want from me as a priest is to know I care about them.

Rick Warren, in his book, *The Purpose Driven Life,* tells us: "You will never grow a close relationship with God by just attending church once a week or even having a daily quiet time. Friendship with God is built by sharing all your life experiences with God." The best selling book on this subject is *Practicing the Presence of God* by Brother Lawrence, a French monk. He tells us to turn to God as often as we can during the day with a short prayer or greeting like a quick phone call to praise God, or to ask for help to affirm our friendship with God and God's love for us. In this way, we both receive God's friendship, and offer our own in return.

Chapter 34

The Diary of Etty Hillesum

She was born to Jewish parents in Holland, January 15, 1914. In grade school, she studied Hebrew and was interested in Jewish affairs. At the University of Amsterdam, she studied law and took her masters in law in 1939. She also studied Russian language and literature, which had a great appeal for her. Soon after that she began a diary, and at the same time, to the surprise of her friends, she gave much thought to spirituality. This is reflected in her diary.

Westerbork was a Nazi transit camp where thousands of Jews arrived before being sent to various concentration camps. Some Jews were allowed to go there as volunteers. Etty volunteered for two terms of several months each. Here she met mothers separated from husbands, children from parents, the elderly, the sick, the aged. She tried to comfort and help to the best of her ability.

In the midst of the pain and sorrow she experienced at Westerbork, she wrote this in her diary on August 18, 1943:

"You have made me so rich, oh God, please let me share out your beauty with open hands. My life has become an uninterrupted dialogue with you, oh God, one great dialogue. Sometimes when I stand in some corner of the camp, my feet planted on your earth, my eyes raised toward your heaven, tears sometimes run down my face, tears of deep emotion and gratitude. At night too, when I lie in my bed and rest in You, oh God, tears of gratitude run down my face and that is my prayer."

On the same day she wrote:

"More and more I tend toward the idea that love for everyone who may cross your path, love for everyone made in God's image, must rise above for blood relatives."

Earlier, on August 8, 1943, she wrote:
"Many people feel their love of mankind languishes at Westerbork because it receives no nourishment, meaning the people here don't give you much occasion to love them. 'The mass is a hideous monster, individuals are pitiful' someone said. But I keep discovering that there is no causal connection between people's behavior and the love you feel for them. Love for one's fellow man is like an elemental glow that sustains you. The fellow man himself hardly has anything to do with it. It is a little bit bare of love here, but I myself feel so inexpressly rich. I cannot explain."

On August 11, 1943 she wrote:
"Most people here are much worse off than they need be because they write off their longing for friends and family as so many losses in their lives, when they should count the fact that their heart is able to long so hard and to be loved so much as their greatest blessings."

My favorite of her prayers was written July 12, 1942:
"Dear God, these are anxious times. Tonight for the first time I lay in the dark with burning eyes as scene after scene of human suffering passed before me. I shall promise you one thing, God, just one very small thing. I shall never burden my body with cares about tomorrow although that takes some practice. Each day is sufficient unto itself. I shall try to help You, God, to stop my strength ebbing away though I cannot vouch for it in advance. But one thing is becoming increasingly clear to me — that You cannot help us, that we must help You to help ourselves. And that is all we can manage these days and also all that really matters, that we safeguard this little piece of you, God, in ourselves. And perhaps in others as well. Alas, there doesn't seem to be much you Yourself can do about our circumstances, about our lives. Neither do I hold You responsible. You cannot help us but we must help You and defend Your dwelling place inside us to the last."

She kept this promise, as is revealed in a letter she wrote to a friend, Christine Van Nooten, on September 9, 1943, as she was about to be sent to the concentration camp where she was murdered November 29, 1943:

> *"Christine, opening the Bible at random, I find this: 'The Lord is my high tower.' I am sitting on my rucksack in the middle of a full freight car. Father, mother, Mischa are a few cars away on the train. In the end the departure was without warning. On sudden special orders from the Hague we left the camp (Westerbork transit camp) singing. We shall be traveling for three days."*

She had refused invitations to go into hiding, choosing to remain with her Jewish people. Said Michael Downey, reviewer, "She discovered beauty amid atrocity. Utterly alert to mystery she faced the truth without flinching. She lived in hope, without a trace of resentment or self pity...her life was poured out as a balm for all wounds. Her words have become a healing salve."

Her reflections on the possibility of death in the gas chamber:

> *"People often get worked up when I say it doesn't really matter whether I go or somebody else does, the main thing is that so many thousands have to go. It is not as if I want to fall into the arms of destruction with a resigned smile — far from it. I am only bowing to the inevitable, and even as I do so I am sustained by the certain knowledge that ultimately they cannot rob us of anything that matters. I certainly do not want to go out of some sort of masochism, to be torn away from what has been the basis of my existence these last few years. But I don't think I would feel happy if I were exempted from what so many others have to suffer. They keep telling me that someone like me has a duty to go into hiding because I have so many things to do in life, so much to give. But I know that whatever I may have to give to others, I can give it no matter where I am, here in the circle of my friends or over there, in a concentration camp. And it is sheer arrogance to think oneself too good to share the fate of the masses. And if God himself should feel that I still have a great deal to do, well then, I shall do it after I have suffered what all the*

> *others have to suffer. And whether or not I am a valuable human being will become clear only from my behavior in more arduous circumstances. And if I should not survive, how I die will show me who I really am." (p. 487)*

Etty Hillesum's relationship to God was truly that of a lover. St. Therese of Avila had a similar love for God. So did St. Therese of Lisieux, France. The latter had great moments of weakness of faith as she lay dying of tuberculosis, at age twenty-four, dealing with the physical and mental illness of her father. But Etty saw human cruelty of an unprecedented nature and did not blame God but was moved to tears at the sorrow God experienced from humans.

To understand this young Jewish woman who read St. Augustine and the New Testament, we should realize her view of God was not a traditional one in Judaism or Christianity. Dr. Francis Collins is the Director of the National Genome and Research Institute. He headed a multi-national team of 2400 scientists who co-mapped the three billion biochemical letters of our genetic blueprint. He wrote "God is beyond our understanding. Jesus assisted us. God is love. He left us one commandment: to love one another."

Dr. Collins is a strong believer in God, but he believes that God cannot be completely contained within nature and therefore is beyond the power of science to reach. Rabbi Heschel said, "There is no proof for God's existence, only witnesses." These witnesses are not necessarily theologians and preachers, but humble, loving people.

I make the above detour to try to explain the attitude of Etty toward God. She expressed it best when she said: "One thing is becoming increasingly clear to me — that You, God, cannot help us — that we must help You to help ourselves." The Medieval theologians had a principle: "Qui facit per alium facit per se." What you do through another you do yourself. Etty saw God giving us the privilege and honor to stand back and be God's agent in reaching out to others — to bring them, through our love, to the love of God. Etty never read the Medieval Christian theologian Meister Eckhar, but she was in tune with his theology that, "Human love is God's love in disguise." Before we reach out to seek the emotional or physical help we need from others, we should regard it as coming from God through others. God is in us inspiring us to share His love. We dishonor God when we refuse to help another in need. Etty realized this when she said: "All that really matters is that we safeguard this little piece of you, God in us." She never blamed God for the inevitable suffering she observed and tried to alleviate. She promised God one thing — she called it "just one small thing:" "I shall never burden my body with cares about tomorrow." She was sustained by her love for people, always distinguishing the person from the evil they did.

Jesus said, "Learn from me, for I am gentle and humble of heart." Etty revealed this gentle, humble side of her when urged by friends to hide and escape from the Nazis. These friends said, "You have so many things to do in life." She refused to leave her people for any reason, not considering herself better than others.

Both Etty and Ann Frank had a spirit of optimism, a belief in a better future that the cruelty and evil of the Nazis could not extinguish. At the end, she was singing on the transport car that took her to the concentration camp. Her parents were on that same train but in a different car, which saved her much anguish. In one of her last letters that she wrote, "I would so much like to live on, if only to express all the love I carry with in me. I feel so light without the least bitterness and so full of strength and love." She does not prove the existence of God but is truly a witness to God's presence in the darkness of Nazi cruelty.

God can never be captured in words and is beyond everything, yet we have burned people at the stake for not accepting some attempt of male theologians to define God. Our religious wars have been fought over different understandings of God and Jesus. Exodus 33 gives us an interesting insight into God. Moses spoke to God, according to the text, and begged God to show his face. God said, "I will make all my beauty pass before you, and in your presence I will pronounce my name, 'Lord'... but my face you cannot see." Then God said, "When my glory passes I will set you in the hollow of the rock and will cover you with my hand until I have passed by. Then I will remove my hand, so that you may see my back; but my face is not to be seen."

This simple story is an attempt to reveal the mystery of God. God is not perceived directly. Jesus showed us how to be the best people God desires. But ultimately, we know God had passed by when we meet courageous, loving people like Etty. All of us reveal the existence of God in our world by extending God's love to others. We need fewer words about God and more acts of kindness and love as Etty teaches us.

Etty Hillesum never heard the phrase "wounded healer." It is attributed to Fr. Henri Nouwen who emigrated from his native Holland to America in the sixties. He served as chaplain to students at Harvard and at other distinguished American universities. He wrote forty books on spiritual topics and was much in demand as a preacher. Yet in his own life he craved affirmation and friendship but was to find, at times, disappointment and abandonment from others which wounded his spirit. He continued his spiritual journey of seeking to help others, calling himself a "wounded healer" until his death in his native Holland on September 21, 1996. He was on his way to St. Petersburg to make a video on the painting of *The Prodigal Son* by Rembrandt. He had written a best selling book on this beautiful painting titled *Return of the Prodigal Son*, wherein he describes love and forgiveness as unconditional.

Etty volunteered to go to Westerbork Concentration Camp to comfort and console others. While doing so she knew rejection and pain of spirit. She was introduced to the New Testament and to St. Augustine by an older man for whom she served as a secretary and at times a lover. She had an abortion along the spiritual journey that led her to a deeper and deeper love for God. I believe, as she comforted those with her in the crowded rail car on their way to death, she would have seen herself as a "wounded healer," reminding us that our wounds, our brokenness, may be how we too come closer to understanding God's love.

A friend sent me the following at Christmas:

Lean on Me. "I am the way. the truth, and the life. No one comes to the Father except through me." John 14:6. During difficult times, I hear God say: "Lean on Me, for I care about you. Let my strength support you, My love carry you. I'm here for you. Lean on Me, and I'll help you through any pain. I'll be your eyes when you feel you have to turn away. I'll be your ears when you can't bear to hear what has to be said. I'll be your heart, always filled with courage and hope. Lean on Me and trust Me. You know I'll be there for you through thick and thin, in the best of times and in the most challenging of times. I am your rock, your fortress, your everything. Lean on Me and discover complete serenity. You are My child, and I will never forsake you. Lean on Me, dear one."

Etty followed this advice by constantly leaning on God.

Chapter 35

Lamps to My Feet

The following persons inspired me by their lives, and I was privileged to share time with them, sometimes as my house guests.

PHILIP BERRIGAN

Phillip Berrigan flew bombing missions in World War II. When he returned, he entered a seminary and was ordained a priest in 1955. Around 1965, he came to Seattle to speak at an anti-war rally and was my house guest at St. Patrick's rectory, Seattle. After leaving Seattle he returned to his home base, Baltimore, and became involved with his brother, Dan, a Jesuit priest, in protests against the Vietnam War and especially nuclear war. He considered the nuclear threat to all of humanity so great that he called for a common international effort against its manufacture and use. He was arrested several times for his anti-war protests, as when he attempted to damage an airplane that carried nuclear bombs and when he poured blood on draft records in Baltimore. It is estimated he spent eleven years of his life in prison for his anti-war protests. He resigned from priesthood and married. He died in December 6, 2002. I found him a gentle, caring person. When I read of his strong anti-war protests, I realized they came from his compassion and love of people, the innocent victims of war. Berrigan wrote a final statement in the days before his death. His final comments included this: "I die with the conviction, held since 1968 at Catonsville, that nuclear weapons are the scourge of the earth; to mine for them, manufacture them, deploy them, use them, is a curse against God, the human family, and the earth itself."

FLOYD SCHMOE

Visitors to Camp Brotherhood will see a statue of St. Francis of Assisi outside the Warren Center which serves as our dining room and office building. The statue was carved from a cedar tree. The artist, Floyd Schmoe, a Quaker, depicted St. Francis kneeling down to place a plant in the soil. This was his understanding of what St. Francis accomplished by his teaching about peace and non-violence in the twelfth century. Floyd Schmoe lived in the spirit of St. Francis as a professor of forestry at the University of Washington. He opted to be an ambulance driver during World War I instead of combat service. He and Rabbi Levine were good friends, and Rabbi introduced me to him on Floyd's eightieth birthday. At that time, he gave me the statue of St. Francis. During World War II, he was beyond the draft age. The dropping of the atomic bombs that wiped out so many thousands of mothers, children and the elderly in Nagasaki and Hiroshima caused him much anguish. After collecting funds from his friends, he set out for Hiroshima in 1948, and with some Japanese volunteers built homes for five years out of the rubble left by the bombs. Newspapers in Japan carried pictures of the caring American. One day, some grade school students came to interview him. One of them, the editor of the school newspaper, asked Floyd Schmoe why he was different from other Americans, as he was the only one who came to help them. Floyd said he was always opposed to war and the killing of people to solve problems and differences. In 1985 on the fortieth anniversary of the dropping of the bomb on Hiroshima, he was the only American invited to the observance. Since his visit there in 1948, he had arranged for many badly burned victims of the bomb to come to Seattle for treatment. Because of his love and concern for the people of Hiroshima, they gave him a gift of $40,000. On his return to Seattle, he went to see the mayor and requested him to match the gift of $40,000 and establish a Peace Park in Seattle. His wishes were carried out later when three blocks of land north of the University Bridge were set aside for the Peace Park. He asked me to give the invocation on the day of dedication and we were joined by people from countries Floyd had helped in some way. There were Russians, Palestinians, Koreans and others. Trees and flowers from these countries were planted. Floyd Schmoe has influenced many people to work for peace. When in Hiroshima in 1985, there was a dinner in his honor. A gentleman at the head table asked Mr. Schmoe if he remembered the grade school children who interviewed him in 1948. He recalled the day. The gentleman said, "I was the editor of the school newspaper and was so impressed by your words that I now represent Hiroshima in the Diet (parliament) and I am the adviser to the prime minister for disarmament." Floyd Schmoe lived to be 105. He was nominated for the Nobel Peace Prize four times.

JOHN T. NOONAN

John T. Noonan was a law professor at the University of California at Berkley and Notre Dame. He came to Seattle in the mid-sixties to give a talk on peace. A mutual friend brought him to my residence. We spent a whole evening discussing the attitude of the Church on usury. Judaism forbade the charging of money on a loan and Christianity followed the same policy. Some, like Professor Rodney Stark in his book, *The Victory of Reason,* trace the change and the rise of capitalism to the medieval monasteries. Some of these monasteries had several hundred monks who engaged in manual labor as part of their vocation. They planted far more crops than they needed for their own use and sold the large surpluses for profit. With the money they received, they made loans with interest to kings and knights in need of money. Some in the church criticized this process, calling it the sin of usury. But the new policy of loaning money for interest continued and is part of western banking, but not of Islam. Professor Stark sees it as the beginning of capitalism. I was fascinated by the analysis of Professor Noonan. He used the attitude of change in the Church in regard to usury to place in perspective the possibility of a change in church policy in regard to contraception, which was then under consideration by Pope Paul VI, who appointed a commission to study it. Professor Noonan subsequently wrote a book titled, *The Scholastic Analysis of Usury and Contraception,* and presently serves as a Federal Judge on the 9th Circuit Court of Appeals in San Francisco. I found him to be a gentle, soft-spoken man with strong convictions, a man who welcomed the changes in the Church introduced by the Vatican Council.

MONSIGNOR WILLIAM BAUM

Monsignor Baum now serves as a Cardinal at the Vatican. In 1965, he was the ecumenical officer of the American bishops in Washington, D.C. As the local ecumenical officer for the Archdiocese of Seattle, I was assigned by Archbishop Connolly to organize the first all-city ecumenical prayer service in January, 1965. Assisting me was a Lutheran pastor and later my colleague on TV, Pastor Oscar Rolander. We selected the Seattle Opera House for the service and extended a general invitation to Seattle churches to participate. About five thousand people attended. An interesting discussion took place between pastor Rolander and myself while preparing for the service. He had decided to bring a King James edition of the Bible. He asked me what edition I would bring. Mindful of the fact that different translations of the Bible aggravated the differences between Christians, I decided on a gesture of unity in regard to the Bible. I suggested that when he finished his reading of the scripture at a lectern on one side of the stage, that he walk across the stage and hand me his Bible for the second reading. Sisters in religious garb and many clergy intermingled with the mixed congregation. I had invited the then Monsignor William Baum to be the speaker. He recognized and affirmed the historic significance of the occasion and was my guest at St. Patrick's, Seattle, for several days. His office had called me in 1962 to be a Catholic representative at a meeting of the American Episcopal Bishops in Seattle. Archbishop Michael Ramsey, the 100th Archbishop of Canterbury and Primate of the Anglican (Episcopal) Church of England, flew from London to address the bishops. I was privileged to meet him and I told Monsignor Baum of an interesting occurrence at the end of their meeting. During a good part of one day the bishops discussed holding a meeting with their Canadian counterparts. They considered a place, a time and an agenda. To my great surprise, I was invited as the Catholic guest to speak at the conclusion of their meeting. I had received no instructions from Monsignor Baum or the Ecumenical Office in Washington, D.C., so I said a brief prayer and spoke extemporaneously, concentrating on my interest in their proposed meeting with the Canadian Bishops. I concluded by saying, "Some day soon I hope there will be a meeting of the American Roman Catholic Bishops and the American Episcopal Bishops." As I walked to my car, a gentleman ran up to me and introduced himself as Bishop Hines from New York, who presided at the meeting. With excitement he asked, "Did you extend an official feeler to us?" Sadly, I said it was a personal statement.

PAT & PATTY CROWLEY

In the exciting years following the Vatican Council, I was friends with some of the leaders of the YMCA in Seattle. At a special anniversary of the founding of the Seattle YMCA in 1966 and honoring the birthday of John R. Mott, founder of the ecumenical movement, John was remembered for teaching and modeling volunteerism and service among young people through his work in the YMCA. I received the unusual honor of being asked to select a Catholic speaker for the occasion. I was a great fan of Pat and Patty Crowley, leaders of the Christian Family Movement in the 50's and 60's. They brought groups of married people together on Sunday evenings for prayer and discussion. I wrote to Pat who resided in Chicago, and invited him to be the speaker. He came with his wife Patty and were my guests at St. Patrick's rectory, where we spent many hours in conversation. Both were members of the Special Commission appointed by Pope Paul VI to study the teaching of the Church on contraception. During their initial discussions they found that most of the clergy and married couples on the Commission were in favor of no change. Before leaving Chicago for Rome, the Crowleys conducted a survey of thousands of Catholic couples in the Christian Family Movement. These were committed Catholics who for the most part supported Catholic education and financially supported the Church and its ministry. The great majority of those dedicated couples voted for a change in the law. Both Pat and Patty shared these findings with their fellow members of the Commission. After studying them, many bishops and laity changed their minds and voted for a change in Church policy. The Commission recommended their findings to the Pope for a change. In an official letter, "Humanae Vitae," published in 1968, the Pope affirmed the traditional teaching. Many who publicly protested, such as Professor Charles Curran, were deprived of the right to teach at a Catholic university. Bishop Shannon, auxiliary bishop of St. Paul, resigned in protest and took up the practice of law. A modification of the law to allow condoms by a partner to help avoid AIDS is under consideration. Some see the Church in the future holding a world-wide conference of married couples to review the current teaching. I believe the Crowleys, who are now deceased, would approve of such a conference.

ROBERT McAFEE BROWN

The sixties were difficult years to be a pastor for the first time. St. Patrick's was an average parish in central Seattle with some who welcomed the changes being introduced as a result of Vatican council, such as English instead of Latin, lay readers, altars facing the people, guitars for music instead of the organ, etc. Others had difficulties with the changes. There was also the tension in the sixties about the Vietnam War. The Archbishop at the time, Thomas Connolly, spoke at a Seattle University graduation about intensifying the war to finish it. Students walked out. The dean of St. Mark's cathedral, a good friend, lost his son in the TET Offensive in 1968.

Many students would not register for the draft and went to Canada. Stories appeared in the press about their inability to find work, their poverty (especially in winter), and in many cases, their need for food and shelter. A group of church people from the Council of Churches decided to have a drive to obtain warm clothing and food for them. They called on me as pastor of a church in the heart of Seattle to offer the parish hall for the meeting. It was the mid-sixties. The opening chapter of the document entitled "The Church Today," approved December 7, 1965, by the Vatican Council just when I became pastor at St. Patrick's Parish stated: "In our times a special obligation links us to make ourselves the neighbors of absolutely every person, and of actively helping them when they come across our path." Mindful of these words, I gave permission for the use of the hall.

Robert McAfee Brown, Professor of Religious Studies at Stanford University, was to be the speaker.

He had written and spoken on ecumenism and I had read several of his writings. He was banned from South Africa for anti-apartheid activities. In 1960 he wrote, *American Dialogue: A Protestant Looks at Catholicism & a Catholic Looks at Protestantism,* co-authored by Fr. Gustave Weigel S.T. I welcomed him as my guest for the evening. He spoke of the occasion as calling us to a true practice of ecumenism when, as members of different churches, we united to address a human need. Several hundred people came, bringing primarily clothes and money to aid the young Americans in Canada who could not bring themselves to take part in the war. As a member of the World Without War Council with Fr. Frank Costello, S.J., then at Seattle University, we helped to provide counselling for conscientious objectors to war. But those in Canada, while not opposed to all war, were against the war in Vietnam.

At the time, public sympathy was not with those who fled to Canada. I received some very negative comments for making the hall available to Dr. Brown. In fact, a prominent lawyer called and said he would like to strip me of my citizenship for helping those "cowards" in Canada, but I felt Robert McAfee Brown spoke in the spirit of the bishops at Vatican Council. More especially, he spoke in the spirit of Jesus asking us to respond as Jesus would.

Chapter 36

St. Paul Writes on Love

One of the greatest chapters on this subject in all of literature.
1 Corinthians, 13.

Paul writes: Love is patient. The word patience has as its root "pati," to endure, in Latin. Love waits and accepts without complaint all manner of challenges, such as from wrongful judgments, poor health, financial reverses, loss of loved ones. Dana Reeve is a great example of a patient, loving person. She set aside her singing career to care for her husband night and day for years after the accident that left him paralyzed. At his funeral she said, "I revise my marriage vows. I promised to love him all our lives. Now that he is dead, I still love him."

Kindness. Putting others first is kindness. Mary, after receiving the announcement of the pending birth of Jesus, walked seventy miles to the home of her cousin, Elizabeth, to minister to her in her pregnancy. Ruth, a non-Jew, left Moab, her native country, to return to Israel with her widowed mother-in-law who sent her to gather wheat in the field of a kind neighbor named Boaz. The kindness of the latter touched Ruth, who married him and made them both part of the ancestry of Jesus.

Love is without Envy. Envy wants what others have and we do not. Modern advertising creates a spirit of envy for physical beauty, material goods, etc.

Love is not boastful or arrogant. Jesus gave us a memorable description of an arrogant person in Luke 18. He tells the story of two men who went to the Temple to pray. One said, "I give thanks, O God, that I am not like the rest of men — grasping, crooked, adulterous — or even like this tax collector." The tax collector prayed, "God be merciful to me, a sinner." The prayer of the latter was heard.

Love is not ill-mannered nor does it seek its own interest. Good manners on the highway, in the home, or at work are like fresh air, wholesome and refreshing.

Love withstands anger and forgets offenses. Corrie Ten Boom, a Dutch woman who survived a Nazi concentration camp due to helping Jews, often quoted from the psalms that God "casts our sins into the depth of the sea." Since she grew up near the sea, she would add her own comment to the words of God by saying, "After God casts our sins into the sea he puts up a sign that reads *No Fishing Allowed Here!* In Matthew 11:29, Jesus said, "Learn from me for I am gentle and humble of heart."

He did not seek His own interest. A "friend" is described in the Bible as the "medicine" of life. A loving friend heals the wounds in us from our own weakness or from the selfishness of others.

Love does not take delight in wrong but rejoices with the truth. The media often concentrates on the personal faults of others. The follower of Jesus should be aware of the good in people. Sunday should be a joyful day as we assist at Mass with others, family members, friends, parishioners, or strangers — all united in loving God. Always look for God in the soul of the other rather than for the faults of others.

Love excuses everything, believes all things, hopes all things and endures all things. The best commentary on these lines is found in *The Living Bible.* "If you love someone you will be loyal to him/her no matter what the cost. You will always believe in him/her, always expect the best of him/her, and always stand your ground in defending him/her.

These three things remain: Faith, Hope and Love, and the greatest of these is Love.

In his farewell message in John 15:9, Jesus said, "As the Father has loved me, so I have loved you, live on in my love." Commenting further in his first letter, Chapter 4:11, John wrote: "Beloved, if God loved us so we must have the same love for one another. No one has ever seen God. Yet if we love one another God dwells in us and His love is brought to perfection in us." Here is Corinthians 13 taken from the Jerusalem Bible:

> *"Love is patient; love is kind. Love is not jealous, it does not put on airs, it is not snobbish. Love is never rude, it is not self-seeking, it is not prone to anger; neither does it brood over injuries. Love does not rejoice in what is wrong but rejoices with the truth. There is no limit to love's forbearance, to its trust, its hope, its power to endure."*

The day-to-day living, the challenge of love as spelled out by St. Paul can be painful but purifying, leading us to a better understanding of God's love.

Some years ago, a well-known Dominican priest in England, Father Bede Jarrett, wrote a letter to a young Benedictine priest, Hubert Van Zeller, about a love relationship in the life of the young priest and a friend. The advice proved helpful, as Van Zeller later had a distinguished and full life as a priest and writer. Here is what Bede Jarrett, the Dominican, wrote to his Benedictine priest friend on how a priest or religious, vowed to God, can have a place for a deep friendship in his or her life:

> *"I am glad [that you have fallen in love with P] because I think your temptation has always been towards Puritanism, a narrowness, a certain inhumanity. Your tendency was almost towards the denial of the hallowing of matter. You were in love with the Lord but not properly in love with the Incarnation. You were really afraid... You were afraid of life because you wanted to be a saint and because you knew you were an artist. The artist in you sees beauty everywhere; the novice in you said, 'Keep your eyes tight shut;' if P had not come into your life, you might have blown up. I believe P will save your life. I shall say a Mass in thanksgiving for what P has been, and done, to you. You have needed P for a long time. Aunts are no outlet. Nor are stout and elderly Provincials."*

In a previous letter Fr. Jarrett had written to Fr. Hubert Van Zeller the following:

> *"If you thought the only thing to do was to retire into your shell, you would never see how lovely God was. You might love [P] and look for God in her. Enjoy your friendship. Pay the price of the following pain for it. Remember it in your Mass and be part of it." Fr. Barry adds, "God is vulnerable indeed, and wants adult friends who work together with God to achieve the dream of a world alive." They will not hurt or destroy on all of my holy mountain, for the earth will be full of the knowledge of the Lord as the waters cover the sea." (Isaiah 11:9)*

As a priest counselor friend of mine, Dom Eugene Boylan, said: "The challenge of life is to accept oneself as we are. This becomes harder as our limitations and insufficiencies become more and more apparent unless we remember that God loves us unconditionally."

Chapter 37

Looking Back at Meeting God

My earliest memory of my introduction to God took place when I was three years old. It was customary in Ireland for the priest to bless a new home. Our home was about five years old when the priest came to perform the blessing. I was the oldest of the four children and had one younger brother at the time of the blessing.

The family assembled in the kitchen. The farm manager was my hero, as I often spent time with him at his work.

On this particular day he joined the family and knelt beside me while the priest read the blessing. Following the blessing, the priest signed and dated a document with the blessing, which was later framed and hung in the kitchen. From the date on it, I calculated that I was three years and three months old. I realized then that prayer was not just in my family but that others prayed also.

At age four, my parents took me to Sunday Mass. I had no idea what was happening and I spent most of the time observing the people around me. Some used beads. Some used prayer books. Some closed their eyes in prayer — or perhaps in sleep! In the middle of the service, a bell rang and the atmosphere changed: there was rapt attention and silence. I concluded that something very important was happening. Then, when I was six and attended school, the religion teacher explained that God came to earth at Mass. She explained that in parts of Ireland the people at that time of the Mass would sing out, "A hundred thousand welcomes, O Lord," a traditional Irish greeting. No doubt my parents had told me about the Mass, but generally it was not discussed in a theological sense.

At age seven, it was explained to me that God would come to me at Mass in a small piece of bread distributed by the priest. The month of my seventh birthday, I received communion for the first time with a very rudimentary understanding of what was happening. As a child, everything I was told I accepted on faith. This applied to what I was told to eat at home, what happened in church, what the appropriate words, actions and behaviors were, etc. Without question, I accepted.

In grade school we had a class in religion every day, taught by a public school teacher. In Ireland, following five hours of secular instruction, religion could be taught. Schools were predominately either Protestant or Catholic. The few Protestants in my school were excused during the last class of the day — religion. They would wait for us Catholics and we all walked home together peacefully.

The religious textbook, written in question and answer form, was called a "catechism" and became more abstract each year. Words and their meanings, not heard in daily conversation, had to be memorized: God the Creator, Sacraments, Trinity, Jesus, Redeemer, Salvation, Grace, Ten Commandments, sin, heaven, purgatory and hell.

Each year, we learned a little more about these subjects, but little was said about God and God's love. We were told about the laws and commandments we had to observe, and were told that if we seriously failed, we committed a mortal sin which separated us from God. If we died in mortal sin we could go to hell forever — and its fire was not pleasant! Those of us who had this introduction to God had a fear of God as Judge.

At age thirteen, I went to a secondary school taught by priests. Like most of the students, I regarded the class in religion as an academic subject because we were graded on it. We studied Bible History, The Life of Christ, The History of the Catholic Church, and we learned much about the laws of the Church. At that time, bible study among Catholics was not encouraged. The sixteenth century separation, introduced by Martin Luther among Christians, turned the Bible into a source-book for quotations to prove others wrong. Fortunately, this has changed.

I regret in my search for God that more emphasis was not given to the Biblical words of Paul to the Romans 13:10, "Love never wrongs the neighbor, hence love is the fulfillment of the law." Instead of emphasizing the laws God wanted us to observe, there was that special law by which all laws were to be observed in all we do and say — the one law or commandment that Jesus gave us: "Love one another."

The intellectual study of God did not bring me as close to God as did everyday life. When a farmer greeted another farmer at work, he said in greeting, "God bless the work" The response was, "And you too." In a time of illness or death, there was a recognition of the presence of God by the words, "Welcome be the will of God."

A promise of a future action always included the words "With God's help." A farewell ended, "Go in the name of God" At noon and six in the evenings, the church bell rang and all paused to turn to God and pray. Thus, God was revealed in the day-to-day conversation of people as friendly, caring, compassionate — more so than the God I learned about in class.

On entering the major seminary at age eighteen to study for priesthood, we again took classes in Church History, and began a deeper study of the teachings of Jesus — on sin, on salvation, and on prayer. My university degrees were in Greek, Latin, and Philosophy. (The seminary is a branch of Dublin University, which today has about three thousand lay students enrolled there.) During the last four years in the seminary, studies concentrated on liturgy, scripture, and on the Catholic Church, which united us to Jesus. Sadly, while God and Jesus had a central place in our studies, we were ever mindful of the exams on our religious studies at the end of the year. Without hesitation, I accepted ordination to serve and endeavor to be Jesus, as a priest, in accordance with what I was taught. The Church had clear-cut regulations for this ministry. I was to be celibate, to be totally obedient to the bishop, and accept without question whatever assignment was given to me. I tried to follow the guidelines for ministry. Soon, I found that the vision I had to be a country priest in Ireland was not to happen. Instead, ministry took me thousands of miles away from home.

At the time of ordination in 1944, during World War II, I took as my motto: "Labor as a good soldier of Christ Jesus." (2 Timothy 2:3) Soldiers were dying in loyalty to their country, which was in a sense impersonal, though very real. As I began my priesthood, my understanding of God revolved around service in loyalty to God — a God who was as abstract to me as "country" was to the young person facing death for love of country.

My introduction to God has been a life-long process, from grade school, high school, seminary and sixty-three years as a priest. I consider my greatest and most enlightening encounter with God as coming from friends. Recently, in the writings of Sr. Joan Chittister, a prominent Catholic nun and author, I came across the following: "Real friends are those who take us into their lives with the ease of family and the warmth of love. Real friends are there for us — no matter the pressure, no matter the pain. It is not that friends justify our failures, it is simply that they do not notice them."

Today, I relate to God as a Friend in the spirit of the words of Sr. Chittister. I have also been helped by a prominent American spiritual writer, Fr. William Barry, S.J., who, as previously mentioned, wrote as recently as October 2, 2006, in the Catholic magazine *America:* "I am convinced that adult members of our churches are not being encouraged to relate to God as adults, and I wonder, if as a result, they lose interest and stop participating in religious activities.

This is a real concern because I believe God is offering a different relationship to mature adults."

I spend two half-hours each day silently in contemplative prayer, inviting God to foster a loving friendship between us, leading to a love such as St. Paul experienced when he wrote, "For I am certain that neither death nor life, neither angels nor principalities, neither the present nor the future, nor powers, neither height nor depth nor any other creature, will be able to separate us from the love of God that comes to us in Christ Jesus, our Lord." (Romans 8:38-39)

Rabbi Abraham Heschel said: " There are no proofs of the existence of God, only witnesses to God by their lives." I am profoundly grateful to the many people who revealed God to me, drawing me closer to God than any books, sermons, or theological teachings ever did. I realize we do not bring God to people but by our actions lead them to an awareness of God already in them.

Chapter 38

Unfinished Business

Life presents or will present all of us with its challenge. I suppose the first time life presented me with unfinished business took place when I was three months old. My paternal grandmother died at that time. My mother told me her last days were spent peacefully with me lying next to her. She longed to see me grow up but it was not to be. She died when I was three months old.

Robert Fine was a colleague on the "Challenge" TV program for two years. He was pastor of the Free Methodist Church at Seattle Pacific University. Death called him in his late fifties. A few days before he died, we had a last visit in his hospital room. We grieved. We prayed together. He expressed his joy at the spiritual closeness we found in spite of our different church membership. Then he said words to me that I have never forgotten. He said "I have in my heart sermons I would like to deliver, books that I would like to write, a wife and children that bind me to life." A few days later I attended his funeral service.

In spite of a long life as a priest I am reconciled to leaving this world with unfinished business. As a Christian, I reflect on the words of Jesus at age thirty-three, dying a painful death in the prime of life, with so much unsaid and unwritten. In John's Gospel, we find his final words. John 19:30, Jesus said, "It is accomplished. Then he bowed his head and gave up the spirit."

I pray that when the time comes, no matter what I feel is unfinished, that I too can say, "It is accomplished...Father, into your hands I commend my spirit."

Chapter 39

Hearts that Are One

The title of the first book that Rabbi Levine and I wrote, *Wild Branch on the Olive Tree,* was selected by me. Aware that it was not what might be called a "catchy" title, I hoped it would promote discussion on Jewish — Christian relations as seen by St. Paul in his letter to the Romans, Chapter 11, verse 17.

A horticulturalist could best explain what Paul had on his mind by grafting one tree to another. Paul was telling us that, as Christains, our foundation rested on Judaism. We Christains need Judaism for our self-understanding. Judaism does not need Christainity for self-understanding.

As a Catholic priest for sixteen years before I met Rabbi Levine, I celebrated Mass every day recalling the life, death, and resurrection of Jesus. Rabbi Levine had been a rabbi for almost 30 years but Jesus was totally absent from his Jewish ministry. He was raised in Czarist Russia until he was about seven years old. Then he and his family came to America. I was raised in Irish Catholicism which had experienced centuries of persecution from a Protestant government that ruled Ireland, leading Catholics to be defensive about their faith and country.

I walked into Rabbi Levine's study in May of 1960, at the request of Archbishop Connolly to discuss a TV program the Rabbi had in mind. He was very disappointed with my apparent inexperience and immaturity which he admits in *Wild Branch on the Olive Tree.*

But in spite of differences in theology, education, age, and life experiences, we discovered a deep unity of heart and mind. When I think of our relationship, I am reminded of a dialogue during the 18th century in Ireland between a Methodist minister and a Catholic priest at the time when there was no dialogue between Catholics and Protestants. In an exchange the Methodist minister wrote to the priest, "If your heart is as my heart, give me your hand and all is well between us."

Rabbi Levine and I had this unity of hearts that lead to 14 years of weekly cooperation on the TV program, "Challenge." We were able to share success and sorrow. He had two children, a boy and a girl. The boy had Down Syndrome and died as a teenager. His daughter, Lori, died of cancer at age 45. Her husband and children requested me to speak at her memorial service.

Rabbi phoned me and asked me to drive him to the service for his daughter. On the way, he was overcome with sorrow and said to me, "I may not be able to speak at the service." But when the time came, he reminded me of one of the great Jewish prophets as he spoke of God, the Giver of Life and the Giver of Love, to whom we commit our lives. I spoke briefly after him.

On the way home during the half hour drive, he was silent. As I reflected on the service, I recalled that sadly there was a time when I would have suffered severely from my Church for participating in a Jewish service. But a scripture message came to mind as vividly as on a screen in front of me. It was from Galatians 6:2, "Help carry one another's burdens, in that way you will fulfill the law of Christ." In helping the Rabbi cope with the grief at the loss of his last child I was being true to the spirit of Jesus who summed up His teaching by telling His followers to " be compassionate" and who was himself "moved with compassion" when meeting human sorrow.

Rabbi was a man who followed his "hunches." By this I mean he was open to follow inspirations of God. Moved with anger at the efforts of those who tried to foster religious bigotry to defeat John F. Kennedy, a Catholic seeking the Presidency in 1960, he followed his hunch to begin a religious dialogue on TV. With the support of WIlliam Warren, manager of KOMO TV, who donated a half hour time slot on Sunday evenings, we began the program in October, 1960, along with Dr. Martin Goslin, a Congregational pastor from Plymouth Church. Dr. Goslin was followed by Dr. Lynn Corson, a Methodist pastor from University Methodist Temple, then Pastor Oscar Rolander, a Lutheran missionary and last, Dr. Robert Fine a Free Methodist pastor.

Rabbi Levine had great experience with Jewish youth camps in California. He had originally intended a camp in the Northwest for Jewish youth and had some real estate friends looking for property. They found a 300 acre farm for sale in Skagit county. When Rabbi saw this beautiful property, he had a change of heart. He decided it should be a camp available to different churches for their own programs but with opportunities for young people to have meals together, sports, dialogue, etc. He wished to offer churches property for a reasonable rental fee.

One morning after a TV program, without any previous discussion about what he had in mind, he invited me to drive to Mt. Vernon with him to "purchase a farm." I said to him, "Rabbi, you know nothing about farming," to which he said, "Come with me and I will explain." On the way over he shared with me for the first time the vision he had and asked if I would support him. Then came *my* "hunch" — a message from the Holy Spirit: "Accept his invitation." I did.

We called on Mr. and Mrs. Goldade, owners of the farm. After both of us explained what we had in mind and our desire to purchase his property, Mr. Goldade, who seemed favorable to our request, said with some sadness, "I am sorry to tell you that a gentleman from California called a few days ago and is on his way to come here to finalize the deal. But if he does not purchase it, I will sell to both of you."

We came home feeling sad. A week later, we phoned Mr. Goldade. He said " The would-be purchaser who was on his way from California had a slight automobile accident in Portland and could not keep his appointment." When I told him what you gentleman had in mind, he told me he would withdraw his offer in your favor." We were very pleased. With the help of some generous friends, we were able to find loans of $22,000 as a deposit on the purchase price of $85,000. This was in November, 1966.

Due to the influence of Rabbi, a luncheon was held at the Washington Athletic Club the last week of December, 1966, where both of us outlined our plans for the property. Those present were some of the leading business leaders in Seattle. They endorsed our proposal which helped with fundraising. The Seattle newspapers carried our story on January 1, 1967.

In 1967, I called on the leaders of the various Protestant religious communities, telling them of our invitation to have them join us in building their own facility for their own faith programs on the property we purchased. All of them "approved" the project but told us they could not afford any new facility. It was then we faced our greatest challenge, and I believe God intervened directly to save the property. In 1967, Mrs. Levine met a professor of architecture, Lee Copeland, at the University of Washington. After learning about our plan, he asked the seniors in his architecture class to design and build a lodge as an academic exercise for which they would be graded. In January, 1968, 14 of them began work on what is known as Fisher Lodge. The students were in class 2 days and at the Camp for 3 days each week, living in the farmhouse and preparing their own meals. It was dedicated by Governor Evans on October, 1968, and thousands have used it since then. Three other lodges, a dining room for 200, and a house of worship have been added.

Rabbi and I had some heart to heart conversations in private especially during his last year. On one occasion, he confessed his sorrow concerning decisions and actions he made which, with growth and wisdom, he regretted. He was specific, and I was deeply moved by his trust in me. As I reflected on these conversations before his death I felt unity of heart with him. As a Christian, I read in the life of Jesus "He grew in wisdom, age, and grace." (Luke 2:40) In my own life, like the Rabbi, there have been actions and decisions which with advanced wisdom, I regret. But he and I, so to speak, reached for the stars as we both grew in maturity.

We accepted our human mistakes and failures because we were in full agreement that the God we believed in loved us unconditionally. I knew Rabbi did not expect me to be perfect and I did not expect him to be perfect. We had a deep love that was not lessened by our human weaknesses and mistakes. The human love we had for each other was divine love in disguise. Knowing that we were loved unconditionally by God was how we both found peace. Our friendship led me closer to God. With his help, I came to a better understanding of the words of the psalmist,"Even though I walk through the dark valley of the shadow of death, I fear no evil for you are beside me."

These words about the dark valley took on a special meaning for me with the Rabbi on two occasions. In May of 1975, I was driving back from Portland with the Rabbi. I had driven down. He was to drive on the return to Seattle. As we approached Olympia on I-5 I fell asleep. I awoke in a field with trees all around me. Rabbi was at the wheel besides me asking "Where are we?" My first thought was "This is not a dream — Have I died?" Rabbi had fallen asleep going 60 miles an hour. The car went over an embankement and ended in a field. When it slowed I began to get out. A state patrolman had watched us disappear and shouted at us not to move in case we were injured. But neither of us suffered even a bruise. Behind us was a tow-truck which pulled us out and the car sustained no damage. Rabbi gave up driving after that experience. But I do recall I woke up to the words of the psalmist not to be afraid, all would be well.

My next experience of the dark valley happened the last Saturday of October, 1985. I had led a tour group to China and arrived home in Stanwood about 9pm. Two parishioners arrived about 10pm, Dick and Dee La Fave. Mrs. Levine had called them to break the sad news to me that Rabbi was very seriously injured in an automobile accident that morning and was in Group Health Hospital. In spite of jet lag I was prepared to go see him, but they persuaded me to wait until the next morning.

When I went to the hospital, I found my dear friend of 25 years unconscious. I prayed beside him to the God we both served as we journeyed our separate paths as soul friends.

The following Sunday, I again visited him with a mutual friend, Mayer Baron, who eventually would become the Chairman of the Board of Directors for Camp Brotherhood for 22 years, and a member for many years at the synagogue that Rabbi Levine led. Each of us took a hand of Rabbi and, though he was unconscious, we promised to do our very best to carry on his vision for Camp Brotherhood.

That weekend, there was a Catholic-Jewish dialogue at Temple De Hirsch Sinai which Rabbi had planned. At the end of the Sunday night service, I was asked to give the Benediction. Standing at the Bema where Rabbi had spoken thousands of times, I gave thanks to God for his life and his leadership in promoting harmony in the human family.

The next morning I received a phone call that he had died. In my mind, I could see him go to heaven in a fiery chariot like the prophet Elijah is in Kings 2:11. Then I realized the kind gesture of the God who assisted us in our differences and united our hearts in that unity where deep calls unto deep. The last prayer recited for Rabbi Levine in the Temple he built was recited by this priest he helped grow in faith. A few days later, I was one of three speakers at his funeral service. I cannot imagine what my priesthood would have been without the influence of the Rabbi.

The preceding chapters tell of my life as a Catholic priest but it is a ministry deeply influenced by my relationship with Rabbi Levine. Blessed be his memory.

Rabbi Levine was the twelfth child in his family. His mother was working in the yard of the family home when the Rabbi decided to enter the family. She hurried to a stable where she gave birth. He often stated this gave him a special regard for Mary, mother of Jesus.

Chapter 40

Encounters with God

An ancient Christian creed composed in 325, and recited on Sundays in Catholic churches, refers to the Holy Spirit of God as "Giver of Life." Therefore, in encountering life in any form, I encounter God.

Recently I visited a friend who has a new home with a magnificent view of the Olympic Mountains and of Puget Sound. But on this occasion both of us stood silently and reverently not looking at the mountains or the water but at two parent swallows flying back and forth to feed five young swallows in a nest beneath the roof of the house. As I watched I wondered at the message given to the parent swallows to fly north from their southern winter home. Then on arrival something told them how and where to build a nest of mud and straw, to lay eggs and hatch them, and then to feed the young. These swallows provided me an encounter with God, the Giver of Life, including the life of the flies captured by the parent swallow to feed their young.

Mother swallow feeding her young

In greeting the thousands of guests who come to Camp Brotherhood I tell them the following. Over millions of years before any Jewish men wrote down their insights concerning their encounters with God, we were given many glimpses by nature of God the Giver of Life. The mighty dinosaurs, the tiniest insects, the sunrise and sunsets, the birds and fishes and tides, the powerful evolution of life forms, in both the animal and humans, all revealed God the Giver of Life. This is another "bible" and I tell our visitors they can have it and 'read' it as they observe the trees and flowers, the deer, the cattle grazing peacefully on our 200 acres and encounter God the Giver of Life present in so many wonderful and varied forms at Camp Brotherhood. This too is a bible for as the psalmist tells us in Psalm 19 verse 2, "The heavens declare the glory of God and the firmament proclaims his handiwork."

A very special and moving encounter with God took place for me as a priest in what is called the Sacrament of Reconciliation. As I listened year after year to story after story of human failures, pain and regret, I was often moved to tears at the sadness in human lives. But I was also comforted in assuring the sad and broken penitents that God's love was healing and unconditional. Then the resolve to begin again with new determination and trust in God's love carried me and the penitent like a current in the river of God's love. The encounter ended on a note of exhilaration making the final moments joyful.

I have been blessed to encounter God in people, in happy couples preparing for marriage, in the grieving family at times of death, in the loyal and devoted parishioners and friends across 63 years in the priesthood. As I reflect on them I recall the words of the English poet William Wordsworth as he reflected on a wonderful experience he had one afternoon watching daffodils dancing with the breeze. He wrote,

"For often when on my couch I lie,
In vacant or in pensive mood,
They flash upon the inward eye
Which is the bliss of solitude,
And then my heart with pleasure fills
And dances with the daffodils."

But love has its pain as well as its great joy. The person who decides to love another must be willing to accept pain which is caused by the pain of the loved one. It may be due to illness in the loved one, to separation due to work, war, study etc. Ultimately the death of the loved one leaves an ache in the heart of the other. Having left all my family and seventy-five classmates in Ireland, having moved to ten different assignments and separation from dear friends in each place, I can speak to the pain that comes with love. But this pain can also lead to a most unique encounter with God. The more you experience pain in love due to allowing another into your heart you begin to realize something of God's love. Scripture and saints keep reminding us of God's love but something is not emphasized, I believe, from these messages. They omit telling us the pain God voluntarily accepts by love for humanity, especially the pain when love offered is ignored and rejected by violence to human life and creation.

Etty Hillesum, a 29-year-old Jewish woman found her love for God tested as a prisoner in a Nazi concentration camp where she met death on Nov. 29, 1943. A few months before her death she wrote in her diary on Aug. 11, 1943, "Most people in the camp are much worse off than they need to be because they write off their longing for friends and family as so many losses in their lives, when they should count the fact that their heart is able to long so hard to love so much as their greatest blessing." She believed God would respond to her loving longing for others in a positive way when Etty felt all she could do is tell God about her loved ones.

In my younger years as a priest I accepted invitations from friends to birthday celebrations, wedding anniversaries, etc. Now, I still love friends but feel in my senior years I do not have the energy to reach out personally to greet my many friends as my heart calls me to do. Now, on behalf of my friends, I ask God's love for them as Etty Hillesum did when she turned over her love for others trustingly to God. When she walked the streets of Amsterdam before her arrest and saw a beautiful flower she would offer it to God, such was her personal love for God, her loving friend. Knowing the concentration camp was drawing closer she wrote, "If I am in a small cell in a concentration camp and just see a cloud pass my tiny window I will present that cloud to you, my God."

Loved ones especially lead me to an encounter with God's love and God's pain. My final encounter with God — death — is drawing closer, at age 88. My mentor and priest friend, Fr. Daniel Walsh assures me in one of his books, "The God who redeems all manner of mistakes and failures will restore eternal life and courage to frightened hearts... because within me is the image and likeness of God, the source of all beauty. Within me and in all of us is a holy place where hands infinitely more gentle than our own once caressed us before we were born, where our souls were kissed before birth, where the fire of love still burns." All our encounters with God in life, in nature and with friends should lead us to the final encounter, when so to speak, we meet God face to face, not with fear but with joy, as a lover meets the beloved.

Part 2
Rabbi Raphael Levine

Chapter 1

In a Russian Ghetto

As I look at the picture of myself with bowed head as my friend Father Treacy is celebrating Mass on an altar which I made for him at his request, I think back to my childhood in Vilna, originally the capital of Lithuania but at my birth belonging to Russia. When I recall the terrible fear I had of Christians, especially of the bearded, black-robed priests associated in my mind with the pogroms and persecutions of my people in their tragic experience in the Russian pale[1] settlements during the 17th, 18th and 19th centuries, and see myself — a rabbi — present at the central act of Christian worship led by a priest, I am amazed at the distance I have traveled from my childhood in the Russian ghetto in Vilna at the beginning of the 20th century to St. Patrick's Catholic Church in Seattle on March 17, 1965.

My first recollections of Christians were of Russian peasants who used to come to our house with their chickens and eggs and loads of bark for the tanneries which my father bought from them and sold in the local market place. Some of them were friendly and kind; but too often when they had indulged too freely in vodka they would become ugly and abusive, calling my father filthy names and heaping contempt upon him and all Jews and Judaism. When at seven I was old enough to go to Russian school I became a special target for the Christian boys to taunt and abuse with their favorite epithet, "Zhid", almost the equivalent of "Sheeny" but worse. It was the Christmas and Easter holidays that were especially trying for Jews in the Russian pale. These were times when Russian peasants, informed by their priests of the Jew's role in the crucifixion of Jesus as sermonically embellished from the New Testament account, became especially ugly in their anger at the Jewish "Christ killers" and made the Jews in their neighborhoods the victims of their holy zeal for revenge. It was at these limes I remember that we would bolt our doors and shutter our windows and stay indoors for fear of the drunken peasants who often terrorized the ghetto. Some of the most tragic pogroms were engineered during these holy days. So my childhood experience with Christianity and Christians was full of fears; and the very word "Christ" became a synonym for tragedy in the Jew's vocabulary, and for me as a child a word which to utter was a grievous sin.

I was born in 1901, in Vilna, the youngest of 12 children of whom four had died before I was born. When I came into the world, four sisters and three brothers were there to greet me. Since no birth records were kept we never really knew the exact date. It was only when I was approaching my 13th birthday and had to go through the ceremony of being inducted into religious manhood as a Bar Mitzvah (Son of the Commandments) according to our Jewish tradition that it became important to fix an exact date. This was necessary to determine what Torah portion I had to read. By diverse family events and relationships at the time of my birth, they calculated that my Bar Mitzvah must occur around the middle of August because my Maftir, which is the portion the Bar Mitzvah boy reads from In a Russian Ghetto 57 the Torah, happened to coincide with the Sabbath nearest August 15, 1914. So I took August 15 as my official birthday and that is what it is to this day. The home in which we lived in Vilna was a wooden, thatched duplex with a balustrade dividing the porch and separating the two dwellings. Our part had two rooms. One was a multipurpose room containing a large brick oven which served as a dining, kitchen, family room and my father's business office; the other was divided by a curtain into two bedrooms, one of them for my maternal grandmother who lived with us. My two nephews and I slept on top of the warm brick oven which extended from the front room to the back wall of the house. The house was lighted by kerosene lamps and the floor was of dirt, covered with sawdust.

I remember how before dawn the peasants would start coming with their products. The walls of our house were white-washed and there was one wall which was used as a kind of ledger where my father would mark down with charcoal strokes the amounts of merchandise each peasant brought. In this primitive way accounts were kept since most of the peasants were illiterate and unable to understand written numbers.

Ever since I can remember, my grandmother lived with us and took care of me while my parents worked. I knew my grandfather only from a photograph, which showed a patriarch with a long, forked beard. He was known as "Lebel the Innndkeeper" in his village of Mushnik, not far from Vilna, and held an office equivalent to mayor. He died at the age of 104 and my grandmother, already in her 80's, came to live with my mother, the eldest of her 15 children.

At a very early age, probably at about four as was the custom among the Jews of the ghetto, I was inducted into my Hebrew education by being taught the Hebrew alphabet. We had a teacher who came to our home to instruct me and my youngest sister, Ida, who was seven years older than I. It was the tradition that when a boy began his first lesson the book was opened and a little honey was placed on the first page to symbolize the sweetness of study. When I was six I went to the Héder, or Hebrew school, where I spent most of the day from eight in the morning to mid-afternoon. I still recall what my first teacher looked like. He was a thin, hunched man, with a scraggly beard and dark, brooding eyes. He wore a long coat, the sleeves of which were greasy with long use as a handkerchief. He was very strict with us children and if we did not know our lessons he would stab us in the shoulder with his two forefingers hard enough to cause considerable pain.

Our home was in the ghetto on the outskirts of the city. Across the road from the house was a large open area with wooded hills. At regular intervals the military garrison at Vilna came here for maneuvers. These were exciting days seeing the military wagons rumbling past our house and the soldiers playing at war in the open fields, shouting as they charged up and down the hills.

The most pleasant memories of my childhood were of the Sabbath and the religious holidays. On Friday my father would come home from work about noon, and my mother, who usually worked right along with him, stayed home all day to prepare for the Sabbath. That was the time when Mother baked the twisted loaves of white bread known as *challah*. White bread was a luxury reserved for the Sabbath and festivals. There had to be at least two loaves to symbolize the double portion of manna which the ancient Hebrews collected on the eve of the Sabbath so that they would not have to collect their daily portion on the Sabbath and so violate the commandment against working on the Sabbath day. Also food had to be prepared not only for the Sabbath eve dinner on Friday but for the entire next day when cooking was prohibited.

The observance of the Sabbath was the high point of every week. My parents did not have to work. There was special food reserved for this wonderful day. Each Friday, my mother would have a peasant woman come to the house to clean and make it spotless. Instead of the usual sawdust on the floor, fine white sand was spread about and the white walls were scrubbed clean, especially the wall that was used for accounting purposes. As Mother began her baking and cooking a heavenly aroma pervaded the whole house. The Sabbath was an occasion when she prepared special dishes including a kind of ravioli called *kreplach* which was filled with ground meat and boiled in chicken soup.

On Sabbath eve the table was set with our best linen, china and silver. There were always two brass candlesticks which were given to my mother as a wedding present by her parents. The two candles had to be lit on the eve of the Sabbath as a symbol of the light and joy which the Sabbath brought into Jewish life. At each place at the table was also a silver beaker for wine used for the *Kiddush* prayer sanctifying the Sabbath.

While Mother was busy preparing the house and the food to honor the Queen Sabbath, as it was called in our Jewish tradition, my father and I would go to the Finnish sauna and take our weekly bath. We had no indoor plumbing at home. We would come home scrubbed clean and put on our best Sabbath clothes, and then my father and I would go to the synagogue for the Sabbath service, which centered on the beauty of the Sabbath and thanksgiving to God for all his bounty to us during the week. At the synagogue we would usually pick up a stranger as a guest to share our Sabbath joy. Strangers, away from home, and professional beggars would come to the synagogue for the Sabbath services knowing that they would receive hospitality from the regular worshipers. Every Jew considered it a privilege to have one or more guests to share his Sabbath joy.

Arriving home, the first thing that father would do was to greet my mother with the traditional poem idealizing Jewish womanhood as found in the 31st chapter of the Book of Proverbs: "A woman of worth, who can find. Her price is far above rubies. The heart of her husband does safely trust in her and she doeth him good and not evil." After greeting Mother, Father would bless each of us children. Then we would sit down to the Sabbath meal that began with the *Kiddush* prayer:

> *Let us praise God with this symbol of joy, and thank Him for the blessings of the past week, for life and strength, for home and love and friendship, for the discipline of our trials and temptations, for the happiness that has come to us out of our labors. Thou hast ennobled us, O God, by the blessings of work, and in love hast sanctified us by Sabbath rest and worship as ordained in the Torah: Six days shalt thou labor and do all thy work, but the seventh day is the Sabbath to be hallowed unto the Lord, thy God.*
>
> *Praised be Thou, O Lord our God, King of the Universe, who hast created the fruit of the vine.*

Then breaking a piece of the challah, Father prayed: "Blessed art Thou, O Lord our God, who brings forth bread from the earth". He cut one loaf into pieces and distributed a piece to each person at the table. With this ritual completed the dinner was served — first the soup, then the entree, usually chicken, then a thick stew of potatoes, carrots and prunes called tzimmes and finally, sponge cake and tea. Before the grace after meals came the zmiros, the singing of selected psalms and traditional Sabbath songs. In the final grace, we thanked God that we had been blessed with the privilege of observing the Sabbath and had been recipients of God's bounty, grateful that we were not dependent on men but always on God for life and everything that enabled us to enjoy it.

By the time the meal was over, and often before it was finished, I was ready for bed, sometimes falling asleep while eating. But the older children and adults remained at the table carrying on conversation which usually turned on a discussion of Torah, instruction from the Bible, or events of the week.

On Saturday morning we were able to stay in bed a little longer. My mother, however, was already up preparing breakfast for my father and me when we got up so that we would not be delayed in going to the synagogue for the morning worship. The synagogue was a wooden structure about a mile from our home. We walked, of course, since riding was forbidden on the Sabbath, because the animals, too, had to have their day of rest. My father took his accustomed place near the Ark, a position given to the more respected members of the community. The service from eight o'clock in the morning till noon was very long for young children and so during the long reading of the weekly Torah portion, we children went outside to play.

Returning home we were greeted by the fragrant aroma of *cholent*, a one-dish meal of meat and vegetables kept warm overnight in the banked oven. After a leisurely midday meal, my father would ask me what I had learned in Hebrew school during the week and examine me to see how much I really had learned. Much of the afternoon I spent in play with my friends. Father would read the Torah portion again and Mother, a translation known as *Tzenah Urenah* which means Go and See — a book prepared for women containing wisdom literature and legends important in Jewish history. Usually my parents would take a nap, a luxury impossible during the busy week. Late in the afternoon, Father and I returned to the synagogue where we sometimes heard a *maggid,* a traveling preacher who went from town to town giving ethical and inspirational sermons. Usually there were men studying Torah or Talmud, the rabbinic commentary on the Bible, led by some of the more learned men of the community if no rabbi was available. By this time the sun was setting and it was time for *Mincha*, the afternoon service, always rather hurried and followed immediately by the evening service, *Maariv.* This ended the Sabbath observance in the synagogue but at home there was still the *Havdalah.*

The *Havdalah* service was mingled with gratitude and sadness. We were very reluctant to see the Sabbath end, with the toilsome week before us for the next six days. Father would take us outside, weather permitting, to watch for the first sign of moonrise, the signal for the beginning of the *Havdalah* service. The ritual included lighting a twisted candle and dipping the candle flame in a saucer of wine. Over each act Father would recite a blessing, thanking God for the creation of light and for the fruit of the vine, and then he would sniff a spice box, symbolizing the fragrance and beauty of the Sabbath, thanking God for creating all kinds of spices. With this ritual completed the Sabbath came to an end and we sat down to the evening meal, which was not so festive as any of the previous meals. The week of toil and trouble lay ahead.

[1] Areas in which Jews were permitted to live without permission were called the pale. Outside the pale only by special permission were carefully selected Jews permitted to dwell and carry on their business or profession.

Chapter 2

Religious Feasts and Fasts

Judaism is rich in festivals and holydays, each with its own special significance and each bringing to my childhood experience new wonders to look forward to through the year. The most glamorous of these was the Passover commemorating the deliverance from slavery in Egypt by Moses. It came in the springtime of the year. Passover was exciting with the whole pattern of life changed. It was a time for cleaning the house of every vestige of leavened bread, a time for the most thorough spring cleaning, for eating unleavened bread, matzo, and the special delicacies reserved only for Passover. A complete set of china was brought out of storage where it had been packed in straw since last Passover to be used only for this festival. In the ghetto where we lived there were several bakeries that specialized in the baking of matzo. It was exciting to go with my parents to the bakery and watch them have our matzo baked and then cart it home in huge white sacks. One part of the house was prepared to receive the matzo. There, in preparation for Passover, some of it would be pounded into flour and what particles were left was used in chicken soup like croutons. It was always a thrill for me when Mother allowed me to help pound matzo into flour with a wooden pestle.

Highlight of the Passover festival was the Seder feast and the night was made for me. For weeks I had prepared to inaugurate the Passover celebration by chanting the traditional four questions, the special privilege of the youngest male child: "Why is this night different from all other nights? On all other nights we may eat either leavened or unleavened bread; why on this night do we eat only unleavened bread? On all other nights we eat all kinds of herbs; why on this night do we eat only bitter herbs?

On all other nights we do not dip herbs in any condiment; why on this night do we dip them in salt water and *haroses*? On all other nights we eat without any special festivities; why on this night do we hold this

Seder service?" Then my father would read through the whole story of how our forefathers suffered as slaves in Egypt and how Moses delivered them by performing wonderful miracles.

One responsibility I always looked forward to was carrying the *haroses*, a paste made of apples, nuts and honey to every family in our neighborhood. My father had the reputation for being the best *haroses* maker in our area and I got to deliver the delicacy for which I was rewarded with a small coin from each recipient. The mud-like appearance of the paste symbolized the mortar which the Hebrew slaves used to make bricks in their forced labor of constructing the cities and monuments for their Egyptian masters.

In the annual cycle of our religious calendar, the festival following seven weeks after Passover was Shabuoth, the Feast of Weeks, a two-day holiday commemorating the revelation of God to Moses on Mount Sinai, a revelation embodied in the Ten Commandments described in the Book of Exodus. Originally, Shabuoth (or Pentecost as it is sometimes called because it occurs 50 days after Passover) was a farmers' festival when the first ripe fruit was gathered and brought as a gift to the Temple in Jerusalem as part of an annual spring pilgrimage to the Holy City. Later it was identified with the revelation on Sinai and commemorates the covenant which God made with our forefathers 3500 years ago. Today it is celebrated in Reform congregations, and increasingly in some Conservative and Orthodox congregations, as a time for the confirmation of boys and girls who at 15 or older wish to publicly accept the faith of their fathers into which they were born and to make their own personal commitment to it.

Another very joyous holiday was Hanukah, the festival of lights. It was celebrated for eight days and commemorated the seemingly miraculous victory in 168 B.C. of the Maccabeans over their Greek overlords who tried to force the Jews to give up their Judaism and to adopt the Greek gods and forms of worship. During the eight days of the festival, candles were lit in the *menorah*, one on the first night, two on the second and one additional candle each night until all eight were glowing.

Legend tells us that after the Maccabees had driven the Greeks out of Jerusalem, they cleansed the Temple of all the pollution the Greeks had caused during their occupation and held a service of thanksgiving and rededication of the Temple to the service of God. Holy oil was required for the service but none was available. A little boy playing in the restored Temple found a tiny jar of oil that still bore the unbroken seal of the High Priest who officiated before the Greeks took over. The jar contained only enough oil for one day but by a miracle it lasted for eight days until new oil could be produced. The eight candles of the *menorah* recall this miracle.

Hanukah was a happy time. We children could look forward to gifts, usually money all our own to spend any way we liked. There were also Hanukah games. My favorite was spinning the dreidel, a small square top made of lead with Hebrew letters on each of the four sides. Each letter represented a word in the sentence "God wrought a great miracle here". If after spinning, the top fell on certain letters, it meant that the spinner had to put one of his Hanukah kopeks (pennies) in the pot; if it fell on others, he was entitled to take a kopek out.

Purim, which occurs about a month before Passover, is another exciting festival for children. It commemorates the deliverance of the Jews of Persia in the reign of Artaxerxes from the evil designs of Haman, prime minister of Persia. The Book of Esther tells how Haman decided that the Jews ought to be eliminated from the Persian empire because their religion was different from the rest of the people and they were an unassimiable group within the body politic. So with the approval of the king he decreed their destruction. However, his nefarious plans were frustrated by Esther, who in a beauty contest was chosen queen of Persia, without the king's knowing that the queen he had chosen was a Jewess. She revealed her identity during this critical period and the king's love for her was so great that he had Haman hanged on the gallows prepared for Esther's uncle, Mordecai, the leader of the Jewish community. Mordecai's and the Jews' divine deliverance was joyously celebrated in the synagogue by reading the story of Esther and by an exchange of gifts. As the story of Esther was read, every time the name of Haman was mentioned there was a stamping of feet and other noise to show contempt for this arch anti-Semite who met his just deserts in that time long ago, and every time Mordecai's name was mentioned there was applause. For us children it was a great opportunity to let go without fear of punishment.

The High Holydays were of special significance. Traditionally the New Year and the Day of Atonement, known as the Days of Awe, were regarded as the time when every person's life was examined and judged by a heavenly court as to whether the individual was to be rewarded or punished for his conduct during the year. The New Year was the day of reckoning; the Day of Atonement, the time when the verdict was rendered. Between the New Year and Day of Atonement were ten days for repentance, for making amends to friends and neighbors for wrongs done to them and asking their forgiveness. Tradition has it that the penitential season will atone only for sins against God, ritual infractions or unfulfilled vows made to God in times of stress. Wrongs committed against one's fellowmen were not forgiven on the Day of Atonement unless the wrongdoer had made every possible effort to right the wrong he had committed by making restitution and seeking the wronged person's forgiveness. I remember my father going out in preparation for the Day of Atonement to every neighbor to beg forgiveness for every wrong he had done knowingly or through oversight or accident.

The Holydays were awe-inspiring for both adults and children; but for me they were a time for new winter clothes in preparation for the approaching Russian winter, in Vilna always very severe. Then there were the special goodies Mother would prepare for the New Year which always included apples and honey to symbolize the hope for a sweet and happy year ahead. Sometimes we even got an orange, a rare treat in the ghetto.

Five days after the Day of Atonement came the Feast of Tabernacles. This was the autumn harvest festival among the ancient Hebrews, when they gathered their grapes, wheat and autumn fruits and vegetables and gave thanks to God that they would have enough food until the next harvest. During the season the Hebrew farmers used to build shelters to protect themselves from the burning midday sun. These were called *succoth* and they became a symbol of the festival and gave it its name Hag Hasuccoth, the Festival of Booths (Tabernacles). To symbolize and commemorate these shelters my father, and every pious Jew in the community, built a wooden hut in his backyard with four walls, a door and a roof of evergreen branches. The idea of the hut was interpreted in later tradition to symbolize the frailty of man and life and his dependence on God.

If the weather was not too inclement we would eat our meals in the *succah* during the eight days of festival. If the weather was bad, my father would take us there for the blessing sanctifying the occasion and then we would go into the house for our meal. It was always exciting to help my father at the end of the Day of Atonement when he came from the synagogue, before he tasted anything after his 24-hour fast, drive a stake into the ground where the *succah* would be erected.

The last day of Succoth was Simchat Torah, rejoicing for the Torah. During Simchat Torah all boys under 13, at the end of the reading of the Torah, were gathered under a large tallit (prayer shawl) and while thus covered by it the blessing over the reading of the Torah was recited on their behalf by the cantor. Boys who had attained the age of 13 and become Bar Mitzvah were already regarded as adults for religious purposes and could wear their own tallit and recite the blessing themselves.

Simchat Torah was the only time of the year that a Jew was allowed to drink strong liquor to the point where he could not distinguish between the need to bless Mordecai and curse Haman, the traditional hero and villain of the Purim story. It was also a time in our ghetto community when the Torahs were carried around the synagogue in a festive procession and we children were given paper flags to carry around as we marched with the elders. Another highlight of the Simchat Torah celebration was the progressive dinner after the morning service when we danced through the streets of the ghetto and went from house to house eating a different course in each house and ending the festival in a kind of carnival spirit.

There were many difficulties to be endured in the Russian ghetto, but there was also much happiness and fulfillment in the festive observances of our religious year.

Chapter 3

America — The Promised Land

When I was five we had a frightening visit from the police. It was during the Russian Revolution of 1905. My brother, Louis, then 23 and a harness-maker by trade, belonged to an organization called the "Bund", a kind of labor union agitating for more rights for the working man. During the Revolution and after, every suspected Bund member was rounded up as a subversive. Louis was arrested in a restaurant where he and some of his friends had gathered, and taken to jail. The police searched the house for weapons and seditious literature. I was very small for my age and one policeman especially was like a towering giant and terrified me. They came during Purim when it is traditional to make a lot of noise and I was playing with a toy cap pistol. The giant grabbed hold of me and said in a gruff voice, "I'm dragging you off to prison. I see you have a revolver and you are a very dangerous person". Then he laughed.

The shock of my brother being in jail with the possibility of being tried as a revolutionary and sent to Siberia was traumatic for the family. For nine months he was in jail awaiting trial. We visited him as often as we could. One day Ida, at that time about twelve, made her way into the city alone to plead with the governor of the province for Louis' release. I really do not know whether it was her plea to the governor or other circumstances that persuaded him to release Louis. But he was released and he and Ida with two of our nephews whose parents were already in America, left Vilna to join them and a married brother, Max.

I was left alone with my father and mother, and the house seemed awfully big and terribly empty. My parents had already decided that they would follow as soon as they were able to arrange their affairs. About two years later they sold everything we had and we set out to join our family going first to Libau, the large Latvian seaport on the Baltic. There we took a ship for England. I was then eight years old.

We landed in Liverpool, England, during the Succoth festival and my father took me to the Orthodox synagogue in Liverpool to worship.

Strange how life deals with us. Twenty-four years later I became rabbi of this same synagogue which my first congregation, the Liberal Jewish congregation of Liverpool, had purchased and transformed into a Reform synagogue.

After waiting about a week in Liverpool, we went to Southampton to board the ship that was to take us to America, and found our place in steerage with other immigrants. Since my family was strictly Orthodox and observed all the dietary regulations we ate no food on the ship that was not kosher. My mother had prepared for the voyage large hampers of food to last the nine days. The only things I remember eating on the ship not brought by my mother were hard-boiled eggs, bread, jam and tea.

We arrived in Quebec and were quarantined, like prisoners, in a wire enclosed stockade. I remember some beautifully dressed ladies from the Jewish community coming to visit us and bringing us fruit and other goodies. After quarantine and customs we boarded a train for Duluth, Minnesota. There, we were greeted by our now American family and it was an intensely emotional experience, a mingling of joy, tears and laughter.

My two nephews, one my age and one three years older, were already quite Americanized since they had been in the country two years and spoke English like Americans. I regarded them with awe. They took me in hand and began my Americanization process. First they gave me an American name. My name in Hebrew is Raphael, but my nephews thought that was no name for an American. The best American names, they told me, were Tom, Dick and Harry. They decided that Harry would be a good one for me. So Harry I became — and remained until I graduated from high school. It was when we were asked to designate how we wanted our names inscribed on our diplomas that I felt sufficiently Americanized to take my real name, though I shortened it to Ralph, using Harry as a middle name. The metamorphosis of my name from Harry to Ralph to Raphael came when I was graduated from the University of Minnesota Law School. I was then already contemplating the possibility of becoming a rabbi. I felt that the name Raphael, which means "God the Healer", was more appropriate for one who had aspirations to be a Jewish religious leader. I still retain the "H" as my middle initial.

Duluth was a city of about 100,000 in 1909. My father, mother and I were settled in a house which Louis and Ida had rented for the family in Chester Park where there were a number of Jewish families. Our wooden house was situated on one of the hills on Sixth Street about three blocks from a lovely wooded area with a creek running through it. To us children this was a wonderland of adventure, eminently suited for our war games since it had a ravine and woods and one could ambush the enemy and hide from him easily.

In Vilna my father had been of some importance, being a petty broker and by ghetto standards, fairly successful. Here in Duluth, handicapped by not knowing the language, already in his 50's and having no particular skill, he had no alternative but to become a junk collector as many immigrants before him had. My mother, of course, could not work as she was even more handicapped by language than he and she had a full-time job taking care of our home.

Peddling merchandise required some capital which we did not have and so each day my father took a sack and went about the neighborhood collecting whatever junk he might get for nothing or for a small sum, toiling up steep Duluth hills toward nightfall with a heavy sack full of junk. After months of this back-breaking work, Louis and Ida bought him a child's coaster wagon, the biggest they could get. My father became a familiar figure in our neighborhood as he dragged his wagon through the streets. In this way he was able to eke out a living which my brother and sister supplemented with their wages, Louis as harness-maker and Ida in a sweater factory. One of the memories that grieves me most is being so ashamed at seeing my father with his wagon that I would take another way home.

I was enrolled in a grammar school about a half mile from our home and supervised by Miss Calverly, a plump, motherly principal whom I shall never forget for her interest in my welfare. She took the little immigrant boy to her heart and helped me during the most difficult first years of American schooling, trying to learn the language and mastering the curricu1um of the primary grades. I was much older than my classmates and through her personal interest I was able to close some of the age gap between myself and them by skipping grades. Even though I did eight grades in five years, I was still older than any of my classmates on graduation While attending grammar school I helped, to supplement the family income by selling newspapers, shining shoes and singing in the synagogue choir. I am very proud that the first suit of clothes I bought in America I paid for with my own earnings as a choir boy. I was paid $2 for my services. The suit I bought, tweed knickerbockers with Norfolk jacket, cost $1.98. I also helped my mother take care of two cows we now owned. My job was to help clean the stable, deliver the fresh milk to our customers and do some chores around the house. My father was doing quite well as a junk dealer and began to take his proper place in the synagogue which we attended.

All through grammar school, Miss Calverly was my staunch friend and confidant. Through her I learned to love America and Americans and the fear of Christians which I brought with me from the Russian ghetto gradually disappeared. I even got to the point of becoming Miss Calverly's personal messenger delivering her Christmas cards and presents to her friends, without feeling that I was betraying my own Jewish faith. During my grammar school years I made a number of Christian friends who also helped me overcome my fears. I began to learn that there were all kinds of Christians that while there were still boys who taunted me as "Sheeny" there were others who were ready to defend me even to the point of fighting with others. I was in America now and this awareness was reassuring and heart-warming.

Chapter 4

Teacher — Lawyer — Rabbi

I was very small for my age and continually haunted by the fear that I would be a dwarf. But I had a strong voice so that even as a child of ten, I was able to recite at our school assembly and make myself heard by large audiences. When at 13 I became Bar Mitzvah and entered into religious manhood, my rabbi wrote a long speech for me, which must have been his philosophy of life, and I delivered it from memory during the synagogue service. You can imagine the astonishment of the congregation on hearing profound religious ideas proclaimed in a booming voice by a little fellow who could hardly reach the top of the podium. This gift for oratory channeled my interest in high school and in college toward becoming a lawyer. My concept of the law as a profession was to stand before a jury and make eloquent pleas for my client. I thought all that was necessary was to have average intelligence, a good voice and, in the vernacular, "the gift of gab". I had all three.

After graduating from high school and completing a two-year teacher training course in Superior, Wisconsin, I went to the University of Minnesota in 1922 to prepare to enter law school. While there I became interested in a Jewish student organization called the Menorah Society. This was a cultural organization which flourished on many campuses in the United States but has since been supplanted by the Hillel Foundation. It was designed to enhance the social and cultural life of Jewish students. In my senior year I became its president and during my term we had a number of debates and symposia discussing Jewish life and Jewish survival. We debated with Menorah societies of other universities and had groups speaking at B'nai B'rith meetings and to other Jewish organizations in Minnesota.

In order to prepare for these debates and symposia, I found it necessary to learn more about Judaism and especially Jewish history, a subject which had been neglected in my Jewish education.

The only Jewish education I had in the Hebrew School was to learn how to read the Hebrew prayer book, to translate the Bible from Hebrew into English, and a little of the rabbinic commentaries on the Bible. The Hebrew school I attended in Duluth five afternoons a week after school emphasized the capacity for speed in reading Hebrew and memorizing prayers. All the canons of education I have learned since were violated. Of the 4000-year history of our people, I knew almost nothing. The little biblical history we got in our Hebrew school was garbled and, to me, had little meaning. So when I had to learn about Jews and Judaism to prepare for the discussions on what it means to be a Jew and the problems of Jewish existence and survival in a non-Jewish world, I found it necessary to begin reading the history of the Jews. My sister, Ida, with whom I lived in Minneapolis during my university years, seeing my interest and need, gave me the classic History of the Jews by Heinrich Greatz, translated into English from German and published by the Jewish Publications Society in a popular edition of five volumes.

I was fascinated by Professor Greatz's vivid style and marvelous capacity for narrative, so that I read the five volumes, one after the other as one reads an absorbing novel. It gave me an insight into Judaism and an understanding of my people I had never had before and this experience changed the course of my life. I continued to study law but I was already beginning to think in terms of devoting my life to Judaism and the Jewish people.

What strengthened this interest leading to my decision to become a rabbi was a conversation I had with the dean of our law school just before graduation. I had enjoyed the study of law and also liked teaching and so I thought I might make teaching law my career. I consulted the dean about the possibility of doing postgraduate work with the aim of becoming a university professor. He was very kind and quite frankly told me that what concerned him was that I was a Jew and while there were some outstanding Jewish law professors, a Jew had to be exceptionally brilliant to attain a professorship at a recognized university law school. This was in 1926.

Fortunately I was enough aware of my limitations to know that while I may have been above average as a student, I was not exceptional. I have never ceased being grateful to Dean Fraser for his honest evaluation of my situation. I finished law school, passed the Bar examinations the first time I took them and returned to Duluth to practice law.

As was the custom among young legal graduates, I tried to get a position with a good law firm and found the going difficult. So I decided to go into private practice with a boyhood friend, Henry Paul (born Polinsky), who had graduated the same year as I had from the University of Michigan Law School.

Henry Paul was a tall, gaunt, Lincolnesque figure of a man with an excellent mind and a fine sense of humor. He was a lovable person — kind, generous to a fault, with a highly sensitized social conscience. We had been close boyhood friends and now that we were both young lawyers on our own, we decided to enter into a partnership to save expenses in operating a law office. Business came very slowly and our practice was largely a matter of collecting debts for our clients, garnisheeing some poor debtor's wages, drawing up an occasional contract or helping in the probate of some small estate of a friend or member of our families. We hardly made enough to pay the modest rent on our office space. Henry had one fault, grievous to me, which was the only flaw in our relationship. He had no sense of time and rarely kept appointments without making the person he was to meet wait what seemed an unconscionable time. I was — and still am — a compulsive time keeper. This became a source of irritation between us, so that while we kept the same office we dissolved our partnership and each carried on his own practice. Our friendship, however, remained close and fast until I left Duluth to study for the rabbinate.

Even while practicing law, my real interests were in working within the Jewish community. I organized study groups among my friends and in the Orthodox synagogue to which my father belonged. These absorbed my attention almost to the neglect of the little law practice that came to me. After about nine months of this conflict of interest between my law work and my teaching, I became convinced that even if I were successful in the law, my heart was not in it. My real interest was in teaching. Law might give me a better living than teaching but what I wanted above everything at that time was personal self-fulfillment which I then felt I could never attain in the law. In Judaism, working with my people for the things which Judaism had taught me were the important values of life for me at least, made me realize that I would be able to find the kind of fulfillment and self-expression I sought only by becoming a rabbi. I cannot say that I received what some feel was a call to the rabbinate, nor as I look back upon my decision to give up the law and to go to a rabbinical seminary was I motivated by any great religious fervor. My faith in God was conventional and rather nebulous; but this I knew with a growing conviction, that in teaching Judaism and in helping my people to understand their heritage I would find my mission in life and the road to self-fulfillment.

As I look back on my decision from the vantage point of 40 years as a rabbi, I can say that if I had my life to live over, knowing everything I now know of the rabbinate with all its difficulties and heartaches, frustrations and disappointments, I would still want to be a rabbi. I am grateful for the choice I made in 1927.

Chapter 5

Hebrew Union College

I decided to go to Hebrew Union College in Cincinnati, the seminary for training Reform rabbis. Although I was reared in the Orthodox tradition, Orthodox Judaism with its rigid dietary discipline and its ultraconservative attitudes toward change no longer appealed to my searching mind. Reform Judaism and the Reform rabbinate offered for me the largest measure of religious freedom in thought and action.

I spent five years at Hebrew Union College. I was 26 when I entered, eight years older than the average freshman who came to the college from high school. The course of study was four years in the preparatory department and four in the graduate, but because of my previous education I spent only one year in the preparatory department. There were about 116 students at the College when I began my studies in 1927, divided fairly equally between the two departments. I was older on entering than most of the seniors that year.

Because I was so much older than my classmates, I was very much alone the first two years. In my third year I met a young woman who had come to Cincinnati from Portland, Oregon, to live with her older sister, Irma Cohon the wife of the professor of theology at the College. She was a graduate of the School of Social Work at the University of Washington. We met through Professor Samuel Cohon who told me that his sister-in-law, Madeline Reinhart, was looking for someone to teach her Yiddish that she might better communicate with many of the clients of the local Jewish social agency where she worked.

I don't know whether I was a successful teacher, but within a few months, Madeline and I became engaged and in 1929 we were married in a simple ceremony in the study of a famous Chicago rabbi, Tobias Schanfarber. After a honeymoon of one weekend mostly atop a sightseeing bus in Chicago, we returned to Cincinnati. I left the dormitory where I had lived my first two years at the seminary and we set up housekeeping in a small apartment. Madeline continued her work in the social agency and I got a position as assistant editor of a new Anglo-Jewish weekly appropriately named Every Friday since it came out every week on the eve of the Sabbath. With the money I earned at Every Friday and what Madeline earned as a social worker, we managed quite well. About a year and a half after our marriage, our daughter Lori Jean was born. Madeline had to give up her work but by then I was a full-fledged editor of Every Friday earning about $2000 a year on a part-time basis. This salary combined with money I earned from Sunday school teaching at a local Temple and a students' bi-weekly congregation at Richmond, Indiana came to about $3000.

I was kept running during the last two years at the College what with editing the paper, taking a full course at the College, teaching Sunday school and holding a student bi-weekly position at Richmond. To keep up this split second schedule, especially between my editorial work and classes, I bought our first car, an ancient Chevrolet for which I paid $150. Often I ate my lunch in the car driving from school to my office and from the office to classes — sometimes a sandwich I brought from home, most often wolfing a hamburger from one of the popular stand-up snack bars which proliferated in Cincinnati at that time.

This kind of hectic daily routine was not conducive to good health, equanimity or good scholarship. Many a time I fell asleep in class, not always from exhaustion. Sometimes it was the soothing drone of some professor's monotonous monologue. However, I managed to survive and even to win a scholarship prize in my senior year. This was due more perhaps to the generosity of one of my professors than to my scholastic achievement. He was Dr. Abraham Cronbach, of blessed memory, to whom I owe more than I shall ever be able to repay, not merely for his kindness but for what I learned from him.

Abraham Cronbach was an unusual man. He was a rabbi, a graduate of the College in which he became professor of social studies. To many of the students he was known as the "autoworker, automatic saint", because he was soft-spoken, ascetic and meticulous in word and action. He was a liberal in thought, even radical, and given to iconoclastic ideas about organized religion. His interpretation of Judaism was in the tradition of the great Hebrew prophets, emphasizing the ethical and moral values in religion above everything. He was probably unique among Jewish religious leaders of his time in that he was an absolute pacifist, and before World War II became the founder of the Jewish Peace Fellowship, a pacifist group within Judaism.

Dr. Cronbach was precise in his speech and most careful in his use of words. From him I learned the importance of the careful use of words to convey their precise meaning. Most of the confusion in the world, he would say, was lack of communication because of the careless use of words so that people rarely understood one another. He decried arguments since they led nowhere because of semantic difficulties. People were using the same words but because of the different connotations each attached to the words he used, there was no meeting of the minds and therefore no real understanding of what they were arguing about. "We are too prone to use words not to illuminate but to persuade", he said, so that such words as good and bad, right and wrong, have little or nothing to tell us about what is good or bad, right or wrong. All that such words describe are the things we like and the things we do not like. When we say a thing is good, it is because we like it or agree with what it connotes for us. When we say it is bad or wrong, we are really saying that it is something we don't like or don't agree with. Most of us, unwittingly perhaps, indulge in what Dr. Cronbach called "propaganda" language and therefore real communication and real dialogue become very difficult to attain.

While at the College I took every course Dr. Cronbach taught. I often accompanied him on his weekly visits to homes for the aged, mental hospitals and other institutions for the poor, the neglected and the forgotten. These visits usually took place on Saturday afternoon after the morning worship in the College chapel.

In addition to taking all Dr. Cronbach's courses in social studies and the psalms, the one I never missed was an extracurricular discussion group over which he presided every Saturday morning for an hour and a half before Chapel. Dr. Cronbach was at his desk punctually at 9 a.m. on Saturdays and any student who cared to drop in was welcome. Sometimes as many as ten came; often I found myself the only one. It was when we were alone that I got to know my teacher best and most intimately and was most enriched by his wisdom and by the sensitivity of his insights. One incident stands out vividly. It was at one of these informal meetings with about seven students in the room. The important news of the week for us seminarians was a story in the New York Times about a very successful rabbi of a large Temple in New York who had decided to leave the rabbinate because he was frustrated by the small attendance at Friday evening services. He gave as the reason for his frustration that he could not compete with the "it" girl, Clara Bow, the movie sex symbol of the roaring '20s. The story in the Times became the subject of that Saturday morning's conversation. The question was whether there was a future for religion in general and for the synagogue in particular since religion and the synagogue could not compete with the distractions of secular entertainment. In the course of the discussion, trying to defend the need for organized religion in spite of the fact that people were abstaining from religious services, I made the statement, "There is no competition in self-effacement". I don't know what I really meant by that statement. Maybe I was trying to say that the rabbi shouldn't try to compete with secular entertainment, that the synagogue was not a playhouse and the service was not a show, that the synagogue had its own role to play, to point up the moral and spiritual ideal whether or not the congregants lived by it, that it was the rabbi's role to express the ideal both by precept and example and not to be frustrated by whether the people followed him or not. Anyway, whatever I was trying to say, Dr. Cronbach took out his little notebook and wrote something in it and tears came to his eyes. I couldn't understand what had happened. The statement seemed to have touched him deeply, but I never knew why until many years later, after I had been a rabbi for 25 years and had gone through some traumatic psychological conflicts myself, that I remembered that morning at the College and I began to understand why Dr. Cronbach was moved to tears by the statement. Self-effacement was for Dr. Cronbach his way of life and unknowingly I had touched the very core of his being.

Chapter 6

Liverpool, England — My First Congregation

Toward the end of our senior year at Hebrew Union College, my classmates and I, almost ready for ordination, were greatly concerned about our future. We were in the midst of the Great Depression and rumors were streaming in that there would be no congregations for any of us; pulpits that were available were offering wages of less than $2000 a year, some as low as $1100. For a single man it might be a survival wage but for a married man with a child, even $2000 was no living wage. I was already earning more from my editorial work, Sunday school teaching and bi-weekly congregation at Richmond. It was during this time of concern that Miss Sachs, the College president's secretary, came into history class one day with the message that Dr. Morgenstern wanted to see me immediately. Suddenly all the sins I had committed at the College rushed to my consciousness. What had I done to be called into the president's office in the middle of a class?

I left my seat and proceeded with trepidation. Dr. Morgenstern's greeting was brusque but his eyes were smiling. Without asking me to sit down he said, "Raphael, how would you like to go to England?" My first reaction was shock that quickly turned into exhilaration. To go to England, to have an opportunity for a religious experience in a foreign land appealed to my spirit of adventure. My immediate impulse was to say, "Yes, I would like to go to England", then I remembered I was not alone. I was married. I had a wife and year-old daughter. How would Madeline take to the idea of leaving her native land, her family and friends to be a rabbi's wife in a land she knew little about? Dr. Morgenstern didn't make it any easier when he interrupted my thoughts with the further statement that he had to know my decision by the next day and that the position would pay 600 English pounds, in those days about $3000. I mumbled some words of thanks for considering me for the position and said I would let him know the next day. I left the office in a daze and returned to my history class. But my thoughts were not on history. They were full of visions of England and of the opportunity for an unbelievable adventure; above all, there was the wonderful feeling of having an offer of a congregation at a wage which in England was considered quite good for a fledgling rabbi.

I went home still exhilarated but when I told Madeline about the offer, it was her turn to be shocked. Her first reaction was what I had feared, very negative. I spent most of the night trying to convince her of how fortunate we were to have such an offer in these times of economic depression. I explained that congregations were few and that some of my classmates were willing to accept positions at $1500 a year or less. Liverpool was the second best congregation that year; the best offer went to a classmate who was single, as assistant rabbi at Temple Emanuel, New York. I appealed to Madeline's sense of adventure, to the opportunity of meeting new people — not in a strange land but rather in the motherland of our American culture and tradition and I emphasized how much this experience would mean to my career. Nothing convinced her and I realized I would need more time to come to a decision. I told this to Dr. Morgenstern and he said, "All right. I'll give you till the end of the week — two more days." I was relieved and immensely grateful.

The next two days were full of excitement, what with discussions with Madeline's relatives and one of my professors, Dr. Sheldon Blank, who had lived for a time in England and had married a fine Englishwoman. They encouraged us to accept the position and felt that I would be able to do a really constructive work in strengthening the Liberal Jewish movement which was yet in its infancy in the British Commonwealth. They told me about the kind of people with whom I would be associated: Dr. Israel Mattuck, an American rabbi who had gone to England in 1912 to be the first American Reform rabbi of the budding Liberal Jewish movement founded by Dr. Claude G. Montefiore, a great biblical scholar, and the Hon. Lily Montagu, daughter of Lord Swaythling, for years the head of the Orthodox Jewish community in England. After her father's death the Hon. Lily, with her sister Marion and inspired by Dr. Montefiore, began the Jewish Religious Union to promote a liberal interpretation of Judaism in England.

Under the leadership of Dr. Mattuck, with the support of Dr. Montefiore, and tireless labors of the Hon. Lily, the Liberal movement grew to three congregations: the Liberal Jewish Synagogue of London of which Dr. Mattuck was senior rabbi; another synagogue in North London, and the Liberal Jewish Synagogue in Liverpool which had been organized two years before I came and which was served by Rabbi Morris Goldstein, also an American. It was Rabbi Goldstein's resignation and return to America that prompted Dr. Morgenstern's offer to me of the Liverpool congregation.

Encouraged by Dr. and Mrs. Blank and their reassuring picture of what life in England was like, Madeline finally agreed to accept Dr. Morgenstern's offer. With the decision made, the rest of the school year passed quickly — finishing my thesis, preparing for ordination and making plans for the new life before us.

Ordination in June 1932 was a beautiful, solemn, happy occasion. I was the only graduate to have his baby attend the service. It was a proud day for the Levine's. I was now a rabbi, authorized to teach Judaism and be a member of the panel of three judges which constituted a *Beth Din*, a court empowered to hear cases and make decisions according to Jewish law on matters both secular and religious affecting Jewish life.

We spent an exciting summer with my family in Duluth making preparations for England — getting passports, buying clothes, attending farewell parties. About six weeks before the Holyday season was to begin, which in 1932 was on October 1, we left Duluth for New York to board the Corinthia for England.

Chapter 7

Toward Brotherhood in Liverpool

The Liverpool congregation had a membership of about one hundred. All were formerly associated with one of the largest Orthodox congregations in the Midlands, the Princess Road Synagogue, founded in the 18th century by Jewish immigrants from Germany, Holland and Alsace Lorraine. Rabbi Frampton was its honored and beloved minister and when I came to Liverpool he had already served the congregation for 40 years. Most of those now of my congregation had demanded some religious reforms which Rabbi Frampton was either unwilling or unable to grant. They decided to leave the Princess Road Synagogue and organize their own congregation aided and abetted by Dr. Mattuck and the Hon. Lily Montagu, an indefatigable proselytizer for Liberal Judaism. Rabbi Frampton was unhappy with this wholesale secession but found himself powerless to stop it. I am sure that Rabbi Goldstein, who was the first Reform rabbi of the congregation, must have had a difficult time but by the time I came two years later, the new congregation was fairly well established and more or less accepted. I tried to make friends with Rabbi Frampton. I found him to be a polite English gentleman but the doors to any closer relationship were kept closed.

I was the lone Reform rabbi in Liverpool with the nearest colleague 200 miles away in London. There were other Orthodox congregations in the city but their rabbis were also cool to my gestures of friendship. The clergy most ready to accept me were the Unitarians who had several churches in and around Liverpool. Through several of their ministers with whom I became friends, I joined the Ministers' Association and found the religious fellowship I needed among the Christian clergy. Shortly thereafter I suggested we ought to have occasional meetings outside the formal Association to discuss religious and social problems of concern to all of us as spiritual leaders. I offered our home as a meeting place and Friday evening seemed to be the most convenient time. It was acceptable to me as we had our worship services on Saturday afternoon at 3 o'clock instead of Friday evening as was the custom in America. The 3 o'clock time had been set before I came and the reason, I was told, was to give those who belonged to Orthodox synagogues an opportunity to visit our worship services if they wished, with the hope of winning them over to Liberal Judaism. I continued the practice during my six-year ministry in Liverpool.

After a few evenings of discussion and fellowship with the ministers group, we decided to formalize our relationship in an organization we called the World Order Group . In time we were joined by ministers of a number of other denominations .including Baptist, Congregational, Methodist and Anglican. Lay people also joined — a writer, teacher, social worker and a young architect, Donald Bradshaw and his wife with whom Madeline and I became intimate friends. The Bradshaw's had belonged to the Church of England and had experimented with other denominations, finally deciding on Christian Science. Donald was a highly sensitive, poetic and spiritually oriented young man a few years younger than I. We discovered a deep spiritual kinship with each other and for the last three of my six years in Liverpool, he and his wife never missed our weekly Friday meetings.

The main purpose of our World Order Group was to try to work out programs that would further the cause of peace and good international relations between Britain and the countries of Europe. A number of the ministers considered themselves absolute pacifists and hoped that through the World Order Group, we might exert some influence upon British attitudes, at least in Liverpool. In the middle '30s, the growing menace of Nazism became the major concern of our group and Hitler's virulent anti-Semitism and organized persecution of Jews brought me to the fore as a spokesman for my people. I was inundated with invitations to speak at the churches of World Order Group members to explain what was happening in Germany, and from all kinds of other non-Jewish organizations who couldn't understand why the Jews should be so singled out for persecution by the Nazis.

In 1938 while president of the Liverpool B'nai B'rith, a Jewish fraternal organization, I persuaded members to sponsor a dinner to which each would invite one or more Christian friends as a gesture of fellowship and brotherhood. I was asked to give the toast to our non-Jewish guests and since it represents my present thinking, I would like to quote a part of it here:

We are living in very troubled times. The number of nations that still retain their political and social sanity is decreasing. In more countries than we like to think, liberty and tolerance and even simple human justice to defenseless minorities — these values which humanity has achieved after so many centuries and at such terrific cost — are being ruthlessly destroyed by an unbridled chauvinism, or are being argued away by a national madness which has become the obsession of rulers and people alike. Democracy and democratic ideals and institutions are being challenged everywhere. We are being told that we are not fit to rule ourselves in freedom, but must be whipped into submission and to blind obedience to the infallible wisdom of a superman, the Fuehrer, who is to be the master of our fate and the captain of our soul.

Against this madness there is no greater bulwark in Europe than this country, founded as it is upon the principle which the dictator states are attempting to uproot from European civilization, namely, that the first purpose of a state is to afford its citizens the maximum opportunity for liberty in their personal life, freedom in their spiritual striving, and justice to all regardless of race, creed or color. This principle of government has through centuries of political and social evolution become part of the British heritage. The spiritual values which it has fostered, liberty, and tolerance and fair play, have become woven into the texture of British character, bred in the bone and ingrained in the soul. My country, too, founded by Britons who carried with them across the Atlantic their British heritage stands in the new world for these self-same ideals. But here in the old world your country stands pre-eminent because of its power and its stability as the champion of democracy and democratic institutions, and as the protagonist of justice and the rights of all men to life, liberty and to freedom to develop their personality in their own way.

Therein lies the source of your power, and your greatness. Because you have learned not merely to tolerate but to respect differences of race and creed, language and culture, you, in your small island, command the loyalties of the most heterogeneous group of peoples ever gathered into one commonwealth of nations. And by that very fact this country stands as the symbol and the promise of that unity which we hope the whole of mankind will ultimately achieve amidst the great diversity of its races and languages, creeds and cultures.

For that is the goal of human striving. The ideal of human brotherhood, which is the cherished hope of us all, does not imply uniformity among men, nor an absence of differences. But it does imply an absence of divisiveness. Differences we want. We would not have it otherwise; for in the diversity of the contributions to civilization lies in its rich beauty and its grandeur. After all, whatever beauty and spiritual quality our civilization has achieved has been made possible because there has been a diversity of genius among individuals and among peoples; because there have been Greeks who were gifted with the power to express their soul in beautiful forms; because there have been Romans with a genius for organization and statecraft, and because there have been Hebrews with a passion for God and righteousness which enabled them to give the Bible to the world.

So the world needs its diversity of races and peoples, its languages and cultures, its religions and its differing ways of life — that by their distinctive contributions to humanity each may add a stone to the cathedral of the spirit which the ages are building — the foundation of which is mutual respect and sympathetic understanding and the tower of which is brotherhood.

Tonight we have met to bear witness to this truth. Here we are — Jews and Christians of several denominations — people of different racial backgrounds and differing faiths, yet we are united in fellowship and moved by the deepest sense of good will toward one another because, in spite of our differences, and they are by no means slight, we recognize an overarching unity implicit in our common humanity and in our common desire to further the ideals and which all of us cherish, and of which the world today stands in such urgent need.

We are not met for mutual admiration; but for mutual respect. We have not come to flatter but to try to understand, and above all to bear witness, in these troubled times, to our faith, in one another and in the future — a future founded upon truth and justice and the spirit of true brotherhood.

And so it is with a profound sense of the high significance of this occasion and conscious of the great privilege bestowed upon me that I propose the toast to our guests, our brethren of other faiths.

The European situation worsened with Hitler's incursions into the Ruhr and the Rhineland and taking over Austria as a German satellite. Now he was making demands upon the allies of World War I, especially France and Britain, for the Sudetenland, then under the control of Czechoslovakia, on the pretext that its population was predominantly German and had belonged to Germany prior to World War I. The British government felt that Hitler had gone too far for continued appeasement. But so great was the desire both in France and Britain to avoid a showdown with Hitler that when Neville Chamberlain, prime minister of Britain, and Edouard Daladier, premier of France, went to Munich to discuss the situation with Hitler, they signed the Munich Pact sacrificing Czechoslovakia's in the interests for what they hoped would be the last of Hitler's demands.

The night before the Munich Pact was signed, in October 1938, our World Order Group met to discuss what to do in the event Chamberlain failed in his mission, and war with Nazi Germany could not be avoided. The whole of that day was tense with activity and rumor. War seemed imminent. Britain had mobilized its fleet. A blackout was ordered throughout the country and gas masks were issued in preparation for possible war. The question before our group was whether if war came we would in the spirit of our pacifist leanings refuse to participate and if necessary claim conscientious objection to any military activity. The absolute pacifists among us said they had no choice. They would under no circumstances do anything to help Britain's war effort should she become involved. I took issue with my friends and tried to convince them that this was not a situation where absolute pacifist principles could be invoked.

Justified as I felt as a Jew to do everything in my power to destroy Nazism — and I admitted my bias — my reasons for participation if war came were moral, not personal. I agreed with the absolute pacifists that moral ends cannot justify immoral means, that moral persuasion is infinitely superior to the use of force to achieve moral ends. However, in order for moral persuasion to operate, there must be a moral conscience to which a moral appeal can be made. In the situation which confronted us at the moment, there was no conscience in any sense that our Judaeo-Christian tradition recognized as moral in Hitler and Nazism to which any moral appeal we might make could or would be understood or accepted. On the contrary, Hitler rejected every aspect of the Judaeo-Christian value system as the morality of slaves, to be rejected and destroyed by the German Herrenfolk, the master race destined to rule the world. To submit to such an evil was in my judgment not only un-Jewish but also un-Christian.

No one really knows what Jesus meant when he said, "You have heard that it is said, 'an eye for an eye and a tooth for a tooth', but I say unto you, do not resist one who is evil. If any one strikes you on the right cheek, turn to him the other also." If he meant, as I believe he did and as many Christian thinkers interpret this non-resistance doctrine to mean, that one must not return evil for evil, blow for blow, insult for insult, but should return good for the evil done him in the hope that this might soften the evildoer, make him contrite and inspire him to turn from his evil ways, then the non-resistance doctrine has a rational, spiritual and psychological validity. This kind of moral power can and often has transformed evildoers into saints. But Hitler and the Nazis had rejected such spiritual power as the weakness of slaves. They relied entirely on the power of the mailed fist. The only way other than complete surrender to an evil such as this was to resist it with every means available to us. So we argued until dawn not knowing whether or not we would have to put our philosophies to the test the next day.

In the morning we got the news that Neville Chamberlain was on his way home with the Munich Pact signed, rejoicing in his assurance that we had achieved "peace in our time". The world was to rue the consequence of the Munich Pact. But that we did not know on the day of reprieve from imminent war, October 1, 1938.

Chapter 8

London and the Blitz

After six years in Liverpool, I received a call to the mother Liberal Jewish synagogue in the St. John's Wood district of London with a congregation of more than 1500.

When Donald Bradshaw and his wife heard the news of our impending departure, they came to our home one night and told me they had decided to convert to Judaism. I was not greatly surprised. During the years of the World Order Group, they had been the most ardent and loyal members and were our closest non-Jewish friends. My first question was, "Why? Why do you want to become Jews?" Donald reminded me that they had been coming to the Friday evening meetings for three years; he said they had come to realize that Judaism was the kind of religion they were looking for.

I pointed out that in discussing Judaism at these meetings, we had concentrated on its ideal aspects, its prophetic tradition, its moral and spiritual values, but that not all Jews were prophets or idealists. They were people with human weaknesses, common to all. I asked the Bradshaw's to reflect on what they would gain — would they be better by changing their label from Christian to Jew; would they have deeper insights than they already had or greater sensitivity? I reminded them that they knew very few Jews personally and that becoming a Jew is more than accepting a creed or theology. It is identification with an historic, ethnic group, a people with a unique experience to which they would always be strangers. Nor is the synagogue merely a religious institution, I said. It is also a social center for the Jewish community. I told the Bradshaw's I would not encourage them to think of any kind of formal conversion to Judaism.

Twenty years later on a sabbatical leave from my congregation in Seattle, I visited Liverpool and called Donald Bradshaw who was then a professor of architecture at the University of Liverpool. He told me how grateful he and his wife were that I had not accepted them into

Judaism when they asked me to. They had gone back to the Church of England; he was a deacon in that Church and both were teachers in the religion school and happy in having rediscovered the religion which was their heritage.

It has always been my conviction that there are two kinds of religion, institutional which is sectarian and represents the cultural heritage of the individual born into a particular religious group and his identification with the group, and personal religion which is the individual's personal commitment to God, the Father of us all. The personal commitment to God is witnessed not by the kind of church a person belongs to but the life he lives which every great religion describes in terms of man's loving relationship with God and with his brother man.

Shortly after I became an associate rabbi of the London congregation, the effect of the Nuremberg laws to dehumanize the Jews in Germany began to be felt in the stream of émigrés from Germany who flooded London on their way to lands of refuge in Ireland, Africa, Australia, South America, Mexico, the United States and wherever else they could find an escape from Nazi persecution. I was assigned the duty of helping émigrés who had belonged to non-Orthodox synagogues in Germany. I organized the Friendship Club where émigrés could meet at the synagogue for social contacts and attend classes in English with volunteer teachers from the congregation. Eventually the Club had more than a thousand members, among them some rabbis who had managed to escape from Germany. To make their sojourn in London a little easier, we helped them to organize into a community of their own under the leadership of their own rabbis and gave them synagogue facilities to carry on their own program. In this way we tried to help these refugees begin anew in England or to endure their exile more easily while they awaited visas and transportation to countries willing to receive them.

By 1939 the European situation was becoming increasingly tense. The Munich Pact gave Hitler time to consolidate his gains. Having swallowed up Czechoslovakia, he now began to make demands on Poland. Britain and France issued a warning to Hitler that any aggression against Polish independence would trigger a European war. Hitler concluded a firm military alliance with Mussolini and three months later, a ten-year non-aggression and neutrality pact with Soviet Russia. Having secured his eastern borders, he struck at Poland with lightning rapidity which foreshadowed the "blitz" technique he was prepared to use.

As I watched the rapidly deteriorating situation, I did not want my family, now with two children, Lori Jean, who was nearly eight, and David, eight months and retarded from birth, to stay in England. I persuaded Madeline to take the children on a vacation to America. If war came they would remain there; if not they could return. Within a few weeks Britain and France were at war with Germany. The synagogue, situated in the heart of London, was vulnerable to air attack since a block behind it was the important Marylebone electric power station, a prime target. However, the synagogue was the most solid brick structure within a radius of half a mile and had a large basement area suitable as an air raid shelter into which it was converted.

After Madeline and the children left, I went to live in the home of an elderly couple — the Goldstein's. The aerial blitz began with daylight attacks which were repulsed by the Spitfires. So nightly raids began and continued for more than a year. Military targets were no longer singled out for attack. Bombing became indiscriminate. Every morning we would hear of civilian casualties caught in their homes and often in the air raid shelters they had built in their gardens or in some of the public shelters to which they went at night for safety. So often people in shelters were killed while their homes escaped direct hits that many began to take a fatalistic attitude toward the bombing. It seemed useless to hide.

People in London tried to carry on during the blitz as normally as possible. During the day they were fairly safe from attack. At dusk everybody prepared for the air raids. Entire families flocked to shelters before dark and every platform and tunnel of the subway was strewn with sleeping forms. One night when I was working in my study at the synagogue later than usual, I decided to spend the night in the air raid shelter. About midnight the wardens came in and ordered everyone to evacuate the basement of the synagogue. A bomb had landed in front of the building and it was not known if it was a dud or a delayed action bomb. I chose to go to an old Episcopal Church about a half mile from the synagogue which also had a shelter in its basement. When the all clear sounded I went into the city for food and saw along the three-mile route some of the havoc which the night's raid had wrought. Most of the buildings were intact except for glass that was strewn through the streets. In town the crowds were already gathered discussing the raid and filling the tea shops that were open. There was no panic or disorder. The people had become so accustomed to these night raids that the raids became a part of their way of life. After another raid, as I was walking from the Goldstein's apartment to the synagogue, I passed a number of shops that had been almost completely demolished. The owner of one had collected the canned goods and groceries he was able to salvage and had piled them neatly in front of his demolished shop. A sign on top of the heap read: "My shop is more open than usual."

I arrived at the synagogue to see a huge crowd gathered; there had been a direct hit. No one in the basement shelter had been injured but my study was in the direct path of the bomb and my books and papers lay with the rubble in the crater below, The main sanctuary had been partially destroyed and gutted and most of the rest of the building was unusable, Several of the ministers of nearby churches, both Catholic and Protestant offered their buildings for Jewish worship and gatherings. The rabbis accepted the offer of Lords Cricket Club across the street from the synagogue which had a large hall that could be used for worship and for almost a year the Cricket Club served as synagogue.

Chapter 9

Return to America

As the war progressed and the blitz failed to cow Britain into submission, as Hitler invaded Russia despite the non-aggression pact, it looked as if the war would drag on indefinitely and I began thinking about returning to America. It had been more than two years since I had seen Madeline and the children. Madeline had made it clear that she would not return to England. I had stayed with the congregation during the entire blitz and hard as it was to leave them, they understood my decision and gave me their blessing.

Travel arrangements were difficult. Because of the menace of Nazi indiscriminate U-boat warfare on all shipping leaving Britain, the American Embassy strongly urged American citizens to travel by air. Besides, if I could arrive in time to take part in the High Holyday services, it would greatly facilitate my getting a new assignment. Things went well in the beginning and by the time my papers were ready I was able to get a flight to Lisbon where I could board a clipper ship for New York. But engine trouble forced an 11-day stop-over in Ireland. I missed the clipper ship in Lisbon and had no money to see me through a two-week wait for the next one. So I exchanged my air ticket for passage on an American Export Lines ship and faced the U-boat hazards.

On arrival I wired Ida, now living in Minneapolis, that I was in New York without funds and she wired me the fare to Minneapolis. On the way I stopped to see Dr. Morgenstern, still president of Hebrew Union College, to whom I had written about a Holyday position. The letter had never arrived but it would not have helped anyway because of the delay. It was now the second day of Rosh Hashanah. Dr. Morgenstern did promise to recommend me for one of the several congregations that were sure to be opening during the year and with that assurance I went on to Minneapolis and then to Portland for a reunion with Madeline and Lori Jean, then living with Madeline's youngest sister. David had been left in Cincinnati in the care of a motherly woman who worked with handicapped children. Later he was moved to the Washington State Custodial School for the Mentally Retarded where he died at the age of 20.

While in Portland I was invited to speak in the Reform synagogue and the Portland City Club about my experiences as a rabbi in London during the blitz. One who heard me was David Robinson, Western Regional Director of B'nai B'rith, who put me in touch with Richard Gudstadt, then head of the Anti-Defamation League in Chicago. It was a time for growing anti-Semitism in America and just a month before Pearl Harbor, and both Mr. Robinson and Mr. Gudstadt thought I should share my experiences and insights concerning the war on a lecture tour of the United States.

Just before the lecture tour was to begin, I received a letter from Dr. Morgenstern informing me that Rabbi Samuel Koch of the Temple De Hirsch in Seattle was retiring and the pulpit committee of the Temple was seeking a successor. He was recommending me, along with five others, for the position. There was also an opening in Lexington, Kentucky and the congregation there would contact me. I was elated. There was no place I wanted more to serve as a rabbi than in Seattle. Madeline had never ceased to extol the wondrous beauty of the Pacific Northwest and especially Seattle. On my one visit there to give a lecture a few weeks earlier, I found it to be all she said it was.

Many months passed before I heard anything at all from Seattle. The Lexington congregation invited me to visit them and I spent two days meeting leading members of the congregation individually and at evening gatherings. Later, while on the lecture tour, I received a letter from them thanking me for my interest but that after considerable discussion they felt that with my experience, I would not remain long in such a small congregation. Their rejection proved a blessing as with so many other frustrated expectations in life.

After the attack on Pearl Harbor, "I Saw London Bombed" took on new urgency, especially in a coastal city like Seattle with all its prime targets. I still had heard nothing from the Temple De Hirsch congregation when I spoke to about 400 businessmen at a Chamber of Commerce meeting. I told of my experiences during the blitz as a fire watcher and air raid worker, trying to give them some idea of the wonderful spirit of the British during their darkest hour. Immediately after the meeting, the chief of the local civil defense asked if I would stay over till the following Monday to address about 2000 police and defense workers at the Civic Auditorium.

The congregation had not yet selected a successor to Rabbi Koch and the reception I got at the Chamber of Commerce meeting impressed members of the Temple Board of Trustees. The next morning I received a call from the chairman of the pulpit committee asking if I was still interested; I was the only candidate now being considered. That Friday evening I conducted the service and gave a sermon tying it in with Passover being celebrated that week with its ideals of freedom, using some of my experiences in London as illustrations of faith in freedom and the willingness to make great sacrifices to preserve it against tyrants who would destroy it.

Within eight days I was elected rabbi of the congregation — as I often said later, half in jest and half in earnest, by the Seattle Chamber of Commerce. My fondest dream had been realized. I was to be rabbi of the one congregation in America that would have been my first choice had I been given the choice. Madeline was supremely happy. I would begin my official duties on June 4, 1942.

My first years in Seattle were very exciting. My honeymoon with the congregation lasted much longer than I had dared hope for. New members came in large numbers so that the congregation grew from 400 to nearly a thousand in ten years and our religion school grew in proportion. I was very active in the Christian community, encouraged both by my congregation in my efforts to build bridges of understanding and by our Christian neighbors' response. I found that seven days a week was hardly enough to do all the things with which I became involved, unfortunately to the neglect of my family. This became a source of tension between Madeline and me, which with other personal problems, led to a deterioration of our relationship and ultimately to a separation in 1953 after nearly 25 years of marriage. It was a traumatic experience for both of us, but at the time it seemed the only way of avoiding even more harmful results.

For six years I lived alone, determined never to marry again because it would be unfair to any woman, married as I was to my work. Then I met Reeva Miller when she was a resident arts and craft teacher at the Camp for Living Judaism in the Santa Cruz mountains near Saratoga, California. I was there as rabbi-counselor and in the process of writing a book. I needed someone to do some art work for the book and Reeva volunteered to do it. We became friends and I used to see her occasionally when I visited Ida who was now living on a cattle feeding ranch in El Centro, California, which she and her husband operated. In 1958 on one of my winter vacations at the ranch, I found Reeva there. She and my sister had been friends for years and she occasionally visited El Centro, especially when she was having difficulties at home. Her marriage had been unhappy almost from the beginning. She and her husband had been divorced once but had later reconciled. Now they were again in the process of getting a divorce, this time irrevocable, and Reeva had come to El Centro for help and encouragement. When her divorce became final, we decided to get married.

Chapter 10

Religious Camping

I had been rabbi of Temple De Hirsch about a year when I received an invitation from the National Conference of Christians and Jews to be a counselor for a week at a Christian religious camp at Seabeck on Hoods Canal. I had never been to any kind of religious camp before. The group was composed of 200 high school students, boys and girls, from all over the state of Washington. It was a joint venture of two denominations, Baptist and Disciples of Christ churches. My assignment was to teach a course in "Building Bridges of Understanding" carrying the brotherhood message which was the NCCJ's basic reason for existence and activity.

To help me in my assignment, the NCCJ gave me a list of 20 questions which I was to put to my class to determine their attitudes toward people of ethnic and religious groups other than their own. The questions were related to their attitudes toward Catholics, Jews and Negroes — whether they would approve or disapprove having one of these minority groups as a member of their athletic teams or social groups; as a teacher or personal friend; whether they would invite one to their homes; elect one as a representative in government or join in any other association involving closer relations with any of them. The answers were to be unsigned.

I gave my class of 25 this questionnaire at our first meeting. The answers did not surprise me. The negative answers to most of the questions were high, about 60 % against Catholics, 75% against Jews, 90% against Negroes. I did not tell the class the results of the survey. That week I conducted my class in human relations trying to give them some understanding of how people needed to learn to get along with others in spite of their differences of race, color or religious faith not only for the welfare of our country made up of all these diverse groups but for their own growth as human beings. I conducted my class informally and tried to help the young people understand the problems of human relations through probing their own attitudes and experiences in a free and open discussion. To work in this way was a new experience for me and one I greatly enjoyed. But more important than the class experience was living with the campers and their counselors, ministers and Sunday school teachers and participating in the program from the early morning watch to the closing friendship circle at night. I was deeply moved by what I saw accomplished as the days went by until toward the end of the week we felt like one united family with a common purpose.

At the end of the week I gave my class the same questionnaire as at the first session to see if their attitudes had changed as a result of the week's experience. No names were to be signed. The answers this time were a surprise. The negative responses against Catholics decreased from 60% to 15%; against Negroes, from 90% to 40%; against Jews, not a single negative answer. These young people were all white Protestant, mostly from small communities where ethnic minorities were rare. Few of them had ever had any personal contact with Jews and hardly any with Negroes or Catholics.

This experience in trying to build bridges of understanding between people convinced me that the best way to combat prejudice was not by preaching brotherhood or lecturing on human relations but by creating the environment in which people of diverse racial and religious backgrounds can meet and work together on equal terms for a common purpose. The camp offered that kind of environment. There was nothing quite like it in any branch of Judaism. This I decided we Jews must have.

How to accomplish it I did not know but it had to be if we were ever to inspire our Jewish youth with loyalty to their faith and their synagogue. At that time there was hardly a synagogue in the country that had any effective program for young people after they were confirmed at 15.

In 1945 I attended a rabbinical conference in Cincinnati and one day called all my colleagues from Pacific Coast states together for a breakfast meeting. At the meeting I suggested it would be helpful for all of us on the Pacific Coast, far from the mainstream of our Reform movement, to organize some kind of association to meet perhaps once a year for discussion of subjects of mutual interest and for fellowship.

Isolated as I was in the Northwest with my nearest colleague in Portland, I keenly felt this loneliness.

The following January ten of us met in San Francisco and formed the Western Association of Reform Rabbis. In January 1947 we held our first full conference at Los Angeles and to the original ten at the organization meeting were added another 15 from Los Angeles and Southern California and their wives. The agenda dealt largely with purposes and goals of our association and programs to implement these goals. During the meetings I told my colleagues of my experience at the Christian youth camp and suggested that our organization undertake as its first project a religious co-educational camping program for our high school juniors and seniors, and perhaps freshmen in college.

The suggestion was received without enthusiasm. There were many who argued that it would never work, that we were not ready for such an undertaking and besides, Jewish youth would not go for a religious camp. "How do you know they wouldn't? Have we ever given them a chance?" I challenged. Rabbi Iser Freund of San Jose had also been a counselor at a Christian camp and enthusiastically supported the idea. I volunteered to organize such a camp if someone would find a suitable site. Rabbi Freund volunteered to find such a place. With these two offers, Association members reluctantly voted to let us go ahead.

I could hardly wait to return to Seattle to inform our Temple Board of Trustees and the boards of the Temple Brotherhood and Sisterhood about the camping program. My enthusiasm was contagious and they promised to help. Rabbi Freund immediately contacted Rev. Peabody, a Christian friend who was associated with a camp at Lake Tahoe, and was able to obtain the Presbyterian conference grounds at Zephyr Cove for our group at a cost of $18 a week for room and meals provided we had 100 campers.

At first young people were dubious about the attractiveness of a religious camp, but the prospect of going to California and meeting boys and girls their own age from other states was alluring enough to overcome doubts. We distributed 20 camper ships among the most promising students of our youth group and these persuaded 20 more to sign up for the program. It was more difficult to interest young people in other areas because of the lack of interest among rabbis, but we finally had 94, six short of the required 100. By counting faculty and their wives we managed to more than fill the quota.

The week's program was a duplicate of the memorable week I had spent at Seabeck, only the content was Jewish. From the waking bell at 7 a.m. to the friendship circle at 10:30 p.m., the day was filled with worship, study, recreation and special interest groups. The climax of the week was the Sabbath worship. We contacted the small Jewish community in Reno, Nevada, and they lent us a Torah, necessary for Scripture reading, and with the Torah came a delegation of their leaders to see what we were doing at a Presbyterian camp. As the service progressed, few eyes were dry under the emotional impact of worship conducted entirely by the young people with the exception of the Torah reading and sermon.

For the second Jewish youth conference there was no difficulty in getting rabbis and campers interested. By the fourth year we had to establish quotas for participating congregations, so great were the demand. During the year Mr. Ben Swig, a San Francisco philanthropist was brought by his rabbi to the YWCA conference grounds near Carmel, California, where the camp was then held to see what we were doing. Mr. Swig was deeply impressed and seeing the potential for religious camping, he decided that we could no longer be dependent on rented facilities. He found a 200-acre estate in the Santa Cruz Mountains near Saratoga, California, and in 1951 Camp Saratoga, the Camp for Living Judaism, was dedicated as the first religious camp in the Reform movement. Today there are nine regional camps throughout the country operated by the Union of American Hebrew Congregations, the national body of Reform Judaism. They have revitalized our youth movement and have become the source of inspiration to many young men and women now being recruited for the rabbinate, religious education and lay leadership.

Chapter 11

Launching of "Challenge"

It was in 1960 when John Fitzgerald Kennedy was nominated for the presidency of the U.S. that I began to receive a rash of hate mail against the possibility of a Catholic president. It reminded me of what happened when another Catholic, Alfred Smith, three-time governor of New York, was nominated in 1928. While many factors defeated Al Smith, not the least of them was the widespread bigotry against Catholics which swept the country. It was after that that Charles Evans Hughes, then Chief Justice of the Supreme Court, along with several friends who were aware of the religious bigotry, decided to do something about it. They organized what later became the National Conference of Christians and Jews to help the American people realize the necessity for religious tolerance and understanding as the basis for survival not only of religion in America, but of America itself.

For some time before Kennedy's nomination I had been interested in organizing some type of TV program in Seattle which would include a Protestant, a Catholic and a Jew to help break down some of the religious barriers which had been dividing people across the centuries into mutually exclusive and often hostile groups. Religion, which I was convinced was intended by God to be a healing balm, uniting mankind in the spirit of love and brotherhood, had become one of its most divisive forces, certainly in the last 1900 years. The religious wars during the Middle Ages, and even into our own time, were to me a blasphemy against the God of love whom the belligerent religionists claimed to worship. In the name of this God of love they slaughtered each other with viciousness unparalleled until the Nazis came with their extermination camps.

I had come to feel that the sectarian faiths of organized religion were an evil in the divisive character that grew out of their imperialistic claims to unique religious revelations and infallible truth. Out of this came the need to proselytize by preaching and often by force as the holy wars of the Moslems, the crusades of the Christians, the wars of the

Reformation and the extirpation of heresies evidenced so tragically through the centuries.

At one time in my rabbinate, disgusted with this kind of divisiveness, I even considered the idea of organizing some kind of universal religion. Fortunately I came to my senses, realizing that even if I were successful, I would only add another sect to the many already in existence. Instead I decided to concentrate on trying to build bridges of understanding, especially between Christians and Jews.

My motivation grew out of the fact that as Jews we were particularly vulnerable and the chief victims of religious prejudice. Living as we do in countries predominantly Christian, the need for understanding the basic unity between Christianity and Judaism in their moral value systems and ethical ideals was vital to our Jewish survival and the only hope for peaceful coexistence with our Christian neighbors.

When I came to Seattle in 1942, anti-Semitism was virulent and widespread in this country. The "Silver Shirts", Father Coughlin's radio program with his insinuations and open attacks on Jews and Judaism, and Gerald K. Smith with his hate campaign against Catholics, Blacks and Jews, made the need for better understanding between Christians and Jews urgent.

I welcomed every opportunity to speak in churches and before Christian groups. I joined the local chapter of the National Conference of Christians and Jews which at that time had lost the confidence of the Catholic Bishop of Seattle, Gerald Shaughnessy, so that he had withdrawn Catholic support from the organization. I went to see him but he felt that the NCCJ with its three-faith program only confused the faithful and would lead to religious indifferentism.

Having no success with Bishop Shaughnessy I had to work within the Protestant community and there I found a warm response from the leaders of the major denominations. One of the relationships I cherished was with the late Stephan Bayne, Jr., Bishop of the Episcopal Diocese of Olympia. He came to Seattle in 1946 and I was invited to participate in his investiture. We became close friends and in the dialogues we frequently had, our faith in the ability of Christians and Jews to enrich one another grew firmer.

To break down barriers and to build bridges of understanding between all faiths, but especially between Christians and Jews, became the dominant thrust of my ministry. In 1952 I suggested to Bishop Bayne the possibility of a TV program and told him I would speak to the Catholic Bishop, the Most Reverend Thomas A. Connolly. Bishop Bayne was enthusiastic about the possibilities for such a program. Bishop Connolly was not. The idea died because the station willing to sponsor such a program was not interested without a Catholic participant.

In 1960 when it looked as if we might have another age of bigotry in America, I again went to Bishop Connolly, now Archbishop, and suggested that at least in Seattle and wherever our influence might reach we would try to avoid the repetition of what happened in the election campaign of 1928. Archbishop Connolly was cool to the proposition. He did not believe that it would be effective or that it would last. However, he agreed to think about it and discuss it with some of his advisers. Several weeks went by and I heard nothing. One night I called him and asked whether he had considered the television program because this time we had a station, KOMO-TV, willing to give us excellent time if we could arrange to have the three faiths participate. The Archbishop said he had thought about it but had not yet come to a decision and would let me know within a week.

I did not even remember having met Father Treacy outside the Archbishop's office when I received a call from him saying that the Archbishop wanted him to see me to discuss the possibility of the television program the Archbishop and I had talked about. I was overjoyed.

When Father Treacy came into my study at the Temple my heart sank. I saw a boyish young man who looked in his mid-twenties, although I later discovered he was past 40, and I wondered if the Archbishop was really serious about the program, sending a boy to do a man's work. How could he send a priest so young and immature to represent the Catholic Church on a television program whose other two members were Dr. Martin Goslin of the largest Congregational Church in Seattle and one of the most prominent ministers in the Northwest, and I who had some stature among rabbis? Anyway, since Father Treacy was chosen as the representative, I resolved to work with him as best I could. We discussed the ground rules on which the program was to be established. There were to be no arguments on theology. There was to be no baiting of one another. The important thing was to discuss those things that our three religious faiths had in common and try to build a better understanding between them. These were ground rules that I had already discussed with the Archbishop because neither did I want religious arguments. I wanted discussion. I wanted dialogue. I did not want arguments. I realized that one cannot argue fruitfully about faith. All we can do is try to understand, not merely with tolerance but respect, the other person's point of view, whether we agree with it or not.

Treacy began fearful of how he would fare in a discussion with a Protestant and a Jew. He was guarded in his comments. He did his homework thoroughly. He was clearly on the defensive. In a way, we all were on the defensive against each other, trying to protect our faith against any possible implication that the others might have something ours did not have. We soon realized that the purpose of the program was not to win debating points for our own faith but to try to under stand each other and our respective faiths.

As the weeks went by and Father Treacy began to feel that we were indeed his friends and colleagues in a common effort toward mutual understanding and good will, his self-confidence grew and we were able to discuss almost anything, no matter how delicate or controversial, with a sensitivity and respect which became the hallmark of CHALLENGE. So on Palm Sunday of the first year of CHALLENGE, we telecast a most delicate discussion, especially between Christians and Jews at that time of the year: "Who Crucified Jesus?"

In 1962 the National Conference of Christians and Jews, influenced especially by this program, presented CHALLENGE with a special national award and in announcing the award at the annual brotherhood dinner of the Washington region, the director said: "It has been the policy of the National Conference of Christians and Jews to select non-clergy to receive awards at the annual brotherhood dinner. However, the service of the CHALLENGE panel is so unique and has had such an impact on the community that the committee felt it must recognize this outstanding contribution to brotherhood; therefore this special award is presented to Rabbi Raphael Levine, Dr. Martin Goslin and Father William Treacy."

As I grew to know Father Treacy more intimately as a person and as a friend, I discovered the great gifts that were his all along and saw him grow in his freedom to use them. His spirit revealed him to be a true disciple of Pope John and led me to apologize on many occasions about how mistaken I was about him at our first meeting. Far from the Archbishop not respecting the television project in sending such a young priest, as I then thought, he had demonstrated great wisdom and understanding when he selected this chancery assistant for so important a mission. Father Treacy had not only the intellectual capacity but he possessed the qualities of heart and spirit to be a most worthy representative of the Church in this stage of the Church's history.

The years of CHALLENGE continued and my relationship with Father Treacy became closer and deeper until I felt toward him as though he were my son and he regarded me as a spiritual father. An eloquent expression of this relationship and the love we felt for each other came when Vatican Council II decreed that at the celebration of Mass the priest should face the congregation rather than stand at the altar with his back to them.

One day Father Treacy came to me and said, "Rabbi, you once promised to make me something if I ever had a parish of my own". My hobby, as he knew, was working in wood and mosaic in the basement of my home. I had made a number of tables, mostly with a chessboard center, on which I had carved some of my favorite quotations. When he asked me to make him something, I thought it was something like a plaque for his study. He reminded me that Mass was now to be celebrated with the priest facing the people. And then he said, "The altar at St. Patrick's is of marble and attached to the wall. It can't be moved. I need a new altar and I must have it within ten days." I was flabbergasted. I knew that the altar was the focal point of Catholic worship, the holiest object in the church, and that he should ask me, a Jew and a rabbi, to make an altar for him touched me deeply. I went to work doing some research on what an altar was and discovered that the least one could use in a church the size of St. Patrick's was a six-foot table.

I worked day and night. The result was an altar of mahogany, birch and walnut. With the help of Reeva, I put on the altar all the symbols that Father Treacy wanted and which meant so much to him, the Chi-Rho in mosaic tile on the center front, and on an ornamental facade at the top, lilies and fish which are ancient Christian symbols.

The altar was completed on the day before it was to be used. Members of his parish carted it to the church and put it in place. A newspaperman from The Seattle Times heard about the altar and decided to do a feature story for the Sunday edition on the day it was to be dedicated and the first Mass in the new form celebrated. The wire news services picked up the story and it was carried in newspapers throughout the United States and beyond. We began to receive letters from all over the world. The response to our simple expression of respect and love was heart-warming and indicated release of something also very deep in other hearts.

It appeared that the impact of this incident touched the lives of many and awakened a hope and a faith that at long last religion which had divided our human family into mutually exclusive and so often antagonistic sectarian groups might bring them together to a spiritual unity as children of God. For had not the Hebrew Prophet Malachi said, perhaps 2500 years ago: "Have we not all one Father? Hath not one God created us all? Why then do we deal treacherously, brother against brother?" (Malachi 2: 15) And did not Jesus quote the injunctions from the Old Testament books of Leviticus and Deuteronomy when he said: "You shall love the Lord your God with all your heart, with all your soul, with all your strength and with all your mind. This is the first and greatest commandment, and the second is like unto it, you shall love your neighbor as yourself'? (Luke 10:27) And Paul added: "On these two commandments hang all the Law (Torah) and the prophets". (Gal. 5:14) How can we show our love of God except as we show love for our fellowman?

I tell the story of the altar to demonstrate the closeness of the relationship which Father Treacy and I had established so that he would not hesitate to ask his friend, the Rabbi, to make for him the holiest religious object in the Roman Catholic Church.

On my part there was no hesitation to do this for him, even though some of my colleagues in the rabbinate thought that it was not the kind of object a rabbi should make even for his dearest Catholic friend. As our friendship grew and deepened we achieved a depth of communication rare even between the best of friends. A severe test of our friendship came when the highly emotional issue of liberalizing our state's abortion laws was being debated by the state legislature. Emotions ran deep between those opposing any attempt to make it easier to terminate unwanted pregnancies and those urging reform in the law.

In spite of the danger of discussing this controversial issue on CHALLENGE we decided that we had a responsibility as leaders of our faiths to put the issue before the public as fairly and as honestly as we could. Father Treacy expressed the position of the Roman Catholic Church and his own on the question eloquently and with a frankness and sincerity that was obvious but also with respect and sensitivity to the attitudes of those like Dr. Corson and myself who held equally deep, equally sincere, but different convictions on the issue, although ours did not represent the views of all Jews and Protestants.

We made two programs on this subject and received many letters, some condemning us for being too tolerant of each other, some disappointed that we could disagree so sharply. So we felt the need for doing a third program which we called "The Spirit of CHALLENGE — The Need to Learn How to Disagree Agreeably", a need we believed belonged to the very essence of true religion and the very foundation of any free, democratic society.

Whether or not we got through to our critics we never knew, but I am confident that fair-minded people obtained a better understanding after this third program of how it is possible, even inevitable, for a religious and deeply committed person to have deep convictions on fundamental issues, especially where faith is concerned, and yet have respect for the different and even opposing convictions held by other people. Father Treacy and I share the opinion that this is religion at its truest and best, and certainly the basis of democracy.

Chapter 12

From Fear to Brotherhood

Long before I met Father Treacy my spiritual odyssey from fear to understanding and appreciation of Christianity as revealed in the life and teachings of Jesus, were gradual steps beginning with the love I had for Miss Calverly, the principal of my first grammar school in Duluth who "mothered" me as a child of eight in my difficult period of becoming Americanized. From her and from some of my early non-Jewish teachers and classmates, I began to learn that there were different kinds of Christians, some good and some bad. This knowledge grew as I came to a more mature understanding of my own religion and other faiths. I began to realize how unjust, unfair and even unintelligent it was to judge religions by any personal experience with only their inadequate representatives or by some of their beliefs and practices which because of my ignorance seemed to me foolish, superstitious, incredible or barbaric.

Dr. Abraham Cronbach, my beloved teacher at Hebrew Union College, helped me more than any other person in that growing understanding of my own religion and other faiths. He taught me how to free myself from stereotype thinking and conditioning, to keep a mind open to new ideas, to suspend judgment upon things that I did not fully comprehend, and above all to guard against generalizing from insufficient experience. The injunction of Rabbi Hillel, who was the spiritual leader of the Jews in Judea when Jesus was but a child, made a profound impression upon me: "Pass not judgment upon your neighbor until you are come into his place", until you yourself have experienced his situation. That insight into the need for empathy was deepened for me by what I learned from Dr. Cronbach and what my personal experience in all the years since has taught me.

This insight, certainly in relation to Christians, grew in my experience as a rabbi in Liverpool. I discovered that the spirit of love and brotherhood which was Judaism as I had come to know it and to expect from Jews, certainly from rabbis, was not practiced toward me nearly so generously by my Orthodox rabbinic colleagues as by some Christian ministers with whom I shared an enriching friendship. I was not angry because my Orthodox colleagues rejected my attempts at friendship with them. I understood their position. I was in their opinion a heretic, a betrayer of Judaism. I did not condemn them, nor did I condemn Orthodox Judaism. I had known Orthodox rabbis in my time and many Orthodox Jewish men and women who were saintly, generous, kind and great-hearted. They were the products of the same Judaism that I had come from. But I became ever more convinced of the need to judge a religion not merely by representatives who were limited by their own personal inadequacies but more by those who tried to witness by their lives the essential idealism and beauty of their faith.

As I studied the Scriptures of other religions, I was amazed at how similar they were, in so many ways, to the ideals and values Judaism proclaimed as man's way to God. I discovered that in all the great religions, and especially in the teachings of Jesus, the door to God could be opened only with the key of love. As a Jew, I had learned from the commandments "to love God with heart and soul and might" and this I recited every day in the Sh'mah — the watchword of my faith (Deut. 6) — and "to love my neighbor as myself", which the holiness code in the book of Leviticus taught me is the way to that love of God. The holiness code I learned is also basic to Christianity, to Islam, to Buddhism, and to other of the great world religions. They expressed it in different idioms and dramatized it in different symbols and forms of worship, but it is practiced with the same varying degree of devotion by their followers as among my own fellow Jews.

These discoveries I made as I followed my beloved teacher's advice to free myself from stereotype thinking about other religions and peoples, to keep a mind open to truth wherever I was able to find it, to free myself as much as possible from the natural human tendency to rationalize my prejudices and call it honest, rational thinking and behavior; and the journey from my childhood fear of Christians and Christianity to a reverent respect for the faith of the Christian friends whom I had grown to love as fellow human beings was fairly uncomplicated.

So when I met Father Treacy, I was ready for the kind of relationship we established across the past 14 years and which we are trying to describe in this book. In Father Treacy's description of how our relationship influenced his life, deepened his insight into his faith as a Catholic and enriched his ministry to his people, he gave undue credit to my part in his spiritual growth. It is true that I may have helped to open windows for him through our CHALLENGE program and through our growing personal friendship. After all, I am 20 years older than he and my experiences have been more varied, but if I claim any credit at all, it was to help him release some of the great potentials of mind and heart and spirit with which God had endowed him from birth.

These potentials and qualities of character he had developed long before I knew him, which he revealed to me almost from the first CHALLENGE program in 1960 and which became clearer and more precious to me as I grew to know him across the years, became a source of strength and enrichment to me. They played a most significant part in a better understanding of my own role as a rabbi and aided me immeasurably in my spiritual odyssey up to now. I say "up to now" because it is yet unfinished and I know will never be finished as long as I live on earth. Through knowing Father Treacy, the dedicated and totally committed priest of his Church as I know him to be, I gained a deeper insight into the Church which helped to make him what he is. The beauty of our relationship is that it has not been one-sided as readers might be led to believe from Father Treacy's version, with me as the giver and Father Treacy as the recipient. It was a relationship in which he contributed to my spiritual growth as much as I to his. It was a relationship in which the beneficial enrichment was mutual and reciprocal, the kind of relationship that transcends all man-made patterns of sectarian differences and touches the core depth of religious communication on a level of love between human beings which God intended all of us ultimately to achieve.

This does not mean that sectarian religion is not important. It is not only important but in my opinion, inevitable. I do not believe that in any foreseeable future, all the different religions of the world will be merged into one world religion, with the same theology and forms of worship and practice. Until the races of the world, languages, cultures, habits of thought and life-styles are merged and all differences in personal growth and maturation are eradicated, I do not see the possibility of one world religion which all humanity will accept and live by. Nor do I think it would be desirable even if it were possible. The very diversity of our human family contributes to the enrichment of human life. It would contribute even more to human fulfillment and happiness if we realized our oneness as a human family bound together into an ever closer relationship on the earth by political, economic and ecological facts of survival on this planet.

So I believe that what Father Treacy and I have discovered in and through each other is a deeper appreciation of the role which sectarian religion can fulfill and become the blessing it has never fully achieved. This was beautifully expressed by Father Treacy's speaking from the pulpit of our Temple on a Friday evening in February 1966. It was our regular Sabbath service which was not altered one iota from our normal Sabbath worship except that Father Treacy's sermon came at the end instead of in the middle of the service as was my normal practice. The large sanctuary was almost full with nearly 900 worshipers of all faiths. Father spoke about some of the far-reaching implications for ecumenism of Vatican Council II and that as a Christian he believed in the incarnation of God in Jesus who in a personal way manifested God's love and concern for human beings. For this reason, he said, he believed that it was in the person-to-person contact that we must come to know each other and love each other. After the service many worshipers, both Christians and Jews, told me they never had felt the presence of God so overwhelmingly as in the spirit of true brotherhood which radiated throughout the service that night. Mrs. Isaac Brown, who was 92 and has since passed away, a founding member of our congregation, told Father Treacy with tears of joy that she thanked God she was privileged to live to see this day. Pope John, of blessed memory, opened windows upon the world to the Catholic Church that had been closed for centuries. In his conception of the Church's new mission he also inspired non-Catholics of all faiths to re-examine their own sectarianism and to realize that by becoming aware that other faiths also had a portion of God's love and truth that they were not being disloyal to their own, only being enriched in their understanding of the deepest insights of their own faith. It is in that spirit that Father Treacy is an authentic disciple of Pope John, even as I believe I am true to the teachings of Judaism at its best. When I say, as I have so often said publicly in lectures and on CHALLENGE, that Judaism is the best religion in the world for me but not necessarily for a Christian, or a Hindu, or a Buddhist, I believe I speak with the authentic voice of Judaism, for I know that 2000 years ago it was said in Judaism, "The righteous among all people shall have a share in the world to come", the rabbinic way of saying all men are accepted and loved by God.

That is why we have written this book together, to show that people as different as an Irish Catholic boy born near a village in central Ireland and a Jewish boy born in a Russian ghetto, so different in ethnic origins and cultural backgrounds, so far apart in our religious faiths, so diverse in our education and experience, and so different in temperament as Father Treacy and I should have met in Seattle and have been able to overcome all our early conditioning to achieve the kind of relationship we have so inadequately tried to describe in this book. This to me is the most convincing evidence that there is a divine Providence that shapes our ends, rough hew them though we may.

Endorsements

Knowing Father William Treacy for the last seven years has been for me a rare privilege and a source of boundless inspiration. He embodies what the Quar'an calls an inner "spaciousness" and he walks on "spacious paths."

In Camp Brotherhood, a unique retreat place that Father Treacy co-founded with Rabbi Levine, Muslims have always felt joyously welcome. I have had the great honor and pleasure of dialoguing with Father Treacy in private and public on the subject of Islam. His deeply appreciative understanding of the Islamic faith and his vision for peace never ceases to amaze and move me.

The Prophet Mohammad said, "The character of a friend of God is based on nothing more than graciousness and generosity." Father Treacy is such a friend of God.

Jamal Rahman
Muslim Sufi Minister
The Interfaith Community Church
Board Member, Camp Brotherhood

Dear Father Bill,

I want to take this opportunity to thank you for your wonderful Christmas greeting, the sermon thoughts you shared with me, and your gracious contribution. I appreciate very much your kindness and thoughtfulness in remembering me at this time of year. As you know, I remember you each day in prayer and I ask the Lord to continue to bless you with health of mind and body.

I thank you especially for the ecumenical information that you sent. You have some wonderful experiences and they should not be forgotten. Thank you for sharing that. I know some of the people that you mentioned in your article. The work of ecumenism has been a great challenge for the Church and the fact that is is still alive owes a lot to people like yourself that worked so diligently in the very beginning to set the foundations.

I hope that everything else is going well at Camp Brotherhood and that you are enjoying living there after spending so many years in helping it become what it is. Please be assured that you are in my thoughts and prayers during this Christmas season, and most especially throughout the New Year 2007.

With warmest regards and wishes, I remain fraternally yours in Christ.

Most Rev. Alex J. Brunnett
Archbishop of Seattle

Father William Treacy is one of the pioneers of interfaith dialogue in the Pacific Northwest. Beginning in the 1960s, the ground-breaking television series called "Challenge" which he led with Rabbi Raphael Levine and some special Protestant ministers brought a deepening of interfaith understanding to hundreds of thousands of households over a 14-year period. Father Treacy's open-hearted approach allows him not only to embrace those on other paths than his own, but to celebrate with them the value of their own traditions. It always appears that his commitment to his own faith deepens through his interactions with those representing other traditions.

Camp Brotherhood, created by Father Treacy and Rabbi Levine in 1966 has grown to be the major interfaith retreat center in the Northwest. Thousands of people — children, adults, couples, families, civic and religious groups — continue to benefit from the farm-like setting outside of Arlington, Washington. The multi-faith chapel there reflects Father Treacy's dream of welcoming those of different traditions and inviting them to deepen their faith through prayer and devotion. Each year a New Year's event brings together leaders of various faiths to share energies of prayer to support a New Year of peace and health.

Camp Brotherhood was the first retreat center to which I brought a group once my family and I had relocated to Seattle in 1993. Father Treacy is a treasured inspiration to me. His teaching imparts a great wisdom, and his presence radiates love and compassion. He models what he teaches.

To read his story is itself inspiring, and I recommend these passages to you. Through them you will meet Father Treacy and you will be touched with his gentleness and his wisdom. It is a privilege for me to introduce his words in this way.

Rabbi Ted Falcon, Ph. D.
Rabbi, Bet Alef Meditative Synagogue
President, Northwest Interfaith Community Outreach

Dear Bill,

I thoroughly enjoyed the various materials you sent me, info about the seminaries and current developments, elements of humor, reflections from Ethna, and above all your own writing. You were the first priest I ever met who entered into communication with a Rabbi on TV and the best at it (since my days in Seattle I have met others who did your type of TV ministry, but none as effective as you were.) I have great memories of my time in the Northwest and you were a significant part of my positive experience.

I'm sorry you can't be at our St. Patrick's celebration, but you would be in big trouble if you were not present at the gathering in your own backyard. I'm sure we can figure out a time to get together. I'll probably be back in Seattle next June for the ordinations of Khan and Bryan. If not then, we'll find another time.

I truly look forward to your new publication. From the three chapters you sent me, I can see that you are right on target with the issues and just as alive as ever. I thoroughly enjoyed your book, *Reflections of a Pioneering Priest.* The new book may turn out even better. Right now, I have no major suggestions. Your outline looks truly engaging. One thought: Will you be including ideas on the need of so many of us these days to develop the gift of awareness, stillness, and sense of presence, all of which can lead to an even keener sense of service and to the bearing of much fruit?

I look forward to a get-together and for ongoing communication.

Have a great Christmas!

Jerry Brown
A Seminary Rector in San Francisco